DISCARD

THE TALK OF THE PARTY

Communication, Media, and Politics

Series Editor
Robert E. Denton Jr., Virginia Tech

This series features a broad range of work dealing with the role and function of communication in the realm of politics, broadly defined. Including general academic books, monographs, and texts for use in graduate and advanced undergraduate courses, the series will encompass humanistic, critical, historical, and empirical studies in political communication in the United States. Primary subject areas include campaigns and elections, media, and political institutions. *Communication, Media, and Politics* books will be of interest to students, teachers, and scholars of political communication from the disciplines of communication, rhetorical studies, political science, journalism, and political sociology.

Recent Titles in the Series

Campaign 2000: A Functional Analysis of Presidential Campaign Discourse
William L. Benoit, John P. McHale, Glenn J. Hansen, P. M. Pier, and John P. McGuire
Strategic Political Communication: Rethinking Social Influence, Persuasion, and Propaganda
Karen S. Johnson-Cartee and Gary Copeland
Inventing a Voice: The Rhetoric of American First Ladies of the Twentieth Century
Edited by Molly Meijer Wertheimer
Communicating for Change: Strategies of Social and Political Advocates
John P. McHale
Political Campaign Communication: Principles and Practices, Fifth Edition
Judith S. Trent and Robert V. Friedenberg
The Rhetoric of Redemption: Kenneth Burke's Redemption Drama and Martin Luther King, Jr.'s "I Have a Dream" Speech
David A. Bobbitt
Reelpolitik II: Political Ideologies in '50s and '60s Films
Beverly Merrill Kelley
New Frontiers in International Communication Theory
Edited by Mehdi Semati
Entertaining Politics: New Political Television and Civic Culture
Jeffrey P. Jones
News Narratives and News Framing: Constructing Political Reality
Karen S. Johnson-Cartee
The Talk of the Party: Political Labels, Symbolic Capital, and American Life
Sharon E. Jarvis

Forthcoming

Presidential Candidate Images
Edited by Kenneth L. Hacker
Leading Ladies of the White House: Communication Strategies of Notable Twentieth Century First Ladies
Edited by Molly Meijer Wertheimer
Bring 'Em On: Media and Politics in the Iraq War
Edited by Lee Artz and Yahya R. Kamalipour
Women's Political Discourse
Molly A. Mayhead and Brenda DeVore Marshall
The 2004 Presidential Campaign
Edited by Robert E. Denton, Jr.
Making Sense of Political Ideology
Bernard L. Brock, Mark E. Huglen, James F. Klumpp, and Sharon Howell
Politeness and Political Debate
Edward A. Hinck, Shelly S. Hinck, and William O. Dailey
Bush at War
Jim A. Kuypers
Media and the Staging of American Politics
Gary C. Woodward
Towel Snapping the Press
James E. Mueller
Covering Rogue States
Michael Parks and Lyn Boyd Judson

THE TALK OF THE PARTY

Political Labels, Symbolic Capital, and American Life

Sharon E. Jarvis

ROWMAN & LITTLEFIELD PUBLISHERS, INC.
Lanham • Boulder • New York • Toronto • Oxford

ROWMAN & LITTLEFIELD PUBLISHERS, INC.

Published in the United States of America
by Rowman & Littlefield Publishers, Inc.
A wholly owned subsidiary of The Rowman & Littlefield Publishing Group, Inc.
4501 Forbes Boulevard, Suite 200, Lanham, Maryland 20706
www.rowmanlittlefield.com

P.O. Box 317, Oxford OX2 9RU, UK

British Library Cataloging in Publication Information Available

Library of Congress Cataloging-in-Publication Data
Jarvis, Sharon E., 1969–
  The talk of the party : political labels, symbolic capital, and American life /
Sharon E. Jarvis.
    p.   cm. — (Communication, media, and politics)
  Includes bibliographical references and index.
  ISBN 0-7425-3856-7 (c.: alk. paper) — ISBN 0-7425-3857-5 (pbk. : alk. paper)
    1. Political parties—United States. 2. Political culture—United States. 3. United
States—Politics and government—1945–1989. 4. United States—Politics and
government—1989– I. Title. II. Series.
JK2265.J37 2005
  324.273—dc22

                                                          2005001114

Printed in the United States of America

∞™ The paper used in this publication meets the minimum requirements of
American National Standard for Information Sciences—Permanence of Paper for
Printed Library Materials, ANSI/NISO Z39.48-1992.

CONTENTS

FIGURES AND TABLES

LIST OF FIGURES

LIST OF TABLES

ACKNOWLEDGMENTS

When Ted Williams, the last .400 hitter, arrived in Boston for his first season, he said, with the openness of a Westerner and the innocence of a 20-year-old, "All I want out of life is that when I walk down the street folks will say, 'There goes the greatest hitter who ever lived.'" Today, if you see Williams walking down the street and you say, "There goes the greatest hitter who ever lived," you may get an argument but you will not get derision. He won 6 batting titles and lost another by one hit. (In 1949 George Kell batted .3429, Williams .3427.) He batted .406 in 1941 and .388 in 1957, when his 38-year-old legs surely cost him at least the 5 hits that would have given him his second .400 season.

The hard blue glow from people like Williams lights the path of progress in any field. . . . Baseball is hard and demands much drudgery. But it is neither romantic nor sentimental to say that those who pay the price for excellence in any demanding discipline are heroes. Cool realism recognizes that they are necessary. As a character says in Bernard Malamud's baseball novel, *The Natural*, when we are without heroes, we "don't know how far we can go."

—George Will, *Men at Work*[1]

There is a team of heroes in my life who have motivated me to go further than I ever imagined. Without them, this book would not have been possible. Because the following chapters are organized around three themes (symbols, power, and the intersection of these forces), the acknowledgments proceed in that order.

I would like to start by thanking a set of individuals without whose symbolic support this project could not have been completed. My colleagues on the faculty in the Department of Communication Studies and undergraduate and graduate students in political communication at the University of Texas have provided an inspiring and encouraging place to think about the meanings of partisanship and party labels. Specific thanks go to Deanna Matthews, Jennifer Betancourt, Barry Brummett, and the staff at the Annette Strauss Institute for Civic Participation for your many kindnesses. Additional and invaluable support has come from Brenda Hadenfeldt and colleagues at Rowman & Littlefield, Cheryl Niekamp, Kristin Johnson, Vanessa Beasley, Kathy Kendall, Kate Kenski, Brian Siegel, Tony Bernal, Stacey Connaughton, and my Phillips family.

Next, I would like to acknowledge a group whose brute force and sheer muscle have inspired and nurtured my desire to study one of America's most powerful institutions. I am grateful to a stellar Master's Advisor and Dissertation Committee, who helped to guide many of the early ideas addressed here: Professors Hank Kenski, John Daly, Maxwell McCombs, and Chuck Whitney. Next, I am indebted to a group who simply do not scare easy: Anne and Dick Duey, Bill Jarvis, Margaret Surratt, Mark Harkrider, Mary Dixson, Kim Hughes, and Meredith Hardy. All of your talents and influences are genuinely appreciated.

Finally, it is impossible for me to think about this book without applauding two commanding influences: Roderick P. Hart and Walter Dean Burnham. Your careers have been bold, your questions fundamental, and your examples inspiring and impeccable. Your humility and gracefulness will prevent you from ever being booed like the power hitters addressed in this book (Ted Williams and Reggie Jackson), but please know that your successes have been equally great and richly noted.

NOTE

1. George Will, *Men at Work: The Craft of Baseball* (New York: Harper Perennial, 1990), 229–30.

Introduction

PARTIES AND POWER

Fans don't boo nobodies.

—Reggie Jackson

Baseball great Reggie Jackson was a polarizing force. On one hand, this flamboyant, self-proclaimed "straw who stirred the drink" with an IQ of 160 offended millions of baseball fans with his all-or-nothing approach to offense and his truly lackluster defense. Jackson—who admitted to being "embarrassed by short home runs"—achieved the title of baseball's all-time strikeout king (fanning 2,597 times, or one out of every four at bats) and is a record holder for "most consecutive seasons leading the American League in errors."[1] For many fans, then, his braggadocio (especially in light of his inconsistent and self-important play) was off-putting. Others, however, did not seem to mind. These fans were thrilled by this power hitter who led three different ball clubs to win ten division titles, six pennants, and five championships and who earned the title "Mr. October" for slugging home runs in four consecutive at bats in the 1977 World Series.[2] For this group, Jackson's Hall of Fame mouth matched his Hall of Fame play.

Although Jackson is primarily remembered as a sports star, he is also a keen rhetorical theorist, as revealed by his aforementioned statement. Indeed, rather than fretting about the fans who responded to him negatively, he advanced a grander rationale for their impolite behavior: their aspersions proved that he mattered.

As is almost always the case, what is true in baseball is true in general, and this study of political parties is inspired by Jackson's principle: to be criticized is to be significant, to be noticed, and to hold power—however fleeting—over one's critics. A parallel can therefore be drawn between

1

Reggie Jackson and the major political parties in the United States: both command attention, even when they are not universally loved.

To date, political scientists have produced an impressive body of literature on the American party system, describing why parties form, detailing what they do, tracing their roles throughout history, and explaining their ideological perspectives. These theorists have conceptualized and measured parties in the United States and abroad as well as theorized about them in explanatory, predictive, and normative ways. Moreover, scholars have debated the "vitality" of parties, applauding and bemoaning their roles in the American body politic. While many researchers have contributed to this debate, few have taken time to stand back and listen to its contours, to learn more about what these discussions mean for the symbolic and political capital of the major parties as well as that for the American party system. Thus, some basic questions remain to be asked, including the following: How have party labels been talked about in public conversations during the second half of the twentieth century? and How have such discussions shaped the ways that Americans understand parties in 2004?

These questions are bigger than they first appear, largely because they tap into an ambivalence Americans have felt toward parties for the past two hundred years. According to political scholar Gary Orren, "the modern political party is a remarkable innovation since political parties had to battle the personal prejudices of the Founding Fathers in order to establish themselves in the political life of the republic."[3] Nevertheless, political parties formed, in Orren's mind, for one simple reason: they were indispensable. Orren writes,

> In no other democracy has there been a greater need for an integrating mechanism like a political party. This need is rooted in two particular characteristics of American politics. First, America retains an archaic, eighteenth century form of government in which power is fragmented within and among many institutions which share authority. The vast number of veto points in this system makes action difficult and inaction easy. Parties serve as a method for aggregating popular choices, tying these conflicts over courses of action to a broader program, and thus making compromise rather than veto the general form of resolution. Second, the demand for widespread popular participation emerged earlier and has proceeded further in the United States than elsewhere. The American public has achieved a greater voice in political affairs through the steady extension of the franchise, increases in the number of public officials subject to popular approval at the polls, and the involvement of citizens in the selection of party nominees. Political parties are needed to

harness the participation of a powerful citizenry and fashion a coherent message out of the din of voices.[4]

Even though parties serve these important functions, Orren reminds us that "in no other democracy does the anti-organizational spirit run deeper." Because parties, as collectives, challenge the individualistic and populist spirit of American culture, a continuing theme in U.S. political history has been a "conflict between the obvious need for political parties and the public discomfit with them."[5]

The following project was inspired by the mixed feelings that Orren describes, the rhetorical wisdom Jackson embodies, and a genuine desire to learn more about the contemporary understandings of party labels in the 2004 campaign. To better understand how party labels have been discussed, this project reports data from an extensive content analysis keying on six pivotal words (*Democrat, Republican, independent, party, liberal,* and *conservative*— and their derivatives) as they appeared in campaign discourse (presidential speeches, and news coverage of these speeches, covering over fourteen elections) and in discussions of governance (debates in the U.S. House of Representatives on race relations—1957, 1964, 1979, and 1995—and depictions in civics textbooks, 1950–1997). The design of this project relies on a set of assumptions: these six party terms serve as the obvious and nonobvious markers of partisanship over the past half century; these sets of discourse represent the remarks of four elite voices who help to manage the meanings of parties in the United States; and these years cover a period of change for the parties, a time between considerable levels of party loyalty and the ascendancy of television and candidate-centered campaigns.

Chapter 1 begins with a discussion of the fate of the term *liberal*. It then reviews theoretical research on the power of naming; explains the intersection of names, labels, and brands; details shifts in the information environment over the past fifty years; and blends work from communication, political science, and marketing to discuss how citizens make sense of brands, labels, and their identities in a crowded message marketplace. To understand the talk of the party in campaign 2004 is to understand these key shifts in American culture.

After chapter 1 sets the stage for the project, chapter 2 provides its conceptual rationale. Specifically, the second chapter makes a case to attend to both the political and symbolic capital of parties. This discussion of the symbolic capital of parties rests on four assumptions: first, citizens come to know politics through discourse (and thus the attractiveness of party labels is consequential);[6] second, citizen discourse is led, but not determined, by elite discourse;[7] third, the uses of labels function as powerful shortcuts in modern life and have been shown to have important psychological effects on citizens;[8] and, fourth, the meanings of political terms shift with time, as meanings may become broader, narrower, or may change entirely.[9]

The next four chapters offer four perspectives on how party labels have been discussed by elites in the United States. Chapter 3 casts the widest net possible, searching for patterns in label use that transcend word, speaker, and year. Specifically, this chapter details how elites have used party labels continually (having employed them at relatively equal rates throughout the past fifty years—despite periods of strength, decline, and resurgence), hierarchically (using tokens to describe partisans as elites), and skeletally (focusing on loose party coalitions, thereby describing "thin" versus "thick" partisanship). In these ways, parties have never been forsaken, have not had their privileged positions challenged, and yet, surprisingly, have not been discussed in detailed ways. This chapter concludes by addressing these themes in light of how such patterns—visibility, elite status, and thin description—affect parties' symbolic capital.

While chapter 3 addresses dominant themes in party language use, chapter 4 looks underneath them for trends over time. Perhaps not surprisingly, the patterns show linguistic support for the key political theories of the periods under study: between 1948 and 1960, party labels were portrayed as collectives (as the pluralist theorists might predict); between 1961 and 1979, they were described as moving from an elite level to a mass level (as critical realignment scholars might expect); between 1980 and 1999, they were associated with frenetic action and a splintered body politic (as contemporary trends of candidate-centered campaigning might forecast); and in campaign 2000, the George W. Bush campaign emphasized a desire to work with "both Democrats and Republicans" (and thus his "uniter not a divider" approach led to a rhetorical resurgence of sorts for party labels, which was picked up in news reports), whereas the Al Gore campaign continued to speak in the niche-marketing style of the earlier era. Chapter 4 closes by observing how W. Bush's approach created symbolic opportunities for him and his party in 2000 and 2004.

The four sets of elites in this study have differing needs for political parties, and chapter 5 presents their idiosyncratic perspectives on partisanship. This chapter details how legislators used party labels to sharpen partisanship and mobilize teamwork, how journalists used these terms in personalized and dramatic ways, how candidates preferred a careful and useful constitution of parties, and how textbook authors celebrated and inflated the language of partisanship. Chapter 5 focuses on the distinct needs for the parties and on the way these needs influence how elites discuss these labels. In doing so, it attends to how these actors use, and in turn are used by, party labels and how their language affects the symbolic capital of these organizations.

Chapter 6 illustrates how elites constitute parties in language and shows how their voices prefer some aspects of partisanship to others. Specifically, the chapter details how these elites have protected the stability of the terms *Democrat*, *Republican*, and *party*; praised the populism associated with the *independent* label; condemned the ideology connected with the word *liberal*; and used the term *conservative* sparingly (until, of course, it was embraced and promoted by Republicans in 2000). This chapter traces how individual labels have shifted in American politics and concludes by commenting on how the relative attractiveness of such terms can have effects on the voting public.

Chapter 7 returns to the context established in chapter 1, and in reconciling the findings presented in chapters 3 through 6, it discusses how Republican candidates and legislators have exercised considerable discipline in demoting the term *liberal*, in placing the *Republican* brand name closer to citizens, and in forestalling critique of the term *conservative*. While neither party can completely control the uses of its words—indeed, cultural and political forces are operating on all of these words at any given time—this project shows how brand consistency has yielded a net symbolic gain for the Republican party as the nation headed into the 2004 presidential campaign. Additionally, chapter 7 details how even though Americans have never loved parties, American elites have a strong tradition of talking about them and have generally used party labels in ways that contribute to their political potency in the United States. Because Americans are more likely to come to know parties through language than through other partisan activities, because elite voices continue to symbolically sanction the two-party system, and because one party has been more organized in its label use than has the opposition, listening to the talk of the party teaches valuable lessons about public understandings of these organizations in the 2004 campaign and into the future.

NOTES

1. See "Errors by Outfielders," *Baseball-Almanac.com*, www.baseball-almanac.com/recbook/rb_ofer.shtml (14 July 2004).

2. "Reggie Jackson," *Baseball-Reference.com*, www.baseball-reference.com/j/jacksre01.shtml (14 July 2004).

3. Gary Orren, "The Changing Styles of American Party Politics," in *The Future of American Political Parties: The Challenge of Governance*, ed. J. L. Fleishman (Englewood Cliffs, N.J.: Prentice Hall, 1982), 4–41, 4.

4. Orren, "Changing Styles," 5.

5. Orren, "Changing Styles," 5.

6. Murray Edelman, *Political Language* (New York: Academic Press, 1977).

7. Phillip Converse, "The Nature of Belief Systems in Mass Publics," in *Ideology and Discontent*, ed. D. E. Apter (New York: Free Press, 1964), 206–61; John Zaller, *The Nature and Origins of Mass Opinion* (Cambridge: Cambridge University Press, 1992).

8. James Pennebaker, Matthias Mehl, and Kimberly Niederhoffer, "Psychological Aspects of Natural Language Use: Our Words, Our Selves," *Annual Review of Psychology* 54 (2003): 547–77.

9. Victoria Fromkin and Robert Rodman, *An Introduction to Language* (New York: Holt, Rinehart and Winston, 1974).

1

POLITICAL BRANDING, 1948–2004

Once upon a time, Democratic presidential candidates were proud of the word *liberal* and even trumpeted the term in their campaign speeches. Consider the following statements.[1]

In 1948, Harry Truman told an audience that he was "happy to pay tribute to the *liberal* spirit of the forces of labor in the United States" and wanted "to reiterate emphatically [his] faith in the *liberal* philosophy of the Democratic party."[2] In 1952, Adlai Stevenson coupled the term *liberals* with those who "do not want to cause harm to the innocent."[3] In 1956, Stevenson went a step further, by praising the "new leadership in the Democratic Party: young, *liberal*, creative" and by closing one of his more artful campaign speeches as follows: "now I bid you goodnight, with a full heart and a fervent prayer that we will meet often again in the *liberals'* everlasting battle against ignorance, poverty, misery and war."[4] And, in 1960, John F. Kennedy even went so far as to connect the term with best business practices, telling voters, "It is sound, *liberal* policy to see that our productive plant is the best and most modern in the world."[5] As odd as these proclamations sound to a contemporary ear, there was a time not too long ago when Democrats associated the *liberal* label with loyal constituencies, electoral victory, cherished ideals, and even sound economic policies.

Times sure have changed. In 1964, Republican presidential candidate Barry Goldwater began to question the term, and his opponent—Democrat Lyndon Baines Johnson—did little, rhetorically, to defend it. By the 1980s and 1990s, Goldwater's instincts and Johnson's reluctance became normalized. In those years, GOP candidates Ronald Reagan, George H. W. Bush, and Bob Dole used the term with increasing regularity and force, and their Democratic opponents avoided it entirely. In the early days of the 2004 campaign, Democratic presidential candidate John Kerry also steered clear of this term (although it is important to note that Republican and conservative actors used it to refer to this "Democrat from Massachusetts"). One of Kerry's biggest supporters, Senator Ted Kennedy, worked to protect Kerry from the label. In an interview with NBC's Tim Russert, for example, Kennedy would not respond yes to the question: "Is Kerry a *liberal?*" Instead, Kennedy responded, "John Kerry believes as I do that labels don't make a lot of sense." These words had barely left his mouth, however, before the senator went on to question President George W. Bush's right to use the *conservative* label, given the president's level of "spending on the Iraq war."[6]

Whether they "make sense" to Kennedy and Kerry or not, labels—particularly the *liberal* one—have a place in contemporary political life. In moments of campaigns and governance, labels are hurled at (and sometimes sidestepped by) politicians; they are promoted and decried by surrogates; they are manufactured and disseminated by movements and interest groups; and they are watched closely by the modern-day press. Are they newsworthy? Someone behind a news column appearing in the *New York Times* during the summer of 2003 seemed to think so. At that time, readers were presented with the following discussion, a story entirely devoted to the *liberal* label for its news value:

> Even as the Democratic presidential contenders wrangle over their places on the political spectrum, Republicans see them as pretty much the same. Consider how the Republican National Committee on its Web site described the would-be presidents:
> Howard Dean: "an ultra-*liberal* on social issues who is out of the mainstream and wrong for America"
> John Edwards: "An unaccomplished *liberal* in moderate clothing"
> Richard A. Gephardt: "Keeper of the *liberal* flame"
> Bob Graham: "A tax-and-spend *liberal* in moderate's clothing"
> John Kerry: "A Massachusetts *liberal* out of touch with America"
> Dennis Kucinich: "A flip-flopping *liberal* extremist"
> Carol Moseley Braun: "A controversial *liberal* who was rejected by her own state"
> The Rev. Al Sharpton: "A *liberal* Democrat out of touch with America"
> Somehow, Joseph I. Lieberman escaped similar portraiture. He is described instead as an equivocator on a "journey from populist, to moderate, to moralist and back again." At least he's not a *liberal.*[7]

While the material featured in this column departs somewhat from some of the most rudimentary definitions of what journalists look for in news—the who, what, where, when, and why of a situation or an event—the focus and adornment of the *liberal* label does complement another type of news value: the drama inherent in horse-race coverage. Much of campaign reporting at the close of the twentieth century, scholars have argued, has focused on who is ahead, behind, and catching up. In the aforementioned instance, the demotion of a label features a sense of loss—a loss legitimated through newsprint. Due to some clever name-calling, the *liberal* label is in trouble here; so much trouble that it got its own news story.

Of course, the *L* word is not the only term to drift in contemporary American politics. The term *independent* has shifted considerably over the past half century, too, although the movement surrounding this term may be less noticeable because it has been slower and the rhetorical ground gained has been more gradual. Indeed, it may have been difficult to fully appreciate the symbolic purchase of the term *independent* at the time this book was written, for American citizens appeared to have been in the midst of the term's cultural peak. But consider for a moment how the term was bantered about sixty years ago in campaign news coverage. In the 1950s, for instance, the term *independent* most often appeared as a mere demographic marker in print news ("the so-called independent vote").[8] When independent voters were described, they were often constructed as individuals who frustrated the efforts of the two major party nominees to get elected. In a sense, then, they were depicted as a destructive force rather than a constructive force, as in this clause from the *Washington Post* in 1960: "In both Mississippi and Louisiana *independent* electors are expected to draw support away from the Democratic ticket."[9] Although this may appear to be a modest sentence, it is telling of how independents were once treated in the news. That is, when loyalty to the two major parties was more common, independents were discussed as actors outside the political drama, annoying siphons on the political scene.

By the 1980s, however, the tone and role of the depiction of this label had improved. In that year, John Anderson's run for the presidency as an Independent Party candidate lent the term some institutional purchase at the elite level, even if many of the discussions of his label continued to be associated with limited resources ("the *independent* candidate's establishing the validity of his campaign, already troubled by a lack of funds and declining support in some states"),[10] a losing candidacy ("John B. Anderson, the *independent* candidate, was not leading in any states"),[11] and a position outside of the major contention of American politics ("*Independent* John B. Anderson is no longer a viable candidate").[12] Nonetheless, a set of factors helped to promote the *independent* label from one of nuisance to genuine curiosity, including the public nature of his candidacy (as well as his relative centrism and prior status as a U.S. representative), changes in news norms, an increase in split-ticket voting, an alignment of many traditionally Democratic voters with Republican Ronald Reagan, and a combination of these elements. These factors may have put the independent on the journalistic beat in a new way, and by 1984 independent voters were no longer feckless frustrations that were ignored and devalued. Notice how the following independent voters add to the campaign narrative; rather than disrupt the predictability of the process, Mr. Alioto and Ms. Johnson possess agency and autonomy and provide assistance to the system by ultimately supporting a major party candidate:

- "Fruit-stand operator Michael Alioto, an *independent*, arrived undecided, thought Bush was 'intimidated' by Ferraro's strong performance and left undecided—but saying that, if forced to choose now, he probably would pick Reagan."[13]
- "Sanford Johnson's wife, Dian, moved in the same direction as her husband, but went a notch further to the left. She is a professional artist and a political *independent* who went from leaning toward Mondale to falling solidly behind him."[14]

As these clauses preview, the independent voter had blossomed in campaign reporting by 1984. And judging by contemporary coverage—which values the uncertainty associated with these unpredictable voters, as well as the candidate efforts to track them down and court them—the independent voter continues to be a valuable construction, if not the most valued construction, in modern campaign reporting (as explored in chapter 6).

Now, in one sense, the ruin of the term *liberal* and the relative ascendancy of *independent* could be regarded as simple stylistic choices. Behavioralist scholars, for instance, might crave a demonstration of the impact of these shifts before such word uses are given serious attention. While the goal of this book is not to directly engage in such empirical assessments, it is important to note at the outset that there have been a set of compelling trends that covary with the ways in which these words have been discussed over time. The trajectory of the word *liberal*, as shown here, shows how a term related to partisanship has amassed meanings over the years that have been largely influenced by one set of strategic actors and, as this book details, that have not been countered by another set of forces. Moreover, the uses of *liberal* correlate with two significant trends in public opinion data: politically, the uses of this term have not flushed out America's desire for state programs that provide assistance to citizens; symbolically, however, these same data show that Americans are less likely to support said policies when the *liberal* label is coupled with them.[15]

In the case of the *independent* label, it seems solidly attached to burgeoning cultural norms in the polity. Americans have long been ambivalent about political parties, but as Michael Schudson's *The Good Citizen* outlines, citizens were far more likely to belong to groups and identify with political parties during the latter part of the nineteenth century and the first half of the twentieth century than they are today.[16] Could such political trends be partially explained by the ways in which journalists have been invoking independent voters in campaign news coverage? Charles Kesler seems to believe so. He writes, "Over the course of the 20th century, voters became more and more educated and often what they learned was that partisanship itself was obsolete, selfish and distracting. The intelligent voter, they have learned, is the *independent* voter." Kesler believes that the most important effect of this is the "rise in the independent spirit among all voters." He concludes, "Compared to their counterparts a hundred years ago, few Americans would boast today that they vote a straight-party ticket. Even the strong Republicans and Democrats who do, don't brag about it. That would be, well, déclassé."[17] This rise in independent spirit, interestingly, has not increased the political capital of independent candidates; despite the attractiveness of the term, very few non–major party candidates enjoy electoral success in the United States.

So, how is it that sentiment about the *liberal* label departs from sentiment about liberal policies? How is it that the emerging autonomy of the *independent* label has leapfrogged ahead of its political currency? To use either of these terms is simply to use language, to talk about politics. But, it is also, as the *New York Times* column on liberals illustrates, to engage in name-calling—a process that this book takes seriously, for it is through such acts that words such as *liberal* and *independent* begin to take on or shed meanings for the two political parties.

A central argument of *The Talk of the Party* is that naming is critical in political life. This contention rests on a few assumptions. First, names serve as shortcuts for citizens that help them make sense of politics, particularly as Americans move into an overcommunicated information age. Second, names are dynamic entities for political organizations, ones that can be either positioned successfully and adorned with positive characteristics or repositioned by opponents or the media and saddled with negative connotations. Third, in the United States, naming takes place in a polity that is an heir to one of the most stable party systems in the history of democratic life.

And yet, as the fates of the *liberal* and *independent* labels preview, some of the terms related to partisanship in this stable system are decidedly unstable.

The goal of this book is to listen to how the language of partisanship has been used during an important fifty-year period in American life to learn more about how label use has created and constrained opportunities for politics. Like many books on the subject, this text observes that the major parties continue to have considerable political capital in our system. Unlike other books, though, it comes to this conclusion by tracking parties' symbolic capital and shows how the terms of partisanship have gathered an assortment of connotations over time. As the following chapters show, sometimes these connotations are positive (as in the case of the term *independent*), sometimes they are negative (as in the case of the term *liberal*), and sometimes they are curiously entrenched (as in the case of *party*, *Democrat*, and *Republican*). It is always the case, however, that the ways in which labels are used influence the parties' brand names and, in turn, affect candidates' abilities to connect with voters, to gain elected office, and, ultimately, to govern. For these reasons, the sounds of partisanship merit our close attention.

NAMES, LABELS, AND BRANDS

Figure 1.1 features two *W*s, and both of them have a story to tell. The *W* on the right belongs to a hotel in the Starwood Hotel chain. What, exactly, does this initial represent? A set of things, depending on the marketing materials solicited. According to the hotel's website, "it starts with the name . . . W for warm, wonderful, witty, wired. W for welcome."[18] Early press coverage of the hotel provided a bit of a different description of the *W*. In such coverage, general manager Carlton Hudson of the W French Quarter hotel (in New Orleans) is quoted as saying, "W stands for Wonderful . . . Worldly. Witty. Warm. Whimsical . . . Why hasn't anyone done it before. Whatever. Whenever." Another set of promotional materials mentioned in coverage of the chain emphasizes the terms in a different order: *W* to "witty, warm, wonderful, worldly and welcoming."[19]

This *W* brand began in 1998 and was spearheaded by CEO of Starwood Hotels, Barry Sternlicht. The first hotel in the chain was the W New York, whose success led to the opening of four additional hotels in a two-year span (Sydney, Los Angeles, Honolulu, and New Orleans). These venues, which purportedly combine the "the personality and style of an independent hotel with the reliability, consistency and attentive service of a major business hotel,"[20] have become one of the most successful new hotel

Figure 1.1.   W the brand in 2004
Source: "W the President," www.george
wbushstore.com/w_pres.htm; "W Hotels," www.starwood.com/whotels/
index.html.

brands in the United States since 1998. No small feat, this, for it means that the hotel weathered (1) a downturn in the economy between 2000 and 2004, (2) post–September 11 travel concerns, and (3) the SARS outbreak— all of which have decreased travel and spelled complications for rival hotels during this period.[21] This *W*, then, has picked up business share against other hotels, which, at a lower price point, should be enjoying greater success in a post–September 11 market. Going into campaign 2004, this *W* was a winning brand.

The *W* on the left surfaced in the year 2002 and became more visible during the summer of the 2004 campaign. As the campaign heated up, this *W*, followed by the words *the President*, began to be spotted on square black signs in the audience of President Bush's campaign events. It also appeared on his campaign website, where citizens could purchase a variety of items featuring the letter, including bumper stickers, T-shirts, coffee mugs, tote bags, ball caps, squeeze bottles, and even a silver belt buckle. This *W* was designed by Ted Jackson, CEO of English Emprise. Jackson's work on the *W* became the fodder of an academic article published by rhetorical scholar Dion Dennis, who observes how the *W* emblem departed from earlier merchandising efforts in that it represented a movement away from "kitsch and chum."[22] In Dennis's mind, this *W* represents an effort to invent a sophisticated and integrated new brand: the brand of George W. Bush.

Why would Jackson (on behalf of the Bush campaign) move in this direction? Dennis answers this question by citing materials written by Jackson himself and by inserting the words *citizens* and *politicians* at the appropriate spots. The advertiser notes:

> "Today's society is undeniably brand conscious. We're attracted to brands that project messages we like. . . . Forward-thinking companies [politicians] understand that if their brand carries a message, it carries equity. Companies [politicians] now are using that equity to deepen relationships with customers [citizens] by offering supporting products

that reflect the personality of the brand. It's called relationship marketing, and it works.

"By using a brand strategy, you can help your customers [citizens] stand out in a crowded field of competing messages—which makes you stand out among your competitors. . . . While rarely increasing cost, branded products carry a higher perceived value than unbranded products. . . . Customers [citizens] enjoy receiving high-quality products of a company [politician] they like or recognize."[23]

Jackson sums by suggesting that all of these steps can bring an audience closer to the product or the politician and that they can encourage long-term relationships with the target of identification.

Jackson's *W* did not just garner scholarly attention. Others noticed the *W*, too, and one such column was quick to point out the similarities between the *W the President* label and the *W* brand of Starwood Hotels. The column comments as follows on the similarity of the symbols:

Paging the attorneys who represent Starwood Hotels: it might be time to mail a cease and desist letter to the White House. The folks who manage George Bush's online campaign have unveiled their latest creation, a website that seems to borrow heavily from W Hotels. The same black and white design. The same all-black merchandise with a small "W" logo in the corner. (The only difference is that the word "Hotels" has been replaced with "The President.") And the confusion's probably deliberate, too. You can totally imagine Bush staffers sitting around trying to come up with ways to make W gear more appealing to a younger, hipper audience. But considering that Barry Sternlicht, the CEO of Starwood, is a Democrat, we're guessing that the similarity might not be appreciated.[24]

The presidential *W* also made the *New York Post* gossip column, of all places, where it was observed how the *W* might affect the brand position of the hotel chain.

The W hotel chain is aggressively laying claim to the letter W, no matter what President Bush's nickname is. The group behind the chain, Starwood Hotels & Resorts Worldwide Inc., has fired off legal letters to two political merchandisers, demanding they remove the letter W—as in George W. Bush—from "apparel and accessories" they are selling. The offending items include baseball hats and T-shirts "that mimic the trade dress of the W hotels, which has the effect of eroding the unique brand identity developed in the W logo."[25]

A citizen from Texas, too, got in on the act of commenting on the *W*. During the summer of 2004, Gerald L. Horst wrote a letter to the editor of the *San Antonio Express News* in response to a letter from another Texan (Mr. Looney), who had suggested that referring to the president as *W* was disrespectful.[26] Wrote Mr. Horst,

> *Re: the letter "Lack of respect for America" by Stephen W. Looney (July 25):*
> Mr. Looney writes, "Every time someone refers to our president as 'Dubya' they are showing themselves for the lowlifes they are."
> Mr. Looney needs to lighten up a bit. Perhaps a visit to the official George W. Bush web site, www.georgewbush.com, where the campaign is selling ball caps, tote bags and T-shirts with the "W" logo, would show President Bush and his closest supporters (lowlifes, I think not) call him "W" and Dubya. It is not necessarily a term of disrespect.
> There is also www.GoDubya.com, which points you to the www .georgewbush.com web site.

As campaign 2004 wore on, attention to *W*s and concerns that Sternlicht might take on the campaign quieted, most likely because of the close nature of the final days of the campaign. This quietening does not negate the initial interest in the *W*s—an interest that transcended profession and space. So, what was it about the *W* that caught the attention of scholars, journalists, gossip columnists, and letter writers? What encouraged Dennis to analyze it, a columnist to point out that the CEO of Starwood Hotels probably would not support it, a gossip page to comment on whether the hotel chain would contest it, and a citizen to stand up for the integrity of the letter? What was it about a white letter on a black square that made these individuals pause, prompt them to speak, and put the *W* in a variety of news contexts? One simple answer to all of these questions is that *W* is a name—a brand name—and in 2004, as observers from all walks of life know, that is serious business.

That is, in a society with twenty-four-hour news, a proliferation of cable news channels, constantly updated Internet sites, and insurgent blogs, political observers and pundits are constantly searching for topics to fill their air time and columns. The "strategy" of the candidates and campaigns, of course, becomes safe fodder for discussion and lends itself to incessant chatter. This was particularly the case in 2004. Not only was this a close campaign surrounded by concerns of a polarized electorate and division between the "red" and "blue" states, but it also followed the split outcome of the 2000 presidential election (in which Al Gore won the popular vote and George W. Bush the electoral vote) and a set of politically charged 2002 midterm campaigns (in which the Republican party had a strong showing in the first election after the 2000 recount and after the September 11 terrorist attacks). One topic that received considerable attention—and that may have helped to make the *W the President* so notable—is a story about Republicans' success in studying, mastering, and managing their message in campaigns 1994–2004: in branding both their president and their party label. This narrative has been both praised and bemoaned in an unprecedented number of books, memoirs, columns, and commentaries, and many of these stories applauded and critiqued a perceived Republican advantage in language and strategy as well as the construction of an information infrastructure to disseminate their message.

A variety of stories have appeared on the topic of Republican language, and one of the most visible ones has focused on the successes of wordsmith Frank Luntz. Luntz had become an oft-cited wordsmith by 2004, but it was his symbolic efforts ten years earlier that really promoted him to the public eye for journalists and political junkies. In 1994, Luntz researched and wrote *Language of the 21st Century*, a document produced for Speaker Newt Gingrich and the newly elected Republican majority in the U.S. House of Representatives. In his cover letter to the document, Luntz explains that Speaker Gingrich had challenged him to "find the words and phrases that would enable Republicans of all stripes to define their vision and explain their politics to the American people." And in that document, Luntz delivered.

The materials that he created in response to this challenge featured a savvy and accessible read of many of the best practices of social scientific understandings of language patterns, and these materials did something that many academic reports have yet to do: get in the hands of politicians and directly affect contemporary campaign strategies and the policy debate. Specifically, advice emanating from polling data, focus groups, and Luntz's acclaimed ear included the following: avoid references to "inside-the-Beltway words and programs" (noting "Our constituents don't talk like this, and neither should you"); phrase statements as optimistically as possible (calling attention to how Americans are much more willing to "not give" than to "deny" something); be mindful that Americans are "rights conscious" and "choice oriented" (emphasizing that winning messages do not make the audience feel as is they are making a complicated decision or are forced to compromise); and be careful about how issues are framed (revealing how polling data show that "by 2 to 1, Americans think too much is spent on welfare, but by 10 to 1, Americans think too little is spent on aid to the poor").

Luntz concludes the introduction to *Language of the 21st Century* by calling for a "calmer and quieter political discourse," encouraging Republicans to "understand public anger without overly expressing anger yourself" and to "express emotion without being loud." This is advice that he repeated in 1996 (when he urged House members to soften their sound after his data showed that many voters believed that the "government-bashing" of the new Republican majority was not in sync with their desires) and again in 1999 (when polls showed that millions of Americans were angrier at Republicans in Congress and independent prosecutor Kenneth Starr than they were at President Bill Clinton, who had been impeached one year prior). Moving into the 2000 campaigns, Luntz advised that Republicans use "power adjectives" (such as "able" and "American") that evoke "strong, positive, emotional responses in all demographic groups," and he was quoted in the *Wall Street Journal* as saying, "The tone is off," encouraging Republicans, once again, to communicate emotion without getting angry.[27] Perhaps because of his efforts and achievements or perhaps because of coverage of a wordsmith makes for terrific "strategic coverage," Luntz's tactics have caught the attention of popular presses, magazine columnists, the cable news channel MSNBC (where he holds his own program), and strategists on the Left (namely, linguist George Lakoff, who has credited Luntz's ear and ability to frame the policy debate).[28] A first aspect of the narrative going into campaign 2004, then, was that a force on the Right was attending to language use and crafting a powerful message for the Republican Party.

A second aspect of the narrative was that another force was working more specifically for President George W. Bush: Karl Rove. Introduced to the national political stage during the 2000 presidential campaign, Rove had considerable roots in Republican politics and with the Bush family.[29] He first met George H. W. Bush in 1973 when a controversy surrounding a race for chairman of the College Republicans broke out: H. W. Bush was then chair of the Republican National Committee; Rove was one of the candidates for chair; a memo surrounding the conflict was leaked to the press (on behalf of the other candidate); Bush named Rove the winner; and, according to media reports, a loyal bond was then formed. Rove also met W. Bush in 1973, and reports have it there, too, that a second loyal bond formed.

A former student of the University of Utah who journeyed around the country working on campaigns, Rove made his way to Texas and campaigned for, and then became, chief of staff of Governor Bill Clements in 1978—a lone Republican in a state that, at the time, was still dominated by Democratic statewide officeholders. While in Texas, Rove founded a direct mail company, which many believe has affected his political mind-set.

Whereas general message consultants work to develop a theme that will resonate across a broad array of potential voters, direct mail consultants focus on under-the-radar marketing strategies and on efforts to carve up a district and then mine the groups for potential likely voters. Rove's company enjoyed initial success in Republican politics, suffered a setback in 1986 when a slate of Democrats captured office, but then began to thrive in the 1990s when GOPs increasingly began to dominate statewide spots in Texas.

It was as his other Republican clients were winning that Rove courted W. Bush as a potential gubernatorial candidate in 1990. As accounts go, Bush declined, given his father's position as president. Four years later, though, there was no hesitancy. Bush ran, Rove managed, Bush won, and the pair became a story in the Lone Star state. During Bush's term as governor, Rove reportedly brought several high-profile Republican figures down to Austin to discuss a bid for the presidency. Once Bush became a candidate, and Rove a presidential campaign advisor, the national press attended to Rove more intently. Books appeared, old stories rehashed. Rove did not hide, and his "never deny anything" strategies set the tone for campaign 2000, the first term, and the 2004 campaign.[30] A set of nicknames emerged for Rove, including King Karl, Bush's Brain, Killer Karl, the Controller, Rove Rage, and Boy Genius, to name a few. Unlike other campaign managers, Rove did not sidestep the svengali treatment. Oddly enough, it was as if his tactical maneuverings and instincts added to the Bush bravado. It certainly added to the campaign capital that the team enjoyed in the press.

In a sense, the Republicans' entrepreneurial approach to language, their mastery of message, and their visible strategist all became part of the story of the 2004 campaign, particularly following the news frame in campaign 2000 that the election was "Al Gore's to lose." It was not just George W. Bush running for president in 2004, the subtext of many columns reported; it was George W. Bush the Republican candidate, buttressed by a party that had more control over its words, phrases, and message.

Another element buttressing George W. Bush's candidacy made the news in 2004—and that was the organized movement spreading language patterns like those advised by Luntz. Here, it was not just Republicans' individual efforts that gave the Republican Party a rhetorical edge; it was also a broad information infrastructure that aided their ability to disseminate their message. Much of the buzz started in books written by public intellectuals on the Left, and some of their comments received media attention and were responded to by members of the intellectual Right.

A first book that focused on a conservative information infrastructure was David Brock's *The Republican Noise Machine: Right Wing Media and How*

It Corrupts Democracy.[31] In this text, Brock—a former conservative journalist who wrote critical pieces on Anita Hill and Hillary Rodham Clinton—advances a critique of the burgeoning right-wing information industry, a composite of talk radio, cable television stations, websites, think tanks, and publishing houses. In doing so, he unveils the benefactors of these programs, questions the integrity of the scholarship emerging from conservative-funded think tanks, suggests that these entities have engaged in a seamless propaganda machine (such that claims from one outlet "echo" through others), and argues that the mainstream media, too, contribute to the echo when they air charges of "liberal" bias (in the name of "balance") rather than investigate such accusations. Eric Alterman's *What Liberal Media?* was a another book in this vein, similarly alleging a powerful and, in his mind, all-too-often-overlooked conservative bias in major media outlets.[32] Alterman's title serves as a response to conservative former CBS producer Bernard Goldberg's 2002 best-seller *Bias: A CBS Insider Exposes How the Media Distort the News,* and a central tenet of Alterman's work was that the media are too quick to cover conservative concerns with media bias (and in doing so legitimate the concerns rather than investigate or question them). Alterman voices concern that, after charges of liberal bias have been repeated, they take on a sense of truth; moreover, their repetition lead many networks to take more conservative positions on issues, a pattern that, in his mind, compounds the problem. A third piece to focus on conservative control of the media was director Robert Greenwald's film *Outfoxed,* which emerged during the heat of the 2004 campaign and forwarded a similar critique to the charges of overt and hidden conservative bias in news. For his part, Greenwald focuses specifically on FOX news, and he created a film that features interviews with media watchdogs and former FOX employees, as well as news clips, examples of footage of Democratic and Republican officials, and management memos encouraging certain types of words, topics, and perspectives.

But it was not only folks from the Left and center that contributed to the discussion of the powerful information infrastructure on the Right. Conservative Richard Viguerie's *America's Right Turn: How Conservatives Used New and Alternative Media to Take Power* offers a powerful and unapologetic discussion of the Right's efforts to gain access to the microphones of the country.[33] Specifically, he details how conservatives worked to bypass the media monopoly and traditional gatekeepers in spreading their conservative message to citizens, and he describes how conservatives imagined themselves in the business of building a long-term movement. This communication marathon of sorts started by going straight to people's homes via direct mail in the 1960s and 1970s; then it shifted to conservatives' investing in conservative groups on college campuses, building and funding think tanks to research their message and outframe their opponents, and training conservative journalists to spread their message. In this text, Viguerie comments on how conservative voices have been successful on talk radio (especially because of Ronald Reagan's repeal of the fairness doctrine in the 1980s), on the Internet, and on cable and network news programs (again, particularly because of the financial successes of FOX news—a factor that he, too, believes has led other news programs to add overtly conservative sources, voices, and journalists to their news reports).

The buzz around Republican language use and the formidable information infrastructure that disseminates these messages may be unique to campaign 2004; scholars, however, have focused on the importance of words, naming, and labels in understanding politics for quite some time. Indeed, researchers from a host of academic disciplines believe that the relative strength and connotations of names, labels, and brands play an important role in how people come to understand institutions as well as their places in any given society.

First, take sociolinguists. A central tenet of their field is that only named entities can be shared. For these scholars, language helps individuals come to understand their social situations,[34] and the process of naming entities and using names serves to shape personal thoughts.[35] As Gunther Kress and Robert Hodge explain,

> Language, which is given by society, determines which perceptions are potentially social ones. Those perceptions, fixed in language, become a kind of second nature. We inevitably impose our classifications on others, and on ourselves. Language plays a vital role in what has been called the "social construction of reality."[36]

Moreover, the process of using language, Kress and Hodge elaborate, helps to manage the unfolding construction of reality. Because they believe that "normal perception works by constant feedback," which comes to individuals through language, the space that separates the empirical world from that which is constructed is, in their minds, constantly shrinking. As a result, they contend, individuals can only see, experience, and share things that they can say.

Edward Sapir's work has been especially influential on this score. Sapir has argued that the structure of a culture's language determines the behavior and habits of thinking in that culture. In his words, human beings do not live in the objective world alone, nor alone in the world of social activity as ordinarily understood, but are very much at the mercy of the particular language which has become the medium of expression for their society. It is quite an illusion to imagine that one adjusts to reality essentially without the use of language and that language is merely an incidental means of solving specific problems of communication or reflection. The fact of the matter is that the "real world" is to a large extent unconsciously built up on the language habits of the group.[37]

A fascinating aspect of Sapir's contention is that the "language habits of a group" that "unconsciously" build up understandings of public life are dynamic. Because subtle adjustments in language use—especially those that are not immediately noticed—can build to create new habits for a group, it is critical to keep an eye on word use over time. On this point, Victoria Fromkin and Robert Rodman observe that all languages change with time because the meanings of words can expand (by taking on new meanings), contract (by shedding old meanings), or shift (by drifting to new meanings) from their original moorings.[38]

Michael Schudson has also attended to the process of naming and—more specifically—to the impact of labels in cultural and political life. He has gone so far as to argue that "little is more important than naming, marking, and reminding."[39] In his mind, individuals learn culture by observing how things are named, and people learn the importance of things, given how often they are reminded to think about such things. Because attention is a "scarce resource that culture organizes and directs," prominent, familiar, and visible names enjoy a sense of cultural authority in a given society. For Schudson, this is especially the case when specific names become so familiar that they escape notice, so normalized that they appear benign, so common that they do not call attention to themselves. And because individuals learn culture constantly, Schudson continues, the names that get used on a daily basis are made actionable in a cultural system. They "become backed with the authority of a society" and do a type of work on citizens by focusing a public's attention on one given direction as opposed to another.[40]

Kathleen Hall Jamieson has similarly attended to the power of names, and in her case she has illustrated how the process of naming can be used for political gain.[41] In an analysis of the 1988 presidential campaign, she details how the George H. W. Bush team was able to rename a criminal (from "William Horton" to "Willie Horton"), to label his actions (from rape and murder to "torture" and "terrorize"), to define a political policy (a furlough program became "weekend passes" and a "revolving door"), and to entice the media to include such phrasings in their news reports. The Bush campaign's proactivity in these rhetorical matters shifted the ways in which Americans came to know an issue ("the furlough program"). What is more, the Bush team's discipline in sticking to this language increased the likelihood that citizens heard these terms again and again.

Murray Edelman, too, has focused on the role of names and understandings of politics—an innovative perspective when his seminal *Symbolic Uses of Politics* was first published in 1964 in the field of political science. A set of his key arguments from that text and others merit mention here. Like many sociolinguists, Edelman saw a vital connection between naming and knowing. In *Symbolic Uses of Politics*, he observes how naming becomes a way of understanding things, as "the terms in which we name or speak of anything do more than designate it; they place it in a class of objects, thereby suggest with what it is to be judged and compared, and define the perspective from which it will be viewed and evaluated."[42] He then, like others, gives language a central role in people's understandings of their environments, considering language particularly influential when it "operates unconsciously for the most part, permeating perception, conception and experience."[43] These topics remerge in *Political Language*, where Edelman theorizes, "It is language that evokes most of the political 'realities' people experience";[44] "in politics, as in religion," he continues, "whatever is ceremonial or banal strengthens reassuring beliefs regardless of their validity and discourages skeptical inquiry about disturbing issues";[45] and "language is an integral facet of the political scene: not simply an instrument for describing events but itself a part of events, shaping their meaning and helping to shape the political roles officials and the general public play."[46] Accordingly, he underscores how watchers of language should work to discover how beliefs and understandings become attached to words (and not necessarily the tenability of such beliefs)[47] and to be mindful that citizens' understandings rest on their beliefs that are often tied to word use (whether or not those cognitions are accurate).[48]

In *Politics as Symbolic Action*, Edelman addresses the taken-for-grantedness of political names and places his earlier understandings of the power of even banal linguistic choices in a social context.[49] He forewarns, "Because the pressures are strong to conform to the conventional language style of whatever group one is in, innovative and rebellious behavior is rare." In most cases, he continues, most people do not "consciously decide against being innovative or rebellious. The language they speak makes it unlikely that they will even think of it."[50]

Edelman returns to naming in *Political Language* and details how in the case of poverty, "naming" can aid or prevent the creation of public policy by giving choices to politicians and the public.[51] Specifically, Edelman discusses how when a phrase such as "the deserving poor" is introduced into a policy debate, new choices emerge. Should the government help the "deserving" poor? What should be done with the "undeserving" poor (a rhetorical by-product of the deserving poor)? Do both groups deserve help? The very creation of a symbol for the deserving poor, concludes Edelman, encourages (1) government to do nothing for millions of poor people (after verbally categorizing them as "undeserving") and (2) impoverished citizens to regard other poor people as "undeserving" (siding with governmental elites rather than identifying with those who share their economic condition). In all of these key works, Edelman calls attention to the influence of labels in politics—especially when the process of naming has not been consciously noticed by publics.

Kenneth Burke has also discussed the capacity of language to shape people's thoughts, and like these other scholars, he was particularly intrigued by how messages could influence individuals' subconscious thoughts. In his notion of identification, Burke suggests that at least three types of connections can be made through language: affiliations through a shared substance, affiliations through a common enemy, or affiliations through an unconscious association.[52] Burke argues that this third type is most powerful because it is often unnoticed and, hence, quite persuasive. An example may be helpful here. Suppose a citizen were to say, "We must vote *Republican*—our party needs us." By relying on the pronouns *we* and *our*, this citizen places herself (and potentially anyone else who accepts her statement) in the same group as partisans who donate time and money to their party. In so doing, she makes herself, and others, more involved in the successes of the Republican Party and becomes, in effect, an unpaid (rhetorical) volunteer.

Furthermore, political scholar Richard Merritt has underscored the importance of systematic attention to the conscious and subconscious treatment of political words. In his content analysis of community terms in colonial America, Merritt details how "the unconscious or latent structure" of a column could even "outweigh its manifest content." Specifically, he notes,

> If, for instance, with the passage of time a Tory newspaper in colonial America such as the *Massachusetts Gazette*, devoted an increasing share of its space to news of the American colonies, or if it increasingly identified its readers as "Americans" rather than as "His Majesty's subjects" or

even "colonists," we might say that, despite its pro-British point of view, the latent content of the *Gazette* encouraged its readers to think of themselves as members of a distinctly American community and to turn their thoughts inward toward that American community.[53]

Taken together, then, names and labels are important because they help individuals frame thoughts and share ideas, and they are often beyond conscious control. Moreover, as these researchers observe, names and labels can also shift in understated ways, often without citizens' noticing how such slight changes can influence their thoughts, their understandings of the social scene, and even their identities.

Much of the aforementioned research has examined such concerns at the conceptual level. Scholars have been engaged in similar efforts in the fields of marketing and business, too; however, they have largely used different terminology to do so and have honed in on more practical and pragmatic matters—specifically, tracing the effects of names on employee and consumer behavior. Although rarely cited in political communication research, the study of language in business schools has forwarded important observations on labels and brands, identification and shortcuts, and loyalty (and profit). As the political campaign environment becomes increasingly sophisticated, professionalized, and tied to the best business practices of marketing and advertising, it makes sense to incorporate such understandings into the study of party language.

The enterprise of branding has been regarded as being more specific than marketing yet broader in scope than advertising. Brand names have been defined as labels with special attributes and have been discussed in the following ways. Specifically, the American Marketing Association has defined a *brand* as "a name, term, sign, symbol, or design, or a combination of them, intended to identify the good or services of one seller or group of sellers and to differentiate them from those of the competitors."[54] Marketing scholar Philip Kotler has contended that "a brand is a complex symbol that can convey up to six levels of meaning: attributes, benefits (functional and emotional), values, culture, personality, and user (brands carry with them a picture of their intended audience)."[55] Branding departs from advertising, for researcher John Murphy at least, because branded products and services embrace both tangible and nontangible factors and must possess attributes and values that are coherent, appropriate, distinctive, protectable, and appealing to consumers.[56] Additionally, as branding scholar Daryl Travis contends, brands have class, time-saving, reputation, and relational components.[57] In commenting on the relational aspect of brands, Travis contends that a brand features a set of promises, including an unwritten contract of intrinsic value, an expectation of performance, a covenant of goodness with its users, a sense of predictability, an unwritten warrantee, a presentation of credentials, a mark of trust and reduced risk, a reputation, and a collection of memories.[58]

While the exact definitions of *brand* differ somewhat, marketing scholars seem to agree on the following point: the benefits of brand identification are considerable. It has been estimated that the cost of acquiring a new customer is five times that of maintaining an existing one, and loyal customers account for a disproportionate share of overall sales.[59] Jim Spaeth, president of the Advertising Research Foundation, ups the stakes on brand loyalty, contending that "the holy grail has been the emotional bond, that interpersonal, almost human-like relationship with brands and it's very hard to get at."[60]

While a brand identity is highly desired, marketing professionals advise conceptualizing it as a multilayered phenomenon. This strategic consideration forms an important complement to research on naming and label use from communication scholarship. Scholar Scott Davis, for one, suggests that the desired levels of identification and image of a brand can be imagined in the form of a pyramid. At the bottom of the pyramid, he begins, appear the brand attributes, descriptors of the features of the product or idea. One level up, he continues, appear the brand benefits, a discussion of what the brand can provide. At the top of the pyramid, he sums, reside the brand's beliefs and values, the broadest level of benefits that a consumer can reap from the brand. In detailing this schema, marketing professor Kotler likens the pyramid to the branding of a bar of Dove soap. As he describes, Dove can promote the attribute of "one-quarter cleansing cream" (bottom level of the pyramid); Dove's benefit of "softer skin" (second level); or its value, using the soap and becoming "more attractive" and, perhaps, "happier" and more "lovable" (top level). As Kotler details, the discussion of the ingredients of the soap is least desirable for three reasons: competitors can copy the attributes (and also push a product with a similar recipe); individuals are more often interested in results than ingredients; and the current attributes of a product may move in and out of fashion.[61] It is far more effective, branding theorists contend, to push the higher-level benefits and values of a brand than its attributes.

In his research, Kevin Keller has advanced a report card that can be used to assess how brands are working to connect with consumers. He advises attending to whether or not a given brand excels at delivering the benefits consumers truly desire; stays relevant; is priced commensurate with consumer's perception of value; is properly positioned; is consistent; makes use of and coordinates a full repertoire of marketing activities; is understood by management; is given proper, sustained support; and is monitored to maintain brand equity.[62] While not as systematic as Keller's list, other best practices have included: attending to the emotional impact of the brand (asking how a brand can touch consumers' lives; trigger a universal emotion; create surprise, passion, and excitement; and take an active, positive role in peoples lives),[63] developing a consistent and unforgettable personality for the brand (customizing brand presence to different consumer segments, incorporating brand strategies into product and retail design, and facilitating interactive access to products through the Internet),[64] and working to manage the brand and the branding experience (implementing strategies to stabilize their place in the customer's mind).[65] In all of these ways, successful brands are more than mere names; rather, they are rich and multifaceted symbols designed to connect with audiences, to fulfill them, and to be protected against audience fatigue or the opposition.

Even though these best practices have been made public, scholars are quick to admit that branding is not necessarily an easy process. A handful of major branding mistakes have been noted by marketing guru Jack Trout. Many of these lessons, intriguingly, have less to do with the project being branded and more to do with the competitive context in which they are communicated. Indeed, in his mind, some of the "lessons learned the hard way" are directly related to companies' not paying enough attention to their competition and to culture (an observation in the introduction to this chapter that calls attention back to how Republicans picked up the term *liberal*). As Trout advises, knowing the enemy and oppositional forces help to set the proper strategic direction.[66] Specifically, he suggests that brand managers keep an eye on the communication terrain and the competition in their public communication efforts. Specific steps for brand managers include developing a message that avoids a competitor's strength and exploits its weakness; that is a bit paranoid about the competition; that is aware that competitors will usually get better, if pushed; and that squashes competitors as quickly as possible.[67] Moreover, he contends, if a company is "losing the battle" in managing its brand, he advises that they shift the battlefield (by introducing understressed values of one's own brand) or attack first (if there is concern that a bigger competitor is about to attack, a company should attack first "if for no other reason than to keep [the] competitor distracted and off balance").[68] Trout believes that for one to avoid a major branding mistake, one must stay focused on one's message, the dynamic communication context, *and* the opposition; by keeping an eye on this trifecta, he sums, a brand manager is less likely to be distracted.

While it may seem unholy for some to pair the language of branding with that of politics, the two have been coupled in both academic and popular circles for some time. Examples, here, include the work of Bruce Newman (editor of the *Handbook of Political Marketing* and author of *The Marketing of the President: Political Marketing as Campaign Strategy* and *The Mass Marketing of Politics: Democracy in an Age of Manufactured Images*), Nicholas O'Shaugnessy (*The Idea of Political Marketing*, *The Marketing Power of Emotion*, and *The Phenomenon of Political Marketing*), and Neil Collins and Patrick Butler, who have all examined politics through this lens.[69] Moreover, the *Journal of Political Marketing* has published articles focusing on the rebranding of the Democrats, marketing politics, and European parties as brands.

Popular columns and news coverage make this link as well. Perhaps this is a natural progression in a society well accustomed to dissecting strategy and motive and where journalists and citizens alike are comfortable trafficking in marketing jargon. For instance, notice how reporter Howard Fineman writes the following tongue-in-check column in 2000 for *Newsweek* magazine. There, he discusses how the two major parties should be "rebranded" because, in his mind, they need "names and corporate logos that better reflect who and what they are—and the new fault lines between them."[70] He advances a set of suggestions for such rebranding efforts, including "The Plaintiff's party (Democrats) vs. The Defendant's party (Republicans)"; The Ocean Beach party (Democrats) vs. The Heartland Waterslide Party (Republicans); The Digital Party (Democrats) vs. the Hydrocarbon Party (Republicans); and The Mommy Party (Democrats) vs. the Daddy Party (Republicans)."[71] Also discussed in light of branding procedures is President George W. Bush, this time in a public relations magazine. That discussion focuses on how the Bush team employs three best practices of branding: focusing on the "core customer" (by nurturing, cultivating, and endearing Bush to the social and religious conservatives); staying "on the offense" (keeping on message and on the attack; wearing down competitors by a consistent pursuit of policy objectives); and, occasionally, doing "the unexpected" (catching competitors off-stride by having Bush mention HIV and AIDS in his State of the Union address, placing Democrats in a position where they must agree with him).[72]

Interestingly, the language of branding has been leveled at efforts to build a symbolic case for the Department of Homeland Security (DHS)—an agency formed in response to the September 11 terrorist attacks. According to a *Washington Post* article, Tom Ridge (the director of the department) was talking "a lot about branding" in the early days of this agency. He must do this, the article continues, "in addition to worrying about 170,000 DHS employees, 2,800 power plants, 600,000 bridges, 463 skyscrapers, 190,000 miles of natural-gas pipelines and 20,000 miles of border." Although "nearly all politicians care about branding—just as Procter & Gamble fixates on creating positive 'brand awareness' about Crest, Cheer, Pampers and Pepto-Bismol," Ridge was reported to be the different kind of politician, one who actually used the language of branding publicly, focusing on details of the DHS's visual brand (namely, the creation of DHS logos, patches, and signs). Why did he do so? In the words of one of his assistants to the *Washington Post*, "'brand' is just a jargon word for identity." For the DHS to gain purchase with the public (as well as with the government), it had to attend to the face it was presenting; it, too, needed to manage its image.[73]

It is important to remember that, like other symbols, brand names are rarely static. They, too, are subject to the forces that influence other types of terms and labels, and their potential flexibility is folded into Trout's best practices for their management. In the political realm, this means that party labels as brands could enjoy moments of strength, uncertainty, decline, and resuscitation. Consider how the dynamism and opportunity of party labels are addressed in the *South Florida Sun-Sentinel,* the *Wall Street Journal,* and the *San Jose Mercury News*, respectively.

- In campaign 2004, a group of Democratic state legislators in Tallahassee, Florida, were reported to have formed the Florida Mainstream Democratic Forum to promote how they share the same values (especially patriotism) as those of other citizens of their state. One news article quotes the words of state senator Walter "Skip" Campbell (D-Fort Lauderdale) as being, "Floridians must know that the Democratic party is not made up of ultra *liberals* who want to give away your tax money. We're here because we're fiscally conservative, but we do believe that people have individual rights that need protection."[74]
- Also in 2004, former Reagan speechwriter Peggy Noonan wrote a column in which she muses aloud about how Kerry would present himself (and the *liberal* label) at his convention, asking herself, Is Kerry a *liberal* or a *progressive*? Noonan elaborates by noting how Kerry could help to frame how the country would come to know him: "What is that these days? He could tell us. He might take this opportunity to actually redefine what liberalism is, and rescue it from

its dread L-word status as the thing Democrats are and can't admit. Conservatives aren't afraid to call themselves conservative. They even do this when they're acting like liberals. Mr. Kerry should tell us what liberals intend with regard to domestic policy. Another way to say this is: The past half century liberals have won a great deal— Social Security, Medicare, civil rights, the megastate. What exactly do they want to win now?"[75]

- And in campaign 2002 in California, where even the term *conservative* may be deemed problematic, Republican gubernatorial candidate Bill Simon was reported to have had to take steps toward the political center by saying that the word *conservative* was just a "label" that was "too limited to encompass his ideas for solving California's problems." This statement came after "his opponent, Gray Davis, described Simon as 'pro-life, pro-gun, pro-voucher, pro-deregulation, pre-privatization.'"[76]

In just these three instances, we see how a group of elected officials in Florida receive news coverage for working to reposition their term, how a columnist publicly questions Kerry's terms, and how a challenger candidate is portrayed in the press as entering a campaign setting in which prior understanding of his term had to be addressed. Although, in the case of Bill Simon, he would have probably liked to dismiss the term *conservative* as being just a label that the political conversation forced him to address (as was the instinct of Ted Kennedy with the term *liberal*, noted earlier in this chapter). That he did and that a reporter was there to write about it speaks to the constitutive power of these labels in modern electoral politics.

This Simon case is notable for another reason: it demonstrates that the Republican and conservative priming forces, while largely successful in demoting the term *liberal* and while widely storied in campaign 2004, have not taken hold in all places. Linguist George Lakoff has thought about these Republican symbolic successes and maintains that their influence has been gradual and has depended on a set of smaller moves over the past thirty years.[77] In a discussion that is reminiscent of the books authored by Brock, Viguerie, and others, Lakoff observes that the conservatives

> started back in the 1950s, and after the 1964 election they really got started. For the last 30 to 40 years, they have pumped $2 billion into supporting all of their think tanks and media apparatus. They have built this series of think tanks that started out after the Goldwater debacle, when conservative was a dirty word, when the idea of "tax-relief" could not

be introduced in two words. The phrase would have been meaningless. And what they did was to develop these ideas with very great patience and fortitude, in campaign after campaign, year after year, and invent the right words as the ideas came into popular view. Their success didn't happen overnight. They took a long-term view.[78]

Working with colleagues at the Rockridge Institute in Northern California, Lakoff has crafted notable scholarly as well as compelling publicly minded materials featuring advice about how Democratic and Left-leaning voices could begin to respond to the long-term linguistic efforts of the Right. In these works, he has often turned to one contemporary power phrase of the GOP: "tax relief." As he details, this compact, two-word phrase implies that taxes (and government) are a burden and that citizens need protection from them. While it took time for the Right to distill conversations about taxes to this power phrase, Lakoff observes that whenever it enters the political conversation, Republicans have a net advantage in that the situation has been framed in their favor. For Democrats to fight back linguistically against this advantage, Lakoff prescribes the following steps. First, he advises creating a powerful framing device for the benefits of government. Examples that he provides include saying that "taxes are what you pay to be an American, to live in this country with democracy, with opportunity, and especially with the enormous infrastructure paid for by previous taxpayers—infrastructure like schools and roads and the Internet, the stock market, the Securities and Exchange Commission, our court system, our scientific establishment, which is largely supported by federal money." The next step, in his mind, is to link these benefits to the actions of individuals in the past: "Vast amounts of important, marvelous infrastructure, all of these things were paid for by taxpayers. They paid their dues. They paid their fair share to be Americans and maintain that infrastructure." And his final step pulls these values and actions together (with a dash of cognitive dissonance on top): "And if you don't pay your fair share, then you're turning your back on your country."[79] By taking these steps and by adopting a long-term view, Democrats may begin to control the discussions of their policies and labels in a way that they currently do not.

Even though such steps would take considerable time and focus, there is an optimistic undercurrent to Lakoff's prescriptions: that conservative voices currently enjoy a symbolic edge does not mean that they will continue to own the conversation on taxes or the *liberal* label. It is conceivable, Lakoff sums, that Democrats and the Left could work to build counternarratives to work to reframe some of the ways in which contemporary topics are being discussed. All of this, of course, would have to occur in the busy information environment in which Americans live.

INFORMATION ENVIRONMENT, 1948–2004

According to estimates, the average American was exposed to more than five thousand advertising impressions a day in 2000—a figure that has increased from roughly fifteen hundred in the 1980s and thirty-six hundred in 1998.[80] The American Association of Advertising Agencies suggests that the number is closer to 250 a day, if one counts only television, radio, magazine, and newspaper ads. The advertising industry claims that consumers give 136 of those 250 ads "at least some attention." Heartening news for those who spend money on them, one would suppose, given estimates that advertising is a $250 billion industry.[81]

Much of the money spent on ads goes to television advertising. Perhaps because of the sums spent there, several studies have tracked the effects of these investments on the communication environment as well as on viewers. Some key findings from such works include the following: between 2002 and 2004, the number of television ads that the average man or woman saw each week increased by more than 20 percent; in 2004, the average television ad was thirty seconds long (down from sixty seconds in the 1960s, increasing the sheer number of messages in the marketplace); television is now more cluttered with ads than ever, as between the hours of 10 AM and 4 PM nearly twenty-one minutes of programming each hour goes to ads; and in a comparative study of forty-five countries, U.S. viewers were being targeted by 817 commercials a week, second only to Indonesia (where viewers saw an average of 852 ads a day). How do individuals respond to these ads? One estimate suggests that 64 percent of an audience stays tuned for an ad during an engaging program.[82]

Sixty-four percent is a decent number, but adults can be a fickle audience, and so many advertising efforts are aimed at children—a group that advertising professionals believe is easier to persuade. Research on youth and advertising suggests that in the 1970s, young viewers saw about twenty thousand ads a year, a figure that is estimated to have increased to forty thousand a year by 2004.[83] Other studies show that by the time a child is twenty months old, he will likely start to recognize some of the thousands of brands flashed in front of him each day. Research on marketing firms show that by the time this child is twelve, he will likely have his own entry in the massive data banks of marketers.[84] Advertising critics fear that the number and types of advertisements sent to children each day creates a combination of narcissism, entitlement, and dissatisfaction in the nation's youth.[85] More broadly, critical cultural scholars worry about the constitutive effect of this shower of messages (on youth and adults), arguing that the media in the United States have become vehicles for selling products and that contemporary culture cannot be understood outside of the logic of advertising.

While marketing professionals are typically not concerned with messages that encourage consumption, they worry about the *number* of messages at play, largely because the vast amount of communications generates a competitive marketplace. In their seminal marketing text, Al Ries and Jack Trout contend that this glut of symbols in the contemporary environment creates "an overcommunicated society," one that complicates connecting with an audience, for "there's a traffic jam on the turnpikes of the mind."[86]

Marketers have developed message and placement strategies to break through this clutter. First, consider a set of changes to message types, due to the overcommunication message terrain, several of which involve entertaining the consumers rather than persuading them directly through appeals connected to products.[87] In 2004 alone, some advertisers moved into longer-form narrative films ("advertaiment") instead of commercials; Major League Baseball considered (and then decided against) selling space on the actual bases on some of their fields for ads promoting a summer blockbuster movie; Kentucky Derby jockeys discussed selling ad space on their racing silks; video-game makers worked product placement into their games (indeed, in one game a player has to "drink a Pepsi" to advance to the next round); and even novelists were reportedly selling spaces in their stories.[88] In this election year, some companies, such as Motorola, Ben & Jerry's, and 7-Up, even attempted to break through the clutter by lending their names to endorse MTV's Rock the Vote youth voter mobilization drive—capitalizing on one of the few occasions that has, to date, remained relatively uncommercialized.[89]

Many marketers have also become entrepreneurial with regard to the placement and technological sophistication of their craft. With regard to placement, companies have been known to put ads in unlikely places, such as in restrooms, on ATMs, on fruit in supermarkets, on billboard trucks, in the form of pop-up ads during television programming, on sports stadiums, on digital screens at subway stations, and even behind boats on the San Francisco Bay. In 2004, it was reported that Parent-Teacher Associations accepted money from Coca-Cola in return for allowing this soft drink giant access to their impressionable children. Another marketing behemoth, Mc-Donald's, was an official sponsor of Pope John Paul II's "pray-in" held in May at a Madrid, Spain, airport, leaving many to question if advertising had become too obvious or if even the holiest of institutions had succumbed to marketing pressures.[90]

With regard to technological advances, some innovations include digital billboards that instantly adjust their messages to the passing audiences (many of which can change depending on what radio stations these cars are listening to), digital in-store signs that change messages by time of day as different clienteles do their shopping, and "oscillating" billboards on buses that flip based on the shuttle's location (ads can shift from Spanish-language messages in Hispanic neighborhoods to car-rental ads as the buses approach the airport).[91] All of these technological strategies help to control the dissemination of an ad or a brand's message—an element of brand management critical for marketing researchers.

Given the overwhelming number of ads targeted toward citizens, scholars have begun to trace how they navigate this cluttered message environment. One recent study conducted by Knowledge Networks/SRI shows that some audience members follow the advertising primes whereas others attempt to use technology to shut them out. With regard to the former group, fully half of all television viewers were found to turn on the television with no destination in mind. Concerning the latter group, 78 percent report doing something else while watching television, 33 percent said that network ads disrupted their enjoyment of the program, and 23 percent said the same of cable ads. While marketers are using new technologies to get closer to audiences, individuals appear to be using different technologies to avert such advances. This research also showed that almost 75 percent of viewers reported that they regard the ability to skip a commercial as being important and that many claimed that they would be happy to pay for technologies that would help them do so.[92]

As this discussion illustrates, for-profit companies are competing for the eyes, ears, and, ultimately, hearts of American consumers. Even though such communications occur outside of the realm of politics, these practices are critical to a contemporary understanding of how citizens make sense of parties via language. At least two things occur when so much energy is placed in product advertising: first, the high production values, niche-marketing tactics, and overall attractiveness of these product campaigns become normalized for audiences; second, these appealing messages begin to serve as a (subconscious) baseline against which other types of messages are judged. Consider what happened in a two-year study that compared how two thousand consumers related to a range of sixty brands, from Oreo cookies to Burger King to the Democratic and Republican parties.[93] In that project, researchers found that citizens had "stronger commitments to Clorox" than to America's two major parties. Specifically, the findings revealed that both parties ranked low on trust and other attributes, such as affection and chemistry. Relative to the Democrats, Republicans were perceived as being more attractive among eighteen- to thirty-four-year-olds and slightly ahead on the attribute of price (a judgment most likely linked to the party's record on taxes). In contrast, the Democrats scored relatively higher than the Republicans did in the area of empathy and reciprocity. Both parties, however, fell far behind products such as cookies and bleach—perhaps not an earthshaking finding but one that this book takes seriously.[94]

CONCLUSION

In a *Newsweek* column describing her reaction to Illinois senate candidate Barack Obama's speech to the Democratic Nominating Convention in 2004, journalist Anna Quindlen writes,

> We liberals have fallen on hard times in recent elections. At the very least, like feminists, we are not supposed to say our name. Certainly none of the sanctioned speakers were supposed to describe either John Kerry or John Edwards using the L word. That will be left to the Republicans who will use the description as a pejorative to suggest that the Democratic candidates are out of touch with the moderate values of the American people.
>
> But it's worth remembering that today's moderate values were the *liberal* notions of yesteryear. Social Security. Integrated schools. A war on poverty. In just one generation we have gone from the dark threat of something labeled socialized medicine to the promise of the same thing, called universal health care. We *liberals* have been shamed into thinking our vision failed, when in fact it has simply been absorbed into the national self-portrait. From the idea that a woman ought to have the same legal rights as her male counterparts to the belief that workers should count on being safe from hazardous conditions, formerly *liberal* principles have become bedrock democracy.[95]

This introductory chapter begins by calling attention to the trajectories of two words in the polity: one that has picked up complicated connotations over time, another that has accumulated adornments that place it more solidly inside the campaign narrative. This chapter then moves to discuss the "story" of Republican and conservative successes with symbols and campaign strategy; to detail the power of naming and label use in contemporary life; to address the prominence of brands and branding; and to note how discussions of party labels take place in an overcommunicated society where for-profit branding techniques are pervasive and familiar. All of these factors are critical to understanding Quindlen's concern: a moment in which the symbolic meaning of a favored label has drifted from its political moorings; a moment when the opposition has adorned this label with the "worst practices" of branding discussed here (creating an antibrand out of the term); and a moment when the most visible figures of the Democratic Party dare not utter their label. A moment like this, surely, commands our attention.

The chapters that follow tell a set of stories about the symbolic trajectories of party labels. First, chapter 2 focuses on the political and symbolic strengths of parties and party labels and discusses how the latter can influence the former. Then, chapters 3 through 6 explore how labels have been used between 1948 and 2000 from a variety of perspectives—uncovering uses of labels in broad patterns, over the years, in four different venues, and by individual word. Finally, chapter 7 returns to several of the themes addressed here by culling some of the key patterns from the earlier analyses, and making sense of them in light of research on naming and branding, as well as the patterns in campaign 2004.

Although chapters 1 and 7 refer to Republican successes over the past thirty years in demoting the word *liberal* and in generating buzz about their symbolic and strategic talents, it is important to note at the outset that this book is not all good news for the *Republican* label. As addressed in several places, Democratic candidates and elected officials are more likely than Republicans to use party labels overall, and because of this, the *Republican* label has sometimes been treated harshly (especially in the early years of this study). That organized, consistent, and proactive forces on the Right and in the Republican Party have made the term *conservative* more likeable and have done such damage to the *liberal* label is a multifaceted tale and one, oddly enough, that may hold some hope for Democratic forces hoping to engage in better branding efforts for the Left's terms. Indeed, columns like Quindlen's as well as grassroots efforts in 2004 (to be discussed in chapter 7) may duplicate the early steps taken by the Right in the 1960s to promote the Left's language and Democratic terms. Should the Left organize and adhere to the consistent approach used by Republicans, as described in this book, a more rigorous and balanced talk of the party will surely follow.

NOTES

1. Unless specified otherwise, all italics in quotations were added by the author.

2. Harry Truman, "Radio Address Sponsored by the International Ladies Garment Workers Union Campaign Committee," Washington, D.C. (21 October 1948), Annenberg/Pew Archive of Presidential Discourse, CD-ROM (Philadelphia: Annenberg School for Communication, University of Pennsylvania, 2000).

3. Adlai Stevenson, "Campaign Address Entitled 'Tough Issues,'" Albuquerque, N.M. (12 September 1952), Annenberg/Pew Archive of Presidential Discourse, CD-ROM (Philadelphia: Annenberg School for Communication, University of Pennsylvania, 2000).

4. Adlai Stevenson, "Campaign Address Entitled 'New Politics,'" Palisades Park, N.J. (9 September 1956), Annenberg/Pew Archive of Presidential Discourse, CD-ROM (Philadelphia: Annenberg School for Communication, University of Pennsylvania, 2000).

5. John F. Kennedy, "Campaign Address Delivered at the Biltmore Hotel," New York City, N.Y. (12 October 1960), Annenberg/Pew Archive of Presidential Discourse, CD-ROM (Philadelphia: Annenberg School for Communication, University of Pennsylvania, 2000).

6. Interview between Tim Russert and Senator Edward Kennedy, *Meet the Press* http://msnbc.msn.com/id/4573986/ (15 March 2004).

7. "Wearing Out the L-Word," *New York Times,* 31 August 2003, 26A.

8. "Adlai Defends Tideland Stand in Texas Swing; Charges Carpetbaggers Misstate Position," *Chicago Tribune,* 18 October 1952, 1A.

9. "Nixon Is Acclaimed on 5th Trip South; Kennedy in Chicago," *Washington Post,* 25 September 1960, 1A.

10. "The Main Event," *New York Times,* 7 September 1980, 1A.

11. "Spot Check by NBC News Finds Reagan Is Leading," Associated Press–United Press International wire, 29 September 1980.

12. "Prospects Looking Up for a Head to Head Debate," *Washington Post,* 16 October 1980, 1A.

13. "Debate Changed 1 Mind among 12 Pittsburghers; Backers of Both Camps Voice Disappointment," *Washington Post,* 13 October 1984, 6A.

14. "Group of Viewers Shifts Opinions after TV Debate," *Washington Post,* 9 October 1984, 1A.

15. Robert Reich, *Why Liberals Win Will the Battle for America* (New York: Knopf, 2004); E. J. Dionne, *Stand Up, Fight Back: Republican Toughs, Democratic Wimps, and the Politics of Revenge* (New York: Simon and Schuster, 2004).

16. Michael Schudson, *The Good Citizen: A History of American Civic Life* (New York: Free Press, 1998), 311.

17. Charles Kesler, "Who Needs Political Parties?" *IntellectualCapital.com* (11 May 2000).

18. See "W Hotels," www.starwood.com/whotels/index.html (17 July 2004).

19. Greg Thomas, "W Tries Boutique Hotel Feel at National Chain Level; Offers 'Whatever Whenever' Service," *Orleans*, 17 July 2003, 1F.

20. Thomas, "W Tries," 1F.

21. Diane Brady, "Sleepless at Starwood," *Business Week*, 21 July 2003, 56.

22. Dion Dennis, "Inventing 'W, the Presidential Brand': The Rise of QVC Politics," *CTheory*, www.ctheory.net/text_file.asp?pick=359 (11 December 2002).

23. See Dennis, "Inventing 'W'"; Ted Jackson, "Riding the Coattails of Brand Loyalty," *Promotional Products Business Online*, www.ppai.org/Publications/PPB/Article.asp?NewsID=238 (17 July 2004).

24. "W. Hotels or W. the President?" www.newyorkish.com/newyorkish (6 July 2004).

25. "Gossip," *New York Post*, www.nypost.com/gossip/28411.htm (2 August 2004).

26. Gerald L. Horst, "Letter to the Editor; Focus: President Bush; 'W' Not Disrespectful," *San Antonio Express News*, 1 August 2004, 4H.

27. David Corn, "GOP's New Mouthwash," *Nation* 269, no. 9 (1996): 4–6.

28. Nicholas Lemann, "The Word Lab: The Mad Scientist Behind What the Candidates Say," *New Yorker* 76, no. 35 (2000): 100–108.

29. James Carney, "Hey—Who's That Guy Next to Karl Rove?" *Time*, 23 August 1999, 34; Nicholas Lemann, "The Controller," *New Yorker* 79, no. 11 (2003): 68–84.

30. James Moore and Wayne Slater, *Bush's Brain: How Karl Rove Made George W. Bush Presidential* (New York: Wiley, 2003).

31. David Brock, *The Republican Noise Machine: Right Wing Media and How It Corrupts Democracy* (New York: Crown, 2004).

32. Eric Alterman, *What Liberal Media? The Truth about Bias in the News* (New York: Basic Books, 2003).

33. Richard Viguerie and David Franke, *America's Right Turn: How Conservatives Used New and Alternative Media to Take Power* (Chicago: Bonus Books, 2004).

34. Peter Berger and Thomas Luckman, *The Social Construction of Reality* (Garden City, N.Y.: Doubleday, 1966).

35. Gunther Kress and Robert Hodge, *Language as Ideology* (London: Routledge & Kegan Paul, 1981).

36. Kress and Hodge, *Language as Ideology*.

37. Benjamin Whorf, *Language, Thought, and Reality* (New York: Wiley, 1956), 134.

38. Victoria Fromkin and Robert Rodman, *An Introduction to Language* (New York: Holt, Rinehart and Winston, 1974).

39. Michael Schudson, *Advertising: The Uneasy Persuasion* (New York: Basic Books, 1986). Schudson continues: "But most of the names an adult encounters in a normal day are familiar. *This does not make them unimportant.* Culture works by taking things we already know and *making them actionable*" (xxi–xxii).

40. Schudson, *Advertising*, xxii.

41. Kathleen Hall Jamieson, "The Subversive Effects of a Focus on Strategy in News Coverage of Campaigns," in *1-800 President*, by the Twentieth-Century Fund Task Force on Television and the Campaign of 1992 (New York: Twentieth-Century Fund Press, 1993), www.tcf.org/task_forces/tv_1992_campaign/Jamieson.html (17 July 2004).

42. Murray Edelman, *The Symbolic Uses of Politics* (Urbana: University of Illinois Press, 1964), 131.

43. Edelman, *Symbolic Uses.*

44. Murray Edelman, *Political Language* (New York: Academic Press, 1977), 3.

45. Edelman, *Political Language*, 3.

46. Edelman, *Political Language*, 4.

47. Edelman, *Political Language*, 8.

48. Edelman, *Political Language*, 9.

49. Murray Edelman, *Politics as Symbolic Action: Mass Arousal and Quiescence* (New York: Academic Press, 1971).

50. Edelman, *Politics as Symbolic*, 75.

51. Edelman, *Political Language*, 10.

52. Kenneth Burke, *A Rhetoric of Motives* (Berkeley: University of California Press, 1950); Burke, *Language as Symbolic Action* (Berkeley: University of California Press, 1966).

53. Richard Merritt, *Symbols of American Community* (New Haven, Conn.: Yale University Press, 1966), xiii.

54. Philip Kotler, *Marketing Management*, 11th ed. (Upper Saddle River, N.J.: Prentice Hall, 2003), 418.

55. Kotler, *Marketing Management,* 418–19.

56. John Murphy, "What Is Branding?" in *Brands: The New Wealth Creators*, ed. Susannah Hart and John Murphy (London: Macmillan Business, 1998), 1–12, 3.

57. Daryl Travis, *Emotional Branding: How Successful Brands Gain the Irrational Edge* (Roseveille, Calif.: Prima Venture, 2000), 19.

58. Travis, *Emotional Branding*, 20–21.

59. Patricia Winters Lauro, "According to a Survey, the Democratic and Republican Parties Have Brand-Name Problems," *New York Times*, 17 November 2000, 10C.

60. Winters Lauro, "According to a Survey."

61. Kotler, *Marketing Management*, 419.

62. Kevin Keller, "The Brand Report Card," *Harvard Business Review*, 1 January 2000, 147–57.

63. Marc Gobe, *Citizen Brand: 10 Commandments for Transforming Brands in a Consumer Democracy* (New York: Alworth Press, 2002).

64. Marc Gobe and Sergio Zyman, *Emotional Branding: The New Paradigm for Connecting Brands to People* (New York: Allworth Press, 2001).

65. Jean-Noel Kapferer, *Strategic Brand Management: Creating and Sustaining Brand Equity Long Term* (London: Kogan Page, 1997).

66. Jack Trout, *Big Brands, Big Trouble: Lessons Learned the Hard Way* (New York: Wiley, 2002), 183.

67. Trout, *Big Brands*, 187–89, 191.

68. Trout, *Big Brands*, 191.

69. Bruce Newman, *Marketing of the President: Political Marketing as Campaign Strategy* (Thousand Oaks, Calif.: Sage, 1994); Newman, *The Mass Marketing of Politics: Democracy in an Age of Manufactured Images* (Thousand Oaks, Calif.: Sage, 1999); Nicholas O'Shaugnessy, *The Idea of Political Marketing* (Westport, Conn.: Praeger, 2002); O'Shaugnessy, *The Marketing Power of Emotion* (New York: Oxford, 2003); O'Shaugnessy, *The Phenomenon of Political Marketing* (New York: St. Martin's Press, 1990); Neil Collins and Patrick Butler, "Positioning Political Parties: A Market Analysis," *Journal of Press and Politics* 1, no. 2 (1996): 63–77.

70. Howard Fineman, "Report from LA: Rebranding the Political Parties," *Newsweek*, www.msnbc.msn.com/id/3032542/site/newsweek/ (17 August 2000).

71. Fineman, "Report from LA."

72. Jerry Johnson, "Seeking Votes and Building Brands Have Much in Common," *PR Week*, 26 January 2004, 8.

73. Mark Leibovich, "The Image of Security: Homeland Chief Tom Ridge, Keeping Up His Appearances," *Washington Post*, 22 May 2003, C01.

74. Anthony Man, "Conservative Democrats Challenge GOP's Caricature of their Party," *South Florida Sun-Sentinel*, 23 April 2004.

75. Peggy Noonan, "Will the Real John Kerry Please Stand Up?" *Wall Street Journal*, 22 July 2004.

76. Laura Kurtzman, "California Gubernatorial Nominee Starts to Shy Away from Conservative Label," *San Jose Mercury News*, 7 March 2002.

77. "Interview with George Lakoff," *Alternet.org*, www.alternet.org/story/17574 (15 January 2004).

78. George Lakoff, as cited in "Inside the Frame," *Alternet.org*, www.alternet.org/story/17574 (15 January 2004).

79. Lakoff, "Inside the Frame."

80. Charles U. Larson, *Persuasion: Reception and Responsibility*, 8th ed. (Belmont, Calif.: Wadsworth, 1998), 11; Sut Jhally, *Advertising and the End of the World* [film] (Northhampton, Mass.: Media Education Foundation, 1998).

81. Michael McCarthy, "Critics Target 'Omnipresent' Ads; Advertising Spreads into Non-traditional Venues," *USA Today*, 16 March 2001, 6B.

82. Alastair Ray, "Television—Clearing Up the Commercials Clutter," *Financial Times*, 29 June 2004, 4; David Lieberman, "Studies Show Increase in Television Ads, Promos," *USA Today*, 15 February 2002, 2B.

83. Liz Kowalczyk, "For Kids, a Steady Diet of Food Ads TV, Net Marketing Blitz Studied for Links to Childhood Obesity," *Boston Globe*, 24 February 2004, 1C.

84. David Leonhardt, "Is Madison Avenue Taking 'Get 'em While They're Young' Too Far?" *Business Week*, 30 June 1997, 62.

85. Leonhardt, "Is Madison Avenue?"

86. Al Ries and Jack Trout, *Positioning: The Battle for Your Mind* (New York: Mc-Graw Hill, 2001), 13.

87. Nat Ives, "Putting Out the Message That Registering and Voting Should Have a Place in the Youth Culture," *New York Times*, 13 July 2004, 15C.

88. Bob Keefe, "Advertisers Leaving No Space Unexplored: Spider-Man's Ballpark Gig Joins the Ongoing March of Ad Creep," *Austin American Statesman*, 8 May 2004, 1A, 16A; Ives, "Putting Out the Message."

89. Keefe, "Advertisers Leaving"; Ives, "Putting Out the Message."

90. Sally Beatty, "Bank of America Puts Ads in ATMs," *Wall Street Journal*, 25 July 2002, 8B; Michael McCarthy, "Critics Target 'Omnipresent' Ads; Advertising Spreads into Non-traditional Venues," *USA Today*, 16 March 2001, 6B; Shelley Emling, "Look! Up in the Sky? It's a Bird! It's a Plane! It's an Ad?" *Austin American Statesman*, 20 July 2003, 1J, 6J.

91. Shelley Emling, "Brave New Billboards Arrive; Messages Tailored to Viewers," *Atlanta Journal Constitution,* 16 March 2003, 1G.

92. Joe Mandese, "Consumers Understand, Reject TV Ad Model; Deem Ad-Skipping Indispensable," Media Post's *MediaDailyNews*, www.knowledgenetworks.com (10 March 2004).

93. Winters Lauro, "According to a Survey."

94. Lauro, "According to a Survey."

95. Anna Quindlen, "A Leap into the Possible," *Newsweek*, 9 August 2004, 60.

2

WHAT ARE PARTIES WORTH?

Are political parties powerful in the United States? What about the Democratic Party? The Republican Party? Liberals? Conservatives? Independents? Direct these questions to someone who is involved in American government, and she will likely respond by discussing issues of *political capital*, or resources that can be used to secure desired outcomes. Her list may include such topics as party allegiance on Capitol Hill, relations between the legislature and the presidency, monies raised and spent by the Democratic National Committee and Republican National Committee, successes and defeats in redistricting battles, and patterns of dominance in state legislatures.

But ask a randomly collected group of citizens these questions, and they may respond with entirely different support for their positions. As detailed in chapter 1, the average American is exposed to more than five thousand commercial impressions a day, a figure that increased from roughly fifteen hundred in the 1980s to thirty-six hundred in 1998. Thus, when faced with a question about the power of these labels, survey data have shown that citizens often react in a manner consistent with the symbolic priming forces regnant in their environs, offering such responses as the following: individual candidates are often more visible than the parties are; colorful independents appear more likeable than do candidates of the major parties; the major parties seem more powerful than third parties; and so forth. These types of replies suggest that contemporary understandings of parties may be influenced as much by symbols as by the considerations influencing political sophisticates.

Many important works have already focused on the political might of American political parties. The goal of this chapter is to introduce a rationale

41

to attend to the symbolic worth of parties, particularly as America moves into an overcommunicated society. This discussion rests on four assumptions:

1. Citizens come to know politics through discourse (and thus the attractiveness of party labels is consequential).[1]
2. Citizen discourse is led, but not fully determined, by elite discourse (and thus elite texts hold cues for understandings of party labels).[2]
3. The uses of labels have been shown to function as powerful shortcuts in modern life and to have important psychological effects on citizens (and thus they may act as influential cues and filters to information on the political capital of parties).[3]
4. The meanings of political terms shift with time, as meanings may become broader, narrower, or may change entirely (and thus a rich understanding of these labels and their dynamic nature requires longitudinal analyses and the consideration of several voices).[4]

The following pages, then, provide a backdrop for the inquiry of party labels, first by reviewing discussions of the political capital of parties and then by previewing the conceptual strengths of assessing parties' symbolic capital.

THE POLITICAL AND SYMBOLIC CAPITAL OF PARTIES

One of the more prominent books to come out of political science in the past decade has been Robert Putnam's *Bowling Alone: The Collapse and Revival of American Community*. This work has provided quantitative support for declines in group and civic participation in the United States since the 1960s and has observed that these declines have not been met with new memberships in large-membership organizations, nonprofit service agencies, volunteering, or support groups. This text has brought a set of vocabulary terms to the attention of academic and lay audiences alike. A key term to emerge from such conversations is *social capital*, defined by Putnam as the collective value of all social networks (i.e., the people that individuals know) and the likelihood that individuals in these networks will engage in acts that help each other (i.e., engage in norms of reciprocity).[5] Critical aspects of the definition of *social capital* are that (1) it is not a single thing, (2) it comes in many different shapes and sizes with many different uses, and (3) it is best measured through a triangulation of data sets.[6] An attractive element of this concept is that the emphasis is not on defining the term in a rigid way but in locating multiple resources that put individuals in a place where they might help each other, in searching for moments where relationships create value for people.

Putnam's book has inspired many conversations, the most germane for current purposes is a conceptual one: the analysis of resource (with many shapes and sizes) that helps a person or a set of persons accomplish something. The term *political capital* predates the *Bowling Alone* conversation, but it has certainly gotten more attention because of the buzz surrounding social capital; similarly, political capital can be considered a resource that can be used to achieve an outcome. A set of scholars have examined the concept empirically, attending to how individuals, groups, and organizations acquire it; how social capital can feed into it; how it can be best measured; and how it can be conceived of as having instrumental and structural components.[7] Given recent attention to resources that accomplish goals, questions emerge for parties in the United States, including the following: Do parties have political capital in the American system? If so, what type or types? and Do they merit yet another book addressing them?

If the number and scope of scholarly works analyzing these questions are any guide, the answers appear to be, respectfully, "yes," "a considerable amount," and "increasingly so as the country moves into a more partisan moment." To the first question, some scholars have examined essentialist questions of the parties, and many have suggested that our parties are organic to a democratic state. John Aldrich submits that parties formed naturally in the United States around the "fundamental problem" of the desirable size and scope of the federal government.[8] Joseph Schlesinger has been downright practical in applying this notion to contemporary politics, writing, "We know that the American system is a two party system not only because two parties compete, but because only two parties have a chance at winning any of the significant offices."[9] In arguing that parties are a necessary element of a democratic system, these two observers are not alone. Comparative researchers have also contended that parties are fixtures of all advanced democracies and can be regarded as a definitive component of a democratic state.[10]

Other scholars have focused on the functional and pragmatic inevitability of partisanship, describing parties as

- organized attempts to get power;[11]
- coalitions seeking to control government;[12]
- groups that participate in the political socialization of the American electorate, dominate the recruitment of political leadership, and have full commitment to political activity;[13] and

- institutionalized formal apparatuses that organize our legislatures, campaign organizations, and policy committees.[14]

To the second question, still other researchers have observed the ideological and structural power of party. They point out how parties can stand for principles, as does Edmund Burke when stating that parties promote principles about which all members agree;[15] or for cooperation, as when Joseph Schumpeter advises that parties "are groups whose members propose to act in concert in the competitive struggle for political power";[16] or for discipline, as when Anthony Downs argues that parties encourage candidates to be consistent over time and to advocate policy positions popular with the electorate; and for protection from economic elites, as when Walter Dean Burnham asserts that parties prevent the "concentration of political power, locally or nationally, in the hands of those who already possess concentrated economic power."[17]

The psychological muscle of party has also intrigued scholars. In their seminal piece of survey research on voting behavior, Angus Campbell and colleagues state that "the behavior of the American voter as presidential elector can be described initially as a response to psychological forces."[18] These authors also claim that the stronger one's attachment to a party, the greater his or her psychological involvement in political affairs. In the authors' minds, then, partisanship is an element of identity, a force that has the power to place a person close to or far away from the proceedings of government.

Additionally, party has been regarded as a considerable cognitive cue. In his classic work, Downs contends that partisan cues reduce voters' uncertainty and serve as cognitive shortcuts for their decision making. Samuel Popkin argues similarly, writing that "party identification, viewed from the perspective of low-information rationality, is an informational shortcut or default valve, a substitute for more complete information about parties and candidates."[19] For Downs and Popkin, party cues simplify the political universe for politicians and citizens.

Moreover, some scholars (notably V. O. Key and Burnham) have taken a longitudinal approach to partisanship and have noted the sway that parties have had on American political history. From these widely cited works come the concepts of critical elections (signals of sharp and durable shifts in power), realignment (enduring changes in the relative strengths of parties), and dealignment (a decline in party loyalty and a rise in political independence). A group of scholars has utilized this approach to understand voting patterns, a marked benefit of the historical approach.[20] Another benefit, certainly, is that such a perspective encourages scholars to examine the concept in broader and more sensitive ways. This latter point is underscored by William Chambers and Burnham when they write that the political capacity of parties "can only be understood in their dimension in time."[21]

Some scholars have wondered about the political capital of third-party candidates, studying how and why it is so difficult for them to succeed in politics. Steven Rosenstone and colleagues found that third-party candidates and voters face several major obstacles in our two-party system, including legal and administrative provisions, fewer resources, poorer media coverage, and a lower standard of respect than do major party candidates.[22] Despite these hurdles, some third-party movements and candidates in American history have achieved considerable attention and success—for example, the Liberty Party, Free Soil Party, Know-Nothing (American) Party, Constitutional Union Party, Southern Democrats, Greenback Party, People's Party (Populists), and the Prohibition Party—which can be explained by several factors.[23] These third-party success stories have (1) often resembled the major parties, (2) always tried to work within the major parties before becoming independents, (3) either grew into or out of major parties, and (4) revolved around attractive candidates (e.g, the candidacies of Teddy Roosevelt, Robert La Follette, William Lemke, Henry Wallace, Strom Thurmond, George Wallace, Eugene McCarthy, John Anderson, and H. Ross Perot).[24] While third-party movements have enjoyed occasional successes, they must—as Rosenstone has argued—compete in a two-party system that has codified itself legally and culturally.

Of course, it also has been fashionable to debate the vitality of parties and to compare today's political capital to that of yesterday. Political scientists who have claimed that parties are strong have said such things as the following:

- Party is the single strongest predictor of candidate choice in the public.
- All presidential nominees have won the support of at least a majority of their party in the electorate, no matter how overwhelming their defeat may have been.[25]
- "Parties are organizations that, when they are functioning, mobilize voters, coordinate the activities of leaders, and by recruiting candidates and sponsoring political campaigns, provide some linkage between the two levels of politics (campaigns and governance). . . . It is fair to say that parties still have work to do and were they not to exist, something very like them would have to be invented."[26]

• Parties "are currently conducting a great national dialogue on the purpose of American government and the goals of American community. . . . That dialogue is a societal emblem of the personal and serious conversation that makes political parties essential to meaningful democracy in America."[27]

The flip side has been expressed by those who have advocated the "party's over" proposition, a popular argument between the 1960s and the 1980s. Scholars who have taken this position have asserted that the prominence of split-ticket voting in the United States has led to a weak party system, largely because split-ticket voters seem unburdened by partisan loyalties.[28] Others have claimed that populist reforms of the Progressive Era (e.g., the Australian ballot, mixed-party ballots) as well as Democratic reforms of the early 1970s make it difficult for parties to control the outcome of presidential elections.[29] Still others have suggested that the modern media, namely television, have contributed to the demise of parties, arguing that Americans receive more information from television than from the party (and thus have become less partisan) and devote so much of their leisure time to television that they are left with no time to volunteer for, or become active in, their parties.[30] Moreover, in his analyses of data from 1952 to 1980, Martin Wattenberg has contended that campaigns are becoming increasingly candidate centered instead of party brokered and that citizens have begun to see parties as "less relevant" in solving the most important domestic and foreign policy issues of the day.

Contributions to the "decline of parties" thesis in the 1990s and early twenty-first century have taken on a different tone. An emerging argument has questioned this position, notably supported by Larry Bartels's belief that the conventional wisdom of party decline is badly outdated and by Marc Hetherington's assertion that at the dawn of the twenty-first century, "the measures scholars have used as evidence of mass party decline now point to party resurgence."[31] Additionally, John Petrocik's construct of "issue ownership" might predict that strategic candidates would be motivated to employ partisan messages in presidential campaigns. Specifically, Petrocik contends that parties have reputations for how they have handled issues in the past and that it behooves candidates to call attention to the issues that their party "owns" in order to make such concerns salient to voters and to increase the likelihood that they will regard party loyalists as being more fit for office than opponents in the other party. Of particular relevance to the current project, the notion of issue ownership has been supported in campaign texts, notably analyses of news reports, and in word counts of campaign ads and presidential nomination convention addresses.[32]

In short, scholars have analyzed a number of important reasons why parties have political purchase in the American context. These are all valuable means of responding to the questions posed at the beginning of this section—that is, Do parties have capital? If so, what type? and Do they merit inquiry? Yet in a cluttered message marketplace, these important researches are not the most common ways by which citizens come to understand the purchase of parties; thus, the derived data from such work provide just a part of the answer to the power of parties in an information age.

To gain a fuller answer to the question of what parties are worth, we must look to see how citizens come to know parties through language. The ways in which people talk about party labels can provide insight into their capital in a democratic system. It is important to note at the outset that this project is not the first to address symbols as commodities in public life. To be sure, critical scholars have used the term *symbolic capital* to discuss the currency of symbols in a cultural system as well as how such currency can lead to a variety of outcomes.[33] This project is indebted intellectually to these earlier works, but it borrows the conceptual framework of Putnam in advancing a definition of symbolic capital. In this project, I conceptualize symbolic capital as not a single thing but a dynamic entity that comes in many different shapes and sizes with many different uses.[34] Like social capital, symbolic capital is best measured through a triangulation of data sets and is best understood by attending to the productive value that can be extracted from a term's use. As the following sections show, the symbolic capital of party labels merits our attention, especially as we have moved into an overcommunicated society. This contention rests on four key assumptions.

First, attending to the symbolic capital of parties in 2004 is critical because public communication practices are the primary way modern citizens become involved in public affairs. As Murray Edelman has put it, people are more likely to experience the "language about political events rather than the events themselves."[35] This statement is particularly relevant to political parties, for American voters are more likely to be subjected to the discourse of partisanship than to actual partisan events (e.g., attending party meetings or rallies, studying roll-call votes, or examining campaign donations). Thus, tracking how party labels have been discussed in American political discourse should reveal, to paraphrase Kenneth Burke, how Americans have used such terms and have been used by them as well.

Second, this book pays close attention to how elite voices have discussed party labels. This choice to attend to how elite voices, as opposed to citizen voices, talk about parties may be deemed unpopular or unnecessarily highbrow by some. Nevertheless, as scholars such as V. O. Key, Philip Converse, and John Zaller have observed, elite voices are critical to the development of public opinion, as they help to guide public understandings of politics.[36] Moreover, as Edelman has elaborated, elite constructions of politics significantly structure the expectations people have of such constructions and significantly contribute to the accepting relationship of mass publics to authority itself.[37] In this project I do not make any claims that elite voices determine public opinion (or that any one of the specific voices studied governs how the labels are used). Instead, I have selected to look at four sets of elite discourse (both to increase the richness of the study and to get a sense of how different voices construct the labels in different places), and I maintain that while these voices do not dictate the meanings of labels, they do serve as an important starting place to map the talk of the party.

Third, the uses of labels function as powerful shortcuts in modern life and have been shown to have important psychological effects on citizens. To date, though, these labels have largely been studied in a variety of independent studies; what has been missing has been a project to pull theoretical approaches and empirical findings together to support an analysis of how these labels influence citizens and what such influence might mean for the political capital of the parties. Indeed, the niche that this project fills has been identified by Arthur Sanders, when he writes, "Party identification is a concept which political scientists have studied in great detail over the past several decades. But one aspect of party identification which has not received much attention has been the meaning of party images to people."[38] The meanings of these images are important, Sanders continues, for they are richly influenced by the effects of time and culture. Writing in the late 1980s, he observes how "people's views of the parties are shaped by the political and social environment in which they live," and he sums, "If the parties can, once again, create or develop clearer images, they may be able to increase their ability to influence the nature of political conflict."[39]

In unpacking this third assumption, there is a pair of important aspects to the study of labels as shortcuts in contemporary life: first, broader understandings of how and why citizens take shortcuts in processing political information and, second, more detailed analyses of how individuals respond to specific labels. Concerning the former, it is notable that citizens in the United States are asked to make more electoral decisions than individuals in any other advanced democracy. And, as detailed in chapter 1, Americans are increasingly asked to make these decisions in an overcommunicated society. Given the number of voting decisions citizens are asked to make in light of the number of appeals being sent to them, many have wondered how voters are able to perform their democratic duties.

Two influential works provide heuristic models of how citizens gather and make sense of political information amidst this sea of messages. To begin, in an impressive accounting of the history of citizenship in the United States, Michael Schudson contends that Americans have yielded to a set of forces over time, deferring to elites during an age of assent (1700–1820s), identifying with parties during an era of affiliation (1820s–1920s), becoming more independent during an age of informed citizenship (marked by political reforms and the rise of the mass media, 1880s–present), and becoming more politicized during a moment of right-bearing citizenship (in which politics can be seen as saturating public life, 1960s–present). An outcome of these shifts, in his mind, is the emergence of the monitorial citizen, an individual who "engages in environmental surveillance more than information gathering."[40] Faced with an abundance of data and no longer moored to elites and parties as once was the case, monitorial citizens scan their information environments to develop a sense of "a very wide variety of issues for a very wide variety of ends."[41] From this perspective, citizens respond to the pressures of an overcommunicated society (and their relative independence from elites and parties) by keeping their eyes on the issue environment rather than by mastering the nuances of topics in gross detail.

Next, Samuel Popkin offers the theory of low information rationality to describe what individuals do with this information. Also known as "gut reasoning," Popkin's model "economically incorporates learning and information from past experiences, daily life, the media, and political campaigns."[42] This perspective suggests that individuals use cognitive shortcuts in thinking about politics and rely on proxies—such as a candidate's experiences, campaign competence, and personal character—in making sense of public affairs. Emotions play a role in these shortcuts, for, as Popkin puts it, "one reason that people do not behave like naïve statisticians is that data presented in an emotionally compelling way may be given greater consideration and more weight than to data that is statistically more valid, but emotionally neutral."[43] Consistent with the work by branding theorists, as outlined in chapter 1, Popkin's observations are that emotional cues break through the clutter more effectively than others.

Studies on the effects of specific labels show that these terms can exert a powerful influence on individuals as they make sense of politics. To begin, party labels have been defined as cues that provide simple, direct, and

consequential information in shaping "individual's perceptions and evaluations of political candidates."[44] Moreover, party labels are considered by
many to be the chief cue for millions of Americans as they make decisions
about candidates or issues. The following findings from survey and experimental research outline five aspects of the scope and reach of party labels in
regards to how citizens make sense of politics.

Labels are broadly understood. A set of projects has identified how labels
are understood by citizens of high and low political sophistication as well as
high and low levels of participation. In Richard Herrera's examination of if
and when individuals could identify the meanings of the *liberal* and *conservative* labels, for instance, he found that even though political elites were
more likely to identify the meanings of the *liberal* and *conservative* labels, most
citizens could identify the meanings of these terms. That the meanings are
shared, writes Herrera, points to a quite remarkable linkage between the
mass public and the political elite with regard to political terminology.[45] In
his words, "prior studies may have over emphasized constraint and sophistication as criteria for political engagement by the mass citizenry. In sum, perhaps little is needed to obtain a rudimentary understanding of the language
of politics. . . . The building blocks for a politically informed electorate may
already be in place."[46] Similarly, James Snyder and Michael Ting have observed that citizens are far more knowledgeable about party labels and the
ideological positions of these labels than they are of particular candidates.[47]
These researchers have also explained how voters are far better at discussing
the differences between the major party labels than they are at discussing the
differences between the liberals and conservatives within the parties.[48]

Labels increase the likelihood that citizens will make decisions. Findings from
decision-making research have shown that individuals are more likely to
rely on heuristics when there is a high need for cognitive efficiency.[49] A related finding for party labels has been advanced by Brian Shaffner and
Matthew Streb: a voter is more likely to choose a candidate when partisan
information is provided. As they have explained, "citizens still rely on party
labels a great deal when making decisions on whether and for whom to
vote—especially when they lack other information. This cue helps voters
not only to participate but also to participate intelligently in our political
system. Without the party label, voters become less likely to vote and less
able to link their own party affiliations to their vote choices."[50] Even though
Shaffner and Streb found that highly educated respondents had easier times
selecting candidates to support in the absence of partisan information, the
role of the party label helped all citizens make decisions with confidence
and efficiency. Several projects confirm these patterns that individuals with

fewer political resources are the most likely to take shortcuts; yet, citizens of all levels of sophistication are found to make decisions more efficiently when labels are present.[51] Additionally, this pattern is even more powerful in down-ballot (low-profile) races. Although the lion's share of political science research focuses on presidential and congressional elections, citizens are asked to make decisions on more down-ballot than high-profile contests; in these less-visible races, party cues are critical in whether citizens feel confident about their decisions as well as whether they will even cast down-ballot votes at all.

Labels are viewed through partisan screens. In his work, Arthur Sanders has found that citizens who have an ideological view of the parties are more likely to see differences between them,[52] almost always preferring their parties to the opposition. Pamela Conover and Stanley Feldman have located a similar result for ideological terms, namely, that identification with a party affects how individuals interpret the *liberal* and *conservative* labels.[53] Interestingly, the authors found that symbolic factors seem to have played a more pivotal role than issue positions in determining the evaluation of these labels, having observed that "positive attitudes toward (the *liberal* label) were primarily a function of positive feelings toward the symbols of the radical and reformist left."[54] They also found that while feelings toward capitalism were central to a positive evaluation of conservatism, such feelings were less important toward evaluations of the *liberal* label. They conclude that the two labels derive their meaning from different sources (sometimes from feelings toward the Left, at other times from sentiment about capitalism)[55] and that these ideological identifications constitute a more symbolic than issue-oriented link to the world.[56]

A similar type of screen has been located by Ronald Rapoport, but in this instance the screen is connected to a type of identification with compelling public officials. As his research has uncovered, attitudes toward presidential candidates have both short- and long-term effects on individual-level party identification, so much so that "parties may develop stylistic and trait-like images that are difficult to shake, even in subsequent elections."[57] In a sense, then, the extent to which citizens feel connected to high-profile Democratic and Republican figures can influence how citizens make sense of these party labels in subsequent judgments.

Labels influence how citizens think about candidates. While Rapoport's research suggests that individual cues can influence how citizens regard party labels, Wendy Rahn's studies show the opposite is true as well: when party images have been activated, citizens may not individuate political candidates.[58] More specifically, her studies show that party stereotypes can (1) function heuristically for voters when they are confronted with political information processing tasks and (2) appear to be quite robust cognitive categories with considerable influence in many political information processing tasks.[59] In her studies of how television programming activates or dulls the likelihood that citizens will rely on partisan stereotypes, she has observed that the "busyness" of television can subvert the role of cues in understanding politics. In a study with Kathy Cramer, she found that this was largely the case for citizens who were less engaged in politics (a problem, in the authors' minds, as these are the individuals who are more likely to get their political information from television rather than from the newspapers; thus, the properties of television may make it even more difficult for these citizens to make connections between candidates and the parties).[60] This conclusion may relate to patterns of party cues appearing in the early 1990s—a time when they were less prevalent than they were in the late 1990s; as the data in this project show, if Rahn's study were conducted again in a more polarized environment, the stereotypes that were suppressed on television ten years ago may be more prominent in the new millennium.

Labels are regarded as distinct. Research from a variety of scholars, including Donald Baumer, Harold Gold, Richard Trilling, and Arthur Sanders, all show that citizens see differences between the party labels and are comfortable in identifying a distinct set of stereotypes that separate the two major parties.[61] Specifically, data reveal that citizens have viewed Democrats as those willing "to rely on government intervention, whether to regulate the economy and businesses or to assist the economically disadvantaged"[62] and have regarded Republicans as those opposed to government intervention in the economy, as "champions of low taxes and of bringing businesslike efficiency to government," and as "supporters of entrepreneurial activity."[63] Citizens have also connected these understandings of the parties to favored groups; notably, voters have viewed Democrats as being associated with an array of interests (e.g., labor unions, welfare recipients, gays and lesbians, feminists, and minorities), whereas Republicans have been recognized as business elites and those committed to traditional and conservative values. Additionally, with regard to party philosophies, "the Democrats' dominant image has been one of liberalism, humanism, equality, and support for government activity and social change. The Republican image has been more or less the opposite; it has featured conservatism, anticommunism, property rights, and opposition to government activity and social change."[64] Baumer and Gold observe that on these philosophies, the Republicans did slightly better than the Democrats over the period studied (a pattern that matches trends in label use, described in chapter 6). Baumer and

Gold link these perceptions to reasons why citizens favor one party over the other. In their work, they explain how Democratic voters supported the Democratic Party because they saw it as being compassionate and inclusive and how Republican voters applauded the Republican Party for its efficiency and values.

Labels, then, are influential for a score of reasons: they are accessible; they help citizens make decisions with efficiency (particularly citizens with lower levels of information); they can be influenced by partisan- or candidate-driven predispositions; they can be primed or subverted by communication technologies; and they point to perceived differences between the two major parties in the United States. Because of their prominence and value, these labels also present themselves as desired entities for ambitious candidates, groups, organizations, and movements. For a political actor, there are considerable incentives in working to promote one's label or demote that of the opposition. These incentives give rise to the fourth assumption of labels in this project.

A final contention here is that the meanings of political terms can shift with time, as meanings can become broader, narrower, or can change entirely. As alluded to in chapter 1, sociolinguists believe that naming is a "living process" that offers an

> existing set of classifications, but also a set of operations to enable the individual to further classify or reclassify his reality. The process of classification is never wholly free or wholly constrained. It typically ranges between those two poles or the illusion of these poles. When it seems totally constrained it is susceptible to evasion or change, and when it seems neutral and free the terms of that freedom and the site of that neutrality are prescribed.[65]

Indeed, cultural influences can shift so that names begin to mean less or more than they once did, and antilanguages can emerge to manage realities and counterrealities. Examples of such trends outside of politics can be located in how dictionaries are updated over time and how entries must be added and amended. Consider some of the changes that were made in 2003 to the Merriam-Webster dictionary. In that year, this dictionary added ten thousand new entries, including popular cultural references such as *dot-commer* (a person who has been employed by a company that uses the Internet for business) and *McJob* (an unstimulating, low-paid job with few prospects), as well as *dead presidents* (paper currency), *longnecks* (beer served in a bottle with a long neck) *Frankenfood* (genetically engineered food), and others. Of course, these are the new words, and therefore they may be those most likely to catch our attention. It is critical to know, however, that in addition to these notable new terms, the dictionary also amended over 100,000 of its 225,000 entries in 2003. Although these revisions are subtle and not immediately noticed by citizens who use these dynamic terms, they can have profound effects on how people understand their worlds.[66]

Examples of labels shifting with time can also be found in research on the *Democratic, Republican, liberal,* and *conservative* terms. In Baumer and Gold's work on stereotypes, for instance, the authors have observed that during the Ronald Reagan presidency, "as the economic decline of the 1970s gave way to the apparent prosperity of the 1980s, the Democrats lost what had been an advantage of the promotion of economic prosperity. Democrats were now associated with an inability to manage government and the economy."[67] During these same years, they also found that the Republican Party was increasingly "viewed as being willing and able to crack down on America's enemies, both foreign and domestic, as champions of low taxes and of bringing businesslike efficiency to government, as upholders of traditional/conservative values, as supporters of entrepreneurial activity, and as able stewards of foreign policy"[68] In making sense of these shifts, these scholars observe how the Republican image benefited from changes in the political agenda and environment in the 1980s, so much so that "young citizens who are always less likely to articulate images of either party, disproportionately identified with Republicans in the 1980s."[69] In their 2003 work, James Wilson and Karlyn Bowman describe a similar type of culture shift that benefited the Republican cause. They note that because many contemporary political elites make their ideology more transparent and because of the ideological markers in programming on conservative talk radio and FOX news, many Right-leaning voters, at least, have become more comfortable with the *conservative* label (a comfort, they forewarn, that may bolster their identification with conservative and Republican causes in years to come).[70]

The *liberal* and *conservative* terms, too, have shifted over time. Conover and Feldman have described how the nature of the political environment in the 1960s and 1970s made the word *liberal* more visible and then more salient to citizens, such that it had a stronger impact on decision making than did the term *conservative* during those same years. In the authors' minds, the prominence of the "New Left" and the social issues it championed tended to dominate political discourse in the United States and thus put the *liberal* label more prominently in the minds of many. Writing in the 1980s, however, they note that the emergence of the "New Right" and the concomitant ascendancy of the *conservative* label may mean that this term will have "a stronger impact on self-identification in the coming years."[71] In comparing how citizens made sense of these ideological terms, the authors uncovered two intriguing patterns: first, a positive evaluation of the *liberal* label did not predict a negative evaluation of the *conservative* label; second, a positive evaluation of the Democratic Party did not predict a negative evaluation of the Republican Party.[72] That citizens do not evaluate these terms in a zero-sum fashion is explored in greater detail in chapter 6.

A charming study published in 1936 also shows how labels have changed over time—especially when sociologist Selden Menefree reports that *liberalism* was regarded as a positive term by 83 percent of his sample and that it was the most popular of the eight stereotyped words in his study (other words being *conservatism, fascism, patriotism, pacifism, radicalism, socialism*, and *communism*).[73] In his study of the impact of these terms on students, professors, and other professionals, Menefree comments that these types of words "are being used constantly as an important means of social control." Writing in the 1930s, he details how such labels "are used daily by politicians, newspaper men and others to influence the members of various 'publics,' as for example in the behavior known as 'flag-waving.'" He elaborates how such practices may indicate that these political elites understand that stereotyped words (like *radicalism, socialism*, and *communism*) "are powerful weapons against persons and policies with whom they do not agree."[74] Interestingly, Menefree concludes by asking teachers to educate students to think critically about these charged words as well as how they can be managed by political actors. Writing a full fifty years before many of the branding theorists cited in chapter 1 did, Menefree observes that many of these scare words have stronger emotional connections than rational meanings. He concludes, "By stressing factual and analytical material regarding the movement which these and similar terms represent, [teachers] may inoculate [their] students against irrational behavior in response to stereotyped words."[75]

To sum, then, party labels are more likely to intersect with voters than are other types of partisanship, are managed largely by elite voices, have considerable influence on individuals, and are potentially dynamic. Many scholars have acknowledged such labels' influence, but as Snyder and Ting observe, none have "provided a satisfactory formalization of party labels as brand names."[76] Such a project is important for theoretical reasons, they contend, because it could inform such concerns as when voters actually use party labels in deciding how to vote, what kinds of equilibrium policies result when voters rely on party labels, and the circumstances in which parties try to build and maintain differentiated brand names.[77] While the goal of this project is not to empirically test how citizens or parties react to and modify labels, the current project provides an important first step in such a direction: mapping the ways in which labels have been used over time. The patterns unearthed here are notable for their descriptive value as well as their ability to enrich future empirical analyses.

TRACKING THE SYMBOLIC CAPITAL OF PARTIES

In American politics, party labels are names that can increase or decrease the political opportunities for party organizations. In this sense, then, the symbolic capital of party labels can contribute to the political capital of the groups they represent. In mapping the symbolic capital of these labels, it is important to underscore that, like related topics (e.g., social capital, political capital), symbolic capital is a dynamic construct and best supported through a variety of data sets. My aim in this project is to conduct a type of semantic genealogy, a technique inspired by a host of scholars who have conducted longitudinal studies of language, including Raymond Williams, Richard Merritt, Daniel Rodgers, and Celeste Condit and John Lucaites.[78] All of these researchers have analyzed the meanings of certain key words in public discourse, noting how these terms have changed over time and thereby influenced public life. As Condit and Lucaites assert, people "understand their lives together in large measure through the stories they tell about the past,"[79] and whatever a certain term means, "it is necessarily a function of the interaction between its past and present usages for a particular rhetorical culture."[80] This project searches for such interactions of party labels.

The current design is based on the belief that political parties largely play two important roles in the polity: that of facilitating elections and that of organizing legislatures. Rather than simply listen to how one voice has constructed party labels in one of these venues, I conducted a comprehensive content analysis in this project on how labels are discussed by two voices during presidential campaigns (candidates and the media) and by two voices during periods of governance (legislators and scholars). With regard to the campaign condition, I have examined presidential campaign speeches delivered over fourteen campaigns (1948 through 2000) as well as the newspaper coverage accompanying these speeches. Presidential speeches have been selected primarily because the president is the focus of government for millions of Americans. Presidential speeches are appropriate for this project because presidents are often regarded as the spokespersons for their parties, and these speeches, for the most part, receive more popular and press attention than would speeches delivered by regional or local candidates. I have also watched how newspapers treat these party labels. To draw time comparisons, I have analyzed campaign coverage during the same period as that of the speeches (both texts have been collected from the convention date to election day for the campaigns 1948 through 2000). The newspaper articles come from the *New York Times*, *Washington Post*, *Chicago Tribune*, *Los Angeles Times*, *Christian Science Monitor*, *Atlanta Constitution*, and Associated Press wire stories. These media outlets have been selected for the following reasons: the *New York Times* often sets the national media agenda (and often the agenda of televised nightly news);[81] the *Washington Post* serves as another elite paper on governmental affairs; the *Chicago Tribune*, *Los Angeles Times*, and *Christian Science Monitor* provide regional perspectives while still being widely read newspapers; and the Associated Press wire stories have national influence, as they are regularly picked up in papers throughout the country.[82]

For the governing condition, I have examined congressional debates (in the U.S. House of Representatives) and civics textbooks. Many scholars note that partisanship is more pronounced in the House than in the Senate, largely due to the increased number of members, the committee structure and rules on floor debate, and the amending process.[83] Larry Sabato addresses this point directly when he states, "In no segment of American government is the party more visible or vital than in the Congress."[84] Therefore, to capture how partisanship is treated by a government institution that depends on it, I trace party labels during four debates (two raised by Democrats: one successful, one not successful; and two raised by Republicans: one successful, one not successful) focusing on one issue (civil rights).[85] The topic of civil rights has been selected because it signifies a key division between liberal and conservative approaches to the state—that is, the tension between thinking that the state should act to improve (protect) the lives of citizens and believing that such issues should be left to the people themselves. Admittedly, the parties have altered their stances on civil rights over the years (i.e., a considerable number of Democrats voted against the Johnson-inspired Civil Rights Act of 1964); for this reason, I am careful to interpret the data from these discussions in light of their historical conditions. With regard to civics books, Thomas Cronin writes that most textbook authors see books as having two preeminent functions: to instruct students and to train citizens.[86] As he puts it, these authors see themselves as primary agents in the political socialization of the next generation of citizens. Consequently, it stands to reason that an analysis of civics textbooks should provide a glimpse into what the educational system is teaching Americans to think about parties.

In considering how label use can influence political outcomes in this project, it is important to attend to a set of characteristics of the contexts in which party labels are discussed. This discussion of symbolic capital keys on citizens as ultimate targets of public communications as well as on how political elites have adapted to an information age. Both citizens and elites have special needs and motivations in the contemporary political climate. For their part, U.S. citizens are asked to make more electoral decisions than are voters in any other country, but Americans must do so in the overcommunicated environment already described; to the extent that citizens participate, they need an efficient means of making sense of their political worlds. The elites in this project have somewhat distinct needs and motivations, ranging from getting elected, to passing legislation, to writing news that will attract an audience, to writing books that will train citizens. The ways that groups of elites use party labels combine to form understandings of these words and take place in an overcommunicated society in which many for-profit brands are being carefully managed. On this latter point, as addressed in chapter 1, it is incumbent upon a brand to develop a message that is publicly observable, that inspires attachment, that is taken seriously by the audience and the media, and that can withstand critique from opponents and the press.

The coding scheme featured in this content analysis has been derived from seminal debates in the literature on political parties. In chapters 3 through 6, I present information from these political variables to discuss how the labels have been constructed over time. In chapter 7, I cluster these political variables to interpret them in light of the best branding strategies, discussed in chapter 1 (including the concepts of visibility, potency, and likeability—notions that flatter the shortcuts of the audience and the needs of successful brands).[87] Chapter 7, too, details how these concepts have worked together in the construction of party labels as brands in the past and how they could work together in the future.

CONCLUSION

Are political parties strong? To date, this question has largely been answered through examinations of political data sets. While these are important investigations, they cannot respond to burgeoning concerns in an information age: how party labels have been used, what they have come to mean, and how these meanings influence political capital in the contemporary environment. This project, then, presents a content analysis of how four elite voices have used five party labels from 1948 to 2000. This decision rests on the assumptions that citizens are most likely to encounter parties through language, that elite voices help to manage the meanings of party labels, that labels are key shortcuts with psychological effects, and that labels can change with time.

Because we live in culture, it is often difficult to see the work our environment imposes on us daily. However, looking at a study such as Menefree's, which shows an 83 percent positive approval for *liberalism* (far more than for the label *conservatism*), or one such as Baumer and Gold's, which details gains in the Republican image in the 1980s, reveals how dynamic these terms can be and how open theses labels are to organized forces that may wish to reposition them. Clearly, *liberalism* is not a true semantic grandparent of the *L* word, as detailed in chapter 1. Nevertheless, that *liberalism* was far more attractive to citizens than *conservatism* seventy years ago points to how theses terms can change over time—often in profound and gradual ways that escape direct notice.

The task ahead, then, is to begin to unpack the influences of time and culture on party labels in order to better understand their influence on citizens in 2004. A critical task, this, for as Daniel Rodgers reminds us:

> Political words do more than mystify; they inspire, persuade, enrage, mobilize. With words minds are changed, votes acquired, enemies labeled, alliances secured, unpopular programs made palatable, the status quo suddenly unveiled as unjust and intolerable. Through words, coalitions are made out of voters who, stripped of their common rallying cries and slogans, would quickly dissolve into jarring fragments.[88]

Rodgers continues, "We use words, and we are often used by words. To be wise to the forces of politics is not only to keep one's eyes peeled but one's ears open."[89] And so the following chapters shall.

NOTES

1. Murray Edelman, *The Symbolic Uses of Politics* (Urbana: University of Illinois Press, 1964); Edelman, *Political Language* (New York: Academic Press, 1977).

2. Philip E. Converse, "The Nature of Belief Systems in Mass Publics," in *Ideology and Discontent*, ed. David E. Apter (New York: Free Press, 1964); John Zaller, *The Nature and Origins of Mass Opinion* (Cambridge: Cambridge University Press, 1992).

3. Jaime Pennebaker, Matthias Mehl, and Kimberly Niederhoffer, "Psychological Aspects of Natural Language Use: Our Words, Our Selves," *Annual Review of Psychology* 54 (2003): 547–77.

4. Victoria Fromkin and Robert Rodman, *An Introduction to Language* (New York: Holt, Rinehart and Winston, 1974).

5. Robert Punam, *Bowling Alone: The Collapse and Revival of American Community* (New York: Simon & Schuster, 2000).

6. Putnam, *Bowling Alone*, 21, 415.

7. John A. Booth and Patricia Bayer Richard, "Civil Society, Political Capital, and Democratization in Central America," *Journal of Politics* 60, no. 3 (1998): 780–800; Regina Birner and Heidi Wittmer, "Converting Social Capital into Political Capital: How Do Local Communities Gain Political Influence? A Theoretical Approach and Empirical Evidence from Thailand and Colombia," presented at "Constituting the Commons: Crafting Sustainable Commons in the New Millennium," the eighth conference of the International Association for the Study of Common Property, Bloomington, Indiana, 31 May–4 June 2000, http://dlc.dlib.indiana.edu/archive/00000221 (17 July 2004). Ester R. Fuchs, Lorraine C. Minnite, and Robert Y. Shapiro, "Political Capital and Political Participation," unpublished manuscript, www.sipa.columbia.edu/RESEARCH/Paper/99–3.pdf (17 July 2004).

8. John Aldrich, *Why Parties? The Origin and Transformation of Party Politics in America* (Chicago: University of Chicago Press, 1995).

9. Joseph A. Schlesinger, "The New American Political Party," *American Political Science Review* 79 (1985): 1152–69, 1154.

10. Juan J. Linz and Alfred Stepan, *Problems of Democratic Transition and Consolidation* (Baltimore, Md.: Johns Hopkins University Press, 1996); Phillipe Schmitter and Terry Karl, "What Democracy Is . . . and Is Not," in *The Global Resurgency of Democracy*, ed. L. Diamond and M. Plattner, 2nd ed. (Baltimore, Md.: Johns Hopkins University Press, 1996).

11. Elmer Eric Schattschneider, *Party Government* (New York: Holt, Rinehart and Winston, 1942).

12. Anthony Downs, *An Economic Theory of Democracy* (New York: Harper, 1957); Joseph A. Schlesinger, "The New American Political Party," *American Political Science Review* 79, no. 4 (1985): 1152–69.

13. Frank Sorauf and Paul Allen Beck, *Party Politics in America*, 6th ed. (Glenview, Ill.: Scott, Foresman, 1988).

14. Roger Davidson and Walter J. Oleszek, *Congress and Its Members*, 4th ed. (Washington, D.C.: Congressional Quarterly Press, 1993), 38.

15. Edmund Burke, *Works*, vol. 1 (London: G. Bell and Sons, 1897).

16. Joseph A. Schumpeter, *Capitalism, Socialism, and Democracy* (New York: Harper and Row, 1942), 283.

17. Walter Dean Burnham, "The Changing Shape of the American Political Universe," *American Political Science Review* 59, no. 1 (1965): 7–28.

18. Angus Campbell et al., *The American Voter* (New York: Wiley, 1960), 120.

19. Samuel Popkin, *The Reasoning Voter* (Chicago: University of Chicago Press, 1991), 14.

20. Richard Niemi and Herbert Weisberg, *Controversies in Voting Behavior* (Washington D.C.: Congressional Quarterly Press, 1984); Norman Nie, Sydney Verba, and John Petrocik, *The Changing American Voter* (Cambridge, Mass.: Harvard University Press, 1979); Helmut Norpoth and Jerry Rusk, "Partisan Dealignment in the American Electorate," *American Political Science Review* 76, no. 3 (September 1982): 522–37.

21. William Chambers and Walter Dean Burnham, *The American Party Systems: Stages of Political Development* (New York: Oxford University Press, 1975), v.

22. Steven J. Rosenstone, Roy Behr, and Edward H. Lazarus, *Third Parties in America: Citizen Response to Major Party Failure* (Princeton, N.J.: Princeton University Press, 1984). With regard to legal obstacles, these authors note that the 1974 Federal Election Campaign Act helps to force out third-party challengers. While major party presidential candidates receive lump sums for their campaigns, third-party candidates "are eligible to receive public funds only after the November election and then only if they appear on the ballot in at least ten states and obtain at least 5 percent of the national popular vote" (26).

23. Rosenstone, Behr, and Lazarus, "Third Parties," 79.

24. Rosenstone, Behr, and Lazarus, "Third Parties," 79.

25. Aldrich, *Why Parties?* 14.

26. Nelson Polsby, *Consequences of Party Reform* (Oxford: Oxford University Press, 1983), 182–83.

27. Gerald M. Pomper, "The Alleged Decline of American Parties," in *Politicians and Party Politics*, ed. John Grey Geer (Baltimore, Md.: Johns Hopkins University Press, 1998), 36; David Broder, *The Party's Over* (New York: Harper and Row, 1972); Morris P. Fiorina, *Divided Government* (New York: Macmillan, 1992).

28. Walter Dean Burnham, *Critical Elections and the Mainsprings of American Politics* (New York: Norton, 1970); Martin P. Wattenberg, *The Decline of American Political Parties, 1952–1988* (Cambridge, Mass.: Harvard University Press, 1998).

29. See Polsby, *Party Reform*; see Sorauf and Beck, *Party Politics*.

30. Robert Putnam, "Bowling Alone: America's Declining Social Capital," *Current* 373 (June 1995): 3–10.

31. Larry M. Bartels, "Partisanship and Voting Behavior, 1952–1996," *American Journal of Political Science* 44 (2000): 35–50; Marc Hetherington, "Resurgent Mass Partisanship: The Role of Elite Polarization," *American Political Science Review* 94 (2001): 619–31, 619.

32. John Petrocik, "Issue Ownership in Presidential Elections, with a 1980 Case Study," *American Journal of Political Science* 40 (1996): 825–50. John Petrocik, William L. Benoit, and Glen J. Hansen, "Issue Ownership and Presidential Campaigning, 1952–2000," paper presented to the annual meeting of the American Political Science Association, San Francisco, 30 August–2 September 2001.

33. Pierre Bourdieu, *The Logic of Practice* (Cambridge: Polity Press, 1990); Pierre Bourdieu, *Outline of a Theory of Practice* (Cambridge: Cambridge University Press, 1977); Edelman, *Political Language.*

34. Robert Putnam, *Bowling Alone: The Collapse and Revival of American Community* (New York: Simon & Schuster, 2000), 21, 415.

35. Edelman, *Political Language*, 142.

36. V. O. Key, *Public Opinion and American Democracy* (New York: Alfred A. Knopf, 1961). John Zaller, *The Nature and Origins of Public Opinion* (Cambridge: Cambridge University Press, 1992); Converse, "Nature of Belief Systems."

37. Edelman, *Political Language.*

38. Arthur Sanders, "The Meaning of Party Images," *Western Political Quarterly* 41 (1988): 583–99, 583.

39. Sanders, "Meaning," 597.

40. Michael Schudson, *The Good Citizen: A History of American Civic Life* (New York: Free Press, 1998), 311.

41. Schudson, *Good Citizen*, 310.

42. Samuel Popkin, *The Reasoning Voter: Communication and Persuasion in Presidential Campaigns* (Chicago: University of Chicago Press, 1991), 212.

43. Popkin, *Reasoning Voter*, 16.

44. Wendy M. Rahn, "The Role of Partisan Stereotypes in Information Processing about Political Candidates," *American Journal of Political Science* 37 (1993): 472–96, 473.

45. Richard Herrera, "Understanding the Language of Politics: A Study of Elites and Masses," *Political Science Quarterly* 111, no. 4 (1996–1997): 619–37, 634.

46. Herrera, "Understanding the Language," 635.

47. James Snyder and Michael Ting, "An Informational Rationale for Political Parties," *American Political Science Review* 46, no. 1 (2002): 90–111, 93.

48. Snyder and Ting, "Informational Rationale," 94.

49. Jeffrey Mondak, "Public Opinion and Heuristic Processing of Source Cues," *Political Behavior* 15, no. 2 (1993): 167–92; Mondak, "Source Cues and Policy Approval: The Cognitive Dynamics of Public Support for the Reagan Agenda," *American Journal of Political Science* 37, no. 1 (1993): 186–212.

50. Brian F. Schaffner and Matthew J. Streb, "The Partisan Heuristic in Low-Information Elections," *Public Opinion Quarterly* 66 (2002): 559–81, 579.

51. Herrera, "Understanding the Language." See also, Wendy M. Rahn, John H. Aldrich, and Eugene Borgida, "Individual and Contextual Variations in Political Candidate Appraisal," *American Political Science Review* 88 (1994): 193–99; Susan T. Fiske, Donald R. Kinder, and Michael W. Larter, "The Novice and the Expert: Knowledge-Based Strategies in Political Cognition," *Journal of Experimental Social Psychology* 19 (1983): 381–400.

52. Sanders, "Meaning," 590.

53. Pamela J. Conover and Stanley Feldman, "The Origins and Meaning of Liberal/Conservative Self Identification," *American Journal of Political Science* 25 (1981): 617–45.

54. Conover and Feldman, "Origins and Meaning," 634.

55. Conover and Feldman, "Origins and Meaning," 636.

56. Conover and Feldman, "Origins and Meaning," 644.

57. Ronald R. Rapoport, "Partisanship Change in a Candidate-Centered Era," *Journal of Politics* 59, no. 1 (February 1997): 185–99, 197.

58. Wendy M. Rahn and Katherine Cramer, "Activation of Political Party Stereotypes: The Role of Television," *Political Communication* 13 (1996): 195–212, 208.

59. Rahn, "Role of Partisan Stereotypes," 492.

60. Rahn and Cramer, "Activation of Political," 209.

61. Donald C. Baumer and Howard Gold, "Party Images and the American Electorate," *American Politics Quarterly* 23 (1995): 33–61; Rahn, "Role of Partisan Stereotypes"; Rahn and Cramer, "Activation of Political"; Sanders, "Meaning"; Richard J. Trilling, *Party Image and Electoral Behavior* (New York: Wiley, 1976).

62. Baumer and Gold, "Party Images," 35.

63. Baumer and Gold, "Party Images," 36.

64. Baumer and Gold, "Party Images," 44.

65. Gunther K. Kress and Robert H. Hodge, *Language as Ideology* (London: Routledge & Kegan Paul, 1981), 64–65.

66. Trudy Tynan, "New Words Define New Times," *Austin American Statesman*, 4 July 2003, 27A.

67. Baumer and Gold, "Party Images," 35.

68. Baumer and Gold, "Party Images," 35–36.

69. Baumer and Gold, "Party Images," 51.

70. James Q. Wilson and Karlyn Bowman, "Defining the Peace Party," *Public Interest* 153 (Fall 2003): 69–79.

71. Conover and Feldman, "Origins and Meaning," 630.

72. Conover and Feldman, "Origins and Meaning," 630.

73. Selden S. Menefree, "The Effect of Stereotyped Words on Political Judgments," *American Sociological Review* 1, no. 4 (1936): 614–21. Specifically, those who rated the words positively ranged as follows: for *liberalism*, introductory sociology students (88 percent), sophomore sociology students (81 percent), advanced sociology students (93 percent), advanced economics students (69 percent), night school students (78 percent), and professors (81 percent); for *conservatism*, introductory sociology students (38 percent), sophomore sociology students (26 percent), advanced sociology students (25 percent), advanced economics students (47 percent), night school students (48 percent), and professors (26 percent) (617).

74. Menefree, "Effect," 621.

75. Menefree, "Effect," 621.

76. Snyder and Ting, "Informational Rationale," 90.

77. Snyder and Ting, "Informational Rationale," 90.

78. Raymond Williams, *Keywords: A Vocabulary of Culture and Society* (New York: Oxford, 1976); Richard Merritt, *Symbols of American Community* (New Haven, Conn.: Yale University Press, 1966); Daniel T. Rodgers, *Contested Truths: Keywords in*

American Politics since Independence (Cambridge, Mass.: Harvard University Press, 1987); Celeste M. Condit and John L. Lucaites, *Crafting Equality: America's Anglo-African World* (Chicago: University of Chicago Press, 1993).

79. Condit and Lucaites, *Crafting Equality*, 1.

80. Condit and Lucaites, *Crafting Equality*, 218.

81. Herbert Gans, *Deciding What's News* (New York: Random House, 1979).

82. D. Charles Whitney and Lee Becker, "'Keeping the Gates' for Gatekeepers: The Effects of Wire News," *Journalism Quarterly* 59 (1982): 60–65.

83. John B. Bader and Charles O. Jones, "The Republican Parties in Congress: Bicameral Differences," in *Congress Reconsidered*, 5th ed., ed. Lawrence C. Dodd and Bruce I. Oppenheimer (Washington, D.C.: Congressional Quarterly Press, 1993).

84. Larry Sabato, *The Party's Just Begun: Shaping Political Parties for America's Future* (Glenville, Ill.: Scott Foresman, 1988), 46.

85. Edward G. Carmines and James A. Stimson, *Issue Evolution: Race and the Transformation of American Politics* (Princeton, N.J.: Princeton University Press, 1992). These debates include discussion of the Civil Rights Act of 1957 (encouraged and signed by President Dwight Eisenhower), the Civil Rights Act of 1964 (encouraged and signed by President Lyndon Johnson), the busing debate of 1979 (introduced by Democrats, did not pass the House), and the welfare reform debate of 1995 (introduced by Republicans, passed the House but was not signed by President Clinton). This counterbalanced design was selected for two key reasons: first, these particular debates feature a mixture of rhetorical advocacy and opposition for the parties; second, the topic of civil rights has been selected because it signifies a key division between the liberal and conservative approaches to the state—that is, the tension between thinking that the state should act to improve (protect) the lives of citizens and believing that such issues should be left to the people themselves.

86. Thomas Cronin, "The Textbook Presidency and Political Science," in *Perspectives on the Presidency*, ed. S. Bach and G. T. Sulzner (Lexington, Mass.: D.C. Heath, 1974), 63.

87. These clusters include the concepts of visibility (the public nature of the labels as measured through the number of times in which a term is used); potency (the perceived strength of the labels as measured through the variables *potency, task, time, position, behavior*); likeability (the public evaluation of the labels as measured through the variables *role, context, position,* and *quality*). See the methodological appendix.

88. Rodgers, *Contested Truths*, 4.

89. Rodgers, *Contested Truths*, 6.

3

THE ENDURING PARTY

Americans have never loved political parties. Yet they have also never ignored them either, a point that was as true in the late eighteenth century as it was during the second half of the twentieth century. Consider, for example, how Thomas Jefferson describes parties in two letters, written in 1824 and 1789, respectively:

> Men by their constitutions are naturally divided into two parties: (1) Those who fear and distrust the people and wish to draw all powers from them into the hands of higher classes. (2) Those who identify themselves with the people, have confidence in them. . . . In every country, these two parties exist.[1]

> I never submitted the whole system of my opinions to the creed of any party of men whatever, in religion, in philosophy, in politics or in anything else, where I was capable of thinking for myself. Such an addiction is the last degradation of a free and moral agent. If I could not go to heaven but with a party, I would not go there at all.[2]

Now, consider how two political scholars, John Bibby and Jack Dennis, refer to them in 1997 and 1975, respectively:

> One of the hard facts of American politics has been the overwhelming electoral dominance exercised by the Democratic and Republican parties since the realignment of 1854–1860. Nowhere else in the world have the same two parties so completely and continuously dominated free elections. This suggests that two-party politics is highly compatible with American society, culture, and governmental structures.[3]

> We may be called upon in the not so distant future to witness the de-
> mise of a once prominent institution of American government and pol-
> itics (parties).[4]

As these statements illustrate, there are times when American elites have believed that political parties are a necessary, if not organic, entity in a democratic state. At other times, however, they have found parties both distasteful and feckless. Two questions, of course, could be asked of such statements:
the political capital question—What made these individuals speak of party
as they did? and the symbolic capital question—What are some of the implications of their speaking about parties in these ways?

Political scientists have plenty of ways to answer the first question.
They might, for example, be inclined to look at a moment in history—say,
that regarding George W. Bush in 2004—and ask if his campaign meant that
parties had become weak or strong, particularly in light of other moments.
In doing so, they could measure the extent to which Republicans in Congress have opposed or supported the second Iraq war (and perhaps compare
this opposition or support to George H. W. Bush's backing on Capitol Hill
for the first Iraq war); they could trace campaign contributions, evaluating
if and how Republicans were able to raise money for W. in 2004 vs. 2000;
or, they could assess GOP grassroots efforts and calculate if the party was
more or less successful in mobilizing support from its base in 2004 than in
elections 2002 and 2000. Any or all of these types of projects would tap the
political prowess of Bush and the Republican Party in 2004.

This chapter focuses on the second question and takes a step back to
analyze the discourse surrounding political parties over the past half century.
The questions, then, are as follows: How often have elites used party labels?
How have they talked about them? What can such talk teach us about American politics? What can it further tell us about American culture? American
history? American institutions? American passions? and the American future? Thomas Jefferson was not required to mention parties in his corre-
spondence, and scholars John Bibby and Jack Dennis could have conducted
research on a plethora of other topics. But all three chose to talk about parties. That must mean something.

Because scholars have yet to listen to discussions of party language,
chapter 3 casts the widest net possible, searching for patterns in label use that
transcend label, speaker, and year. In a sense, then, this chapter presents the
broadest configuration of label use over the years—a baseline that serves as a
comparison for the more specific discussions in chapters 4–6. After running
descriptive statistics on all of the data in the Campaign Mapping Project as

well as in my coding of a stratified sample from that textbase, I found (with few exceptions) three themes: first, party labels have not disappeared (despite periods of strength, decline, and resurgence); second, party labels have not been disregarded (they are regularly described as powerful elites); and, third, party labels have not been interpreted in depth (portrayals have focused on loose coalitions, thereby describing "thin" versus "thick" partisanship). Although these claims may appear modest, they nevertheless invite critical inspection because they represent the hegemonic story of party in the United States, the uniform and stubborn ways in which elites have discussed party terms over the years. Indeed, because of their constancy, these themes are central to an informed understanding of parties in the U.S. political system. This chapter addresses these themes in light of how such patterns—visibility, elite status, and thin description—contribute to parties' symbolic capital.

PARTY LABELS ARE USED CONTINUOUSLY

Simple frequencies from the Campaign Mapping Project data reveal that elites have not stopped talking about parties, as might be predicted by Dennis's statement. Figure 3.1 presents data on all labels in the project over time. There we see that there has been a decline in the use of labels by presidential candidates, but it is important to note that this trend seems to be on a slight rebound after 1988. Specifically, the density ratio of label use in 1992 (ratio = .225) and 1996 (ratio = .282) were higher than that in 1988 (.196), and if one examines only the discourse of George W. Bush in 2000 (ratio = .244), a small but notable sense of label use reappears in the last three campaigns. (For his part, Al Gore used fewer labels than any candidate in this sample [ratio = .121], a tendency that—curiously—is correlated with losing candidacies; see chapter 5). Figure 3.1 also shows that there has been something of a curvilinear pattern of label use in news reports and that the density ratios of label use in the nation's newspapers in 1996 (ratio = 1.14) and 2000 (1.30) are higher than any year since 1960 (ratio = 1.19) and are approaching levels last seen in 1952 (ratio = 1.22) and 1956 (1.33). Moreover, simple frequencies from the congressional debates under examination also show that legislators used more labels per total words in the 1995 congressional debate than in any other year examined in this study.[5] Given concern about the vitality of parties at the close of the twentieth century, the question becomes, What accounts for the persistence of such labels? I advance a simple answer: parties may be far more important to the democratic conversation than is commonly realized.

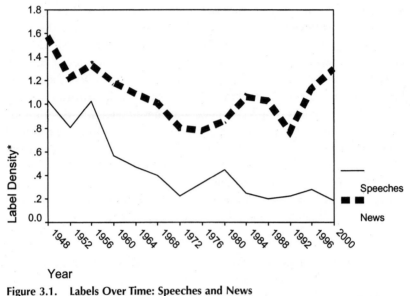

Figure 3.1.   Labels Over Time: Speeches and News
*Label density = label / all words in genre × 100

In examining the qualitative aspects of these trends, I found that one reason why elites continue to discuss parties is that they are consequential, as illustrated by the variables *potency* and *role*. *Potency* was created to measure whether parties were portrayed as "actors" or "recipients of action" in a given sentence. As table 3.1 illustrates, they were considered to be actors 46.8 percent of the time and recipients 30.5 percent of the time. The variable *role* was created to assess the social or political job performed by the parties, and as displayed in table 3.2, we see that party labels were more commonly found to be "part of the solution" (31.8 percent) than "part of the problem" (19.6 percent). Although elites did not always editorialize about parties in these ways, they did portray parties as having a generally positive impact on the political environment. In both of these instances, then, parties were more likely to be discussed as powerful and beneficial than impotent and harmful in American politics.

Textual examples illustrate the patterns found in these figures. Take the following statement made by U.S. representative Bill Richardson (D-NM) on 21 March 1995, whereby Democrats are portrayed as working to improve the lives of welfare recipients, children, and parents. Notice how Richardson constitutes Democrats as being active (tied to such stabilizing verbs as *require, provide, support,* and *maintain*) and empathic (concerned with resources, the safety net, and self-sufficiency). In both obvious and subtle

Table 3.1.   Party Labels by *Potency* Variable (in percentages)

Unclear	21.1
As actor	46.8
As recipient	30.5
Balanced	1.6

Table 3.2.   Party Labels by *Role* Variable (in percentages)

Part of the solution	31.8
Part of the problem	19.6
Unclear/as conflicted	48.6

ways, Richardson constitutes Democrats as being confident and dynamic, up to the task of governance:

> *Democrats* are strong on work. The *Democratic* proposal actually requires that recipients prepare for and engage in work; provide resources for the assistance needed to become self-sufficient, such as education, training, child care, and transportation. *Democrats* support children. *Democrats* maintain the national commitment to providing a safety net for kids, while requiring their parents to become self-sufficient.[6]

Political campaigners also praised party labels, stressing their agency and relevance in the political system. For instance, note the energy and optimism that Adlai Stevenson associates with Democrats when he praises them for their role in suburban growth and home ownership:

> The *Democratic* Party has played a special role in the whole process of suburban growth. This great new development in our life rests essentially on the tremendous social and economic gains which took place under twenty years of *Democratic* government.
>
> It is not just that the *Democratic* Party took over responsibility at a time when the American economic machine had stalled or that twenty years of *Democratic* rule more than quintupled the annual output of goods and services for our people.
>
> Nor is it just that the *Democratic* Party brought back to government a spirit of concern for the ordinary people of the country.
>
> I think, rather, of the basic matter of people owning their own homes and of the contributions of *Democratic* action to home ownership in America.

> We set up the Home Owners Loan Corporation to save people's homes from foreclosure back there in the 1930s. We established the Federal Housing Administration and later the Veterans' Housing Program to bring home ownership within the reach of more Americans. We set up the Federal National Mortgage Association to support the FHA and G 2 home loan programs and thus enable millions of families to buy homes at low interest rates and with modest down payments. We strengthened the Federal Home Loan Banks and established the Federal Savings and Loan Insurance Corporation to help protect home investments.[7]

Republican candidates, too, praised the potency and role of party labels out on the hustings. Unlike Stevenson and other Democrats, GOP candidates often praised their party for standing for principles and ideals—even in the latter years of this project, a time when candidates had been less likely to rely on labels (figure 3.1). Examples, here, include the following. In 1984, Ronald Reagan applauded his party for acting on "a conviction," passing "a resolution concerning Anti Semitism and disassociating the *Republican party* from all people and groups who practice bigotry in any form."[8] In 1988, George H. W. Bush advised an audience to put its "faith in '*Republican* futures,'" for his *party* spent "the last eight years laying the foundation for a better America," "strengthening the peace and ushering in a new era of economic growth."[9] In 1992 Bush praised "the *Republican* election effort this year, so many people doing so much for what I think is good, sound government."[10] In 1996, Bob Dole declared, "The *Republican party* is broad and inclusive. It represents many streams of opinion and many points of view."[11] And in 2000, George W. Bush proclaimed, "We are now the party of ideas and innovation. The *party* of idealism and inclusion. The *party* of a simple and powerful hope. My fellow citizens, we can begin again. After all of the shouting, and all of the scandal. After all of the bitterness and broken faith."[12]

At first blush, these statements seem so cliché-ridden that it is tempting to ignore them—candidates campaign, and part of campaigning is uttering partisan platitudes. Yet in light of Roderick Hart's analyses of the speeches in this data set, these statements honoring the power and benevolence of party labels become more remarkable. Specifically, employing a computerized content-analytic program, Hart has found that presidential speeches are more ebullient than other genres of campaign discourse over this period.[13] In this project, I find a qualified buoyancy in candidate descriptions of party; in these speeches, candidates are more likely to regard party labels as part of the solution (38.5 percent) than as part of the problem (23.4 percent—variable: *role*). There is some variation across the labels, of course, which would be expected (i.e., candidates have consistently seen *party* as being part of the solution rather than part of the problem; Democratic and Republican candidates stand up for their own labels more than they do those of their opponents; and Republican candidates began to disparage the *liberal* label in the campaigns of the 1980s and 1990s). Despite these deviations, however, candidates have largely referred to party labels as being beneficial. This is an intriguing finding, particularly in a time when parties must share the candidate-selection process with the media (largely television) and ambitious politicians (often wealthy ones). Thus, when candidates have spoken of parties, they have spoken of them well.

Textbook authors also stress the potency and positive role of parties and do so more unapologetically than either legislators or candidates. The authors commonly went so far as to equate democracy with the two-party system. In the following examples, note how the authors suggest that the two-party system is emblematic of democracy, thereby encouraging impressionable students to believe that parties are central to the U.S. system:

- "Today's political parties are so much a part of government that it would be hard to imagine government without them."[14]
- "Nearly everyone who gets elected to the House belongs to either the Democratic or the Republican party. Legislators of other parties run for election, but seldom win."[15]
- "Today, Democrats and Republicans similarly dominate the contests for elective office."[16]

Even though legislators, candidates, and authors need different things from parties (a point explored in chapter 5), it is fascinating that they all portray party labels (broadly speaking) as being active and benevolent. It seems powerful that elites with such different job descriptions construct parties in such similar ways.

As table 3.2 also shows, however, parties are not always portrayed positively. Indeed, all four voices sometimes place parties in a negative context (19.6 percent of the time) and in an uncertain or conflicted context (48.6 percent of the time—variable: *context*). Negativity was injected into statements in both direct and obscure ways. First, consider the direct route, as evidenced in these speeches by Michael Dukakis in 1988 and George H. W. Bush in 1992, respectively. Note how Dukakis accuses the Republicans of mismanagement, while H. W. Bush blames Bill Clinton (along with the liberal wing of Clinton's party) for making the wrong choices:

- "After another $25 billion and 8 years of *Republican* mismanagement, our ICBM's [intercontinental ballistic missiles] are more vulnerable than they were in 1980."[17]
- "The *liberal*, McGovern wing of the other party, including my opponent, consistently made the wrong choices."[18]

While complicating statements (like these advanced by Dukakis and Bush) appeared in the data, they were not the most common way for elites to voice disappointment with political parties. Instead, elites—a politically savvy group—were often cautious and measured when critiquing party labels, frequently resorting to "conflicted" statements (ones that feature both positive and negative attributions of partisanship).

In reading the conflicted texts closely, I noticed that much of the tension in these statements took the form of "metacommunication" or "metatalk" (i.e., talk about talk), in which elites open a conversation about party labels even while using party labels.[19] As the following examples show, this strategy helps elites negotiate many of the tensions the party system places upon themselves, including allowing candidates to connect with the voters, legislators to bargain with one another, journalists to write dramatic stories, and textbook authors to address the party system in respectful ways. In a sense, metacommunication seems to have served as a strategic rhetoric for elites wanting to challenge the parties but not willing to forsake the two-party system.

To begin, consider the pressures brought to bear on presidential candidates. In trying to get elected, they know that they must reinforce their base (the loyal party vote) as well as attract the swing vote (often referred to at the end of the twentieth century as the *independent vote*). How, then, should they discuss partisanship? As figure 3.1 shows, they used fewer party labels than did journalists, but they never entirely ignored partisanship. Two candidates—Richard Nixon and Bill Clinton—seemed particularly gifted at using metatalk to establish "common ground" with the country, to position themselves closer to the citizenry than to the traditional party system, and to forge nonpartisan (or extrapartisan) connections with voters.

Nixon's metatalk was quite strategic. Notice how in the following statements he plays party labels off one another, contributing to a kind of partisan ambivalence:

- "In that spirit, I address you tonight, my fellow Americans, not as a partisan of a *party* which would divide us, but as a *partisan* of principles, which can unite us."[20]

- "I'm a *Republican*, but I'm going to tell you tonight that the plea I make is for all of you, whatever you are, *Republicans* or *Democrats* or *independents*, wherever you may be in this great State, to forget for the moment that I am speaking of what your *party* label is and think of this country, and I say that when we select a President of the United States, the country comes first and the *party* label second."[21]

- "What counts today is not our *party*, but this country. And we want the best man for the country whether he's a *Democrat* or a *Republican*. And this is our theme throughout."[22]

Nixon's appeals here would not surprise rhetorician Kenneth Burke. The statements serve as prime examples of Burke's theory of identification, which describes "a condition that occurs when people feel that they are being spoken to in their own language"[23] or "a circumstance in which hierarchical separations have been rhetorically bridged."[24] In these speeches, Nixon uses party labels to elevate himself and his audience to a common place, moving the conversation from a level in which there are divisions (the party/position level—Republicans and Democrats) to a place where there is broader agreement (the principle/valence level—goods that can unite Americans). Leave it to Richard Nixon to use divisive words (i.e., *Democrat*, *Republican*) to unite people.

Bill Clinton also folded metatalk into his speeches, perhaps because he campaigned in the 1990s, a time when candidates, strategists, scholars, pundits, and citizens were savvy to the strategy behind campaigns. As a result, his speeches seemed like unapologetic attempts to voice the dyspeptic logic of late-twentieth-century campaigns. As detailed in chapter 1, *Positioning* authors Al Ries and Jack Trout advise that a key to communicating in an overcommunicated society is to work to place a product in a receptive place in the consumer's mind. Clinton attempted to do just that, playing on a "New Democrat" theme in 1992 and adopting a "Bridge to the Future" mantra in 1996. Like Nixon, Clinton made a case for himself by making a soft case against parties. Unlike Nixon, however, Clinton employed a more specific, future-oriented approach by transporting his audience to the next century and uniting them there, not here. This was both a specific campaign move (capitalizing on his opponent Bob Dole's catastrophic longing for the past) as well as a classic instance of Burke's theory of identification.

Legislators, too, talked about party labels to buy themselves room in congressional debates, often by connecting the meanings of the terms *party* and *partisan* to gridlock and unwieldy behavior. One of Representative Jennifer Dunn's (R-WA) statements in the 1995 welfare reform debate provides an example of this strategy. After listening to Democrats attack the Republican proposal, she denounces partisanship to appeal to the better nature of the legislators when she argues, "Our bill is a mainstream approach, and I urge Legislators not to be deluded by the harsh, *partisan,* intemperate rhetoric they have heard here today. Our bill is tough on bureaucracy, not on kids. Our bill is cruel to the status quo, not the under class."[25]

By talking about the "harsh, *partisan* rhetoric," Dunn elevates discourse and brings partisanship to consciousness (notice how she pits the GOP mainstream plan against the intemperate rhetoric of the Democrats). Here, Dunn decries partisanship roundly, even though in reality her party held a majority in the House and, in the end, her party had enough votes to pass the legislation being debated.[26] Her statement shows that even when a party is in the majority, its representatives may decry partisanship if doing so produces a partisan advantage.

The finding that legislators disparage the *party* label for personal gain is reminiscent of political scientist Richard Fenno's ethnographic work on the campaign strategies of legislators in their districts. Fenno found that "individual legislators do not take responsibility for the performance of Congress; rather, each portrays himself as a fighter against its manifest shortcomings.... Congress is not 'we'; it is 'they.' And legislators of Congress run for Congress by running against Congress. Thus, individual explanations carry with them a heavy dosage of critical commentary on Congress."[27] These data show that this is not just a campaign tactic but a pattern in House discourse as well. Once elected, legislators may stick with this strategy, which benefits them personally, even though it challenges the broader integrity of the institution to which they belong.

Journalists also employ metatalk in their articles, often by playing with the words of the politicians they quote. Consider the following example from the 1956 campaign: "Stevenson told his listeners in Civic Auditorium that 'we must face the fact that every four years the *Republican* candidates talk like Democrats—it is a kind of leap year liberalism. I'm always flattered when they borrow our ideas,' he said."[28] In this story, talk about parties is woven into the very texture of the news article through the remarks of Adlai Stevenson, the candidate. Stevenson's words offer drama and intrigue; accordingly, this particular journalist in 1956 includes them to advance the plot in this campaign depiction.

Textbook authors also engage in metacommunication, and their use of it is more complex than that found in the other genres. This may be true for several reasons: first, scholars write in a more analytical style than do the authors of the other genres examined (having been afforded more time and space to do so); second, scholars attempt to make their portrayals distanced and objective (thereby producing a balanced assessment of where parties are strong and weak); third, textbooks must ultimately meet publishers' needs (which encourages their authors to be careful when describing the political system). This paragraph from political scientist James MacGregor Burns provides a prime example of the ways in which textbook authors use party labels to navigate the tensions of the party system:

> Why this pattern of failure? Why do we stick to a *"two-party"* system when most democracies have multiparty systems? In part because the American people, despite their many divisions over religion, race, and the like, have been united enough that the two big *parties* could adequately represent them. In part it is also because of the nature of our election system. Most of our election districts have a single incumbent and the candidate with the most votes wins. Because only one candidate can win, the largest and second-largest *parties* have a near monopoly of office. The system of election of the president operates in this way on a national scale. The presidency is the supreme prize in American politics: a *party* that cannot attain it, or show promise of attaining it, simply does not operate in the major leagues.[29]

In this paragraph, Burns recognizes the strength of parties, but he does not honor them; he alludes to their power but not in a way that would make a party (or a partisan) proud. The message is clear: parties are strong. The delivery is tense: American citizens stick with parties, despite their pattern of failure. Textbooks, of course, are created to condense material for students. Thus, students reading Burns's text (or the others included in this data set) learn that parties are flawed but nevertheless powerful—a conclusion common to many of the textual examples examined in this chapter.

Frustrations with political parties are not unique to this data set. Revisiting the party decline/resurgence literature is something of a cottage industry in political science research, with a considerable number of books, hundreds of published articles, and myriad conference and seminar papers exploring the ways in which parties have or have not lived up to their potential. So tempting has this line of inquiry been that one scholar has suggested that political scientists have been conducting a "deathwatch" on American parties since the 1960s.[30] So while there is some negativity in the portrayals of parties in this analysis (similar to that witnessed in Dennis's statement at the beginning of the chapter), these moments of critique are rhetorically fascinating because at the very same time that elites are questioning the health of the parties—by virtue of talking about them—these elites prevent, or at least postpone, the parties' death. By not ignoring them, these elites ensure that the construct of party continues to wield influence over their thoughts, conversations, and careers. Although some doubters worry that the breakdown of the party system could lead to "government by the NRA [National Rifle Association] and professional wrestlers" (also known as interest groups and outsiders), these data suggest that this will probably not be the case if legislators, journalists, presidential candidates, and textbook authors have a say in the matter. That they have used party labels continuously over the past half century has kept parties very much alive in the conversation.

PARTY LABELS ARE USED HIERARCHICALLY

Political scholars heretofore have conceived of parties in physical, as well as conceptual, space. One effort to do so, credited first to V. O. Key and then picked up in political scientist Frank Sorauf's textbooks (coauthored with P. A. Beck), locates party in three places: in government, in organizations, and in the electorate.[31] If repetition and widespread use can serve as a guide, this trilogy has been found useful in describing the activities of parties, often appearing in most of the civics textbooks examined here. In the 1990s, however, Gerald Pomper and John Aldrich challenged this schema, preferring to think of parties as groups of "working politicians supported by partisan voters"[32] and creatures "of politicians, the ambitious office seeker and holder."[33] Both Pomper and Aldrich, then, prefer to think of parties as groups of elites, as entities distinctly separated from voters.

These data reveal a similar preference. Over time and circumstance, the voices in this study have constituted parties as elite actors whose paths do not intersect with the people. This finding is not controversial, but its implications may well be. When journalists and textbook authors, as well as candidates and legislators, adhere to a consistent discourse about parties, no official voice exists to challenge the party system.[34] Even though elites do not always celebrate party labels, the data reveal that even when elites do critique labels, they often do so without challenging the labels' place at the bargaining table. The rhetorical treatment of parties, then, may suggest that the privileged position of parties is constantly being upheld in the body politic, at least by the elites in this study.

The elite nature of party labels can be viewed in several ways. The variable *position* was created to trace the party's place in the governmental process as implied by the speaker. As table 3.3 shows, party labels were almost four times more likely to be constituted at the elite level than at the mass level.[35]

Table 3.3. Party Labels by *Position* Variable (in percentages)

Elite	71.2
Mass	18.1
Global/undifferentiated	10.7

Of the four genres, congressional debates saw the highest percentage of elite statements (89.5 percent), often making discourse sound inclusive, at times self-congratulatory. Conceptually, the job of Congress is to represent the public, and theorists have advanced various paradigms of representation, ranging from delegate models (in which representatives voice the desires of their constituencies) to trustee models (in which representatives exercise greater personal judgment in governance). When using party labels, legislators seem to prefer the latter, and so prevalent is this construction that the following sentence, uttered by U.S. representative Jamie Whitten (D-MS) from 1964, instantly sounds familiar: "Mr. Chairman, I can see the coalition of northern *Democrats* and *Republican* leaders on the Judiciary Committee have the votes to defeat us."[36] Behind this familiarity, though, lurk structural markers. This legislator refers to a chairman, a coalition, Democrats and Republicans, leaders, and the Judiciary Committee. All are elite instantiations of party, a common pattern in congressional debates.

The variable *associations* adds to the rhetorical construction of parties as elites. This variable, which measured the entities with which a party label must interact, reveals that labels were most likely to interact with their "own or another party" (38.2 percent), followed by "named politicians" (20.7 percent), "voters" (18.4 percent), "international entities" (2.9 percent), "interest groups" (1.1 percent), and "the media" (0.7 percent), or "other" (5.0 percent) and "none" (13.0 percent). Collapsing these coding categories into two categories ("associations with citizens" and "associations with other entities"), parties were portrayed as interacting just 18.4 percent with "the voters" and 81.6 percent with "other entities." To be sure, there is an inevitable correlation between the *position* and the *associations* variables, for if a political party is seen to be interacting with citizens, chances are that the resulting statements place party at the mass level as well. This correlation does not detract from the overall pattern, though: elites constitute parties as interacting with ordinary citizens less than one-fifth of the time.

Of the genres, candidates (25.6 percent) and journalists (25.4 percent) were more likely to associate parties with citizens than were legislators (13.4 percent) or authors (7.6 percent). These distinctions make sense, considering how the data were drawn (that is, speeches and news reports came from campaign periods; debates and textbooks came, largely, from noncampaign periods). Ronald Reagan, as a candidate and then as president, was particularly known to mention citizens in his speeches. A qualitative read of the data suggests that he also associates parties with citizens more convincingly than did other politicians. Consider how the "Great Communicator" did so in the following speech: "These visitors to that city on the Potomac do not come as white or black, red or yellow; they are not Jews or Christians; *conservatives* or *liberals*; or *Democrats* or *Republicans*. They are Americans awed by what has gone before; proud of what for them is still a shining city on a Hill."[37]

Kathleen Hall Jamieson has written about how Reagan's rhetoric comfortably singles out special groups and individuals for direct address without sounding self-serving.[38] Whether Reagan was speaking directly to the families who lost astronauts in the explosion of the space shuttle *Challenger*, thanking a physician or nurse who had written him a thank-you note following his hospitalization for colon cancer, or referring to his wife as "Nancy" (Jamieson notes that most prior presidents had often referred to their wives as "Mrs."), he placed people in his speeches more intimately than had his predecessors, most likely inviting "affection that prevented him from attack."[39] Probably so, but more important for the current purpose is that Reagan also brought attention to a powerful contraindication: political rhetoric in the United States rarely salutes its subjects.

Nevertheless, Reagan's style, as Jamieson notes, was successful in building both empathy with voters and respectful relations with fellow politicians. Given Reagan's success in including citizens in speeches (and implicitly associating them with party labels), it is possible that parties could deploy these tactics as well. Organized efforts to verbalize the connection to voters could—rhetorically—increase the relevance of parties in the minds of citizens. In a political world with vast sums spent on advertising, market research, and public relations campaigns, dramatizing the connections between party and the citizenry seems like a natural first step for political parties interested in decreasing voter alienation.

Kenneth Burke would find the general pattern of referring to parties as elite entities quite natural. In his writings, Burke contends that humans are "goaded by the spirit of hierarchy (or moved to a sense of order)."[40] This passion for order, writes Burke, encouraged the creation of rules for organizing sentences (grammar), organizing arguments (logic), and cooperation based on identification of speakers with audiences through symbols (rhetoric) as the foundation of human activities;[41] in all of these ways, people craved order so much that they enforced it in places where it did not otherwise exist. This need to categorize—to understand life in terms of hierarchies—offers a helpful perspective in interpreting why parties continue to be seen in an elite frame. That is, for at least the past fifty years, party labels have efficiently reduced uncertainly by rhetorically identifying those in charge, thereby contributing to a narrative of power in the United States.

Murray Edelman, too, has addressed the politics of hierarchy. In his mind, "man cannot live with himself, with his state, or with his state of affairs unless he continuously re-creates his past, his present, and his future in light of his significant symbols." He continues, "The themes a society emphasizes and re-emphasizes about its government may not accurately describe its politics; but they do at least tell us what men want to believe about themselves and their state. These beliefs help to hold men together and help maintain an orderly state."[42] From this perspective, the common theme that parties are "elite actors who do not interact with the citizens" maintains order. Even though this theme may not be entirely truthful, it does reveal the elite's preferred understanding of political parties.

The finding that elites continue to refer to parties in hierarchical terms (even when complaining about them) becomes particularly interesting when considered alongside Michael Nelson's argument about how U.S. citizens juggle ambivalent feelings about American politics. In his article "Why Americans Hate Politics and Politicians," Nelson suggests that when Europeans are asked what makes them most proud of their country, they mention physical beauty or cultural achievements. "Ask Americans what they are proudest of," he continues,

> and they will describe their form of government—democracy, freedom, "all men are created equal," etc. When Americans travel to Washington with their families (which most do who can afford to), they are making pilgrimages of a sort. They visit the city's sacred shrines to Lincoln, Washington, Jefferson, Kennedy, and our fallen soldiers. They gaze upon its sacred texts—the Constitution and the Declaration of Independence—at the National Archives. They visit its temples of law and democracy—the Supreme Court, the Capitol, the White House. Their attitude is serious, even reverential; their gaze open-mouthed.[43]

Why do Americans, then, hate politics? Nelson wonders. He concludes that they have left themselves no alternative. Given a reverence for the Constitution and a loyalty to higher law, Americans naturally focus their frustrations on politics and politicians. In his mind, citizens resolve dissonance not by challenging democracy on a conceptual level but by critiquing how it is practiced and who practices it. This chapter tells a similar story. Although Americans love the party system far less than they love the Constitution, their complaints about parties fall far short of radical or revolutionary change. A similar pattern can be found in these statements. As long as these voices continue to regard party labels as elites do, then party labels' role in government is, in a semantic sense, secure, even if occasionally vilified.

PARTY LABELS HAVE NOT BEEN INTERPRETED IN DEPTH

In the American context, parties have a strong tradition of loose and decentralized ties, the observation of which prompted E. E. Schattschneider to write:

> Decentralization of power is by all odds the most important single characteristic of the American major party; more than anything else this trait distinguishes it from all others. Indeed, once this truth is understood, nearly everything else about American parties is greatly illuminated. . . . The American major party is, to repeat the definition, a loose confederation of state and local bosses for limited purposes.[44]

The disjointed nature of political parties creates special tensions for the elites who must describe them. Specifically, how do elites go about depicting historically loose coalitions? Do they prefer an aggressive approach (one that interrogates deep conflict, exposes tensions, and publicizes disagreement)? Or do they favor a more moderate approach, one that glosses over the conflict, works to prevent future tensions, and ensures requisite room for bargaining and cooperation in the future? In a sense, the question becomes, How partisan are the portrayals of party labels (broadly speaking) in the American political system?

Rather than offer pointed opinions and judgments about parties, my findings show that when we look at all of the labels together, we find that elites often describe parties in "unclear" or "mixed" ways. Qualitative researchers who stress the connection between "thick description" and cultural meanings might be concerned by elites' reluctance to offer clearly delineated portrayals of parties. Indeed, seminal work in ethnography suggests that "thick description leads to thick understanding"[45] and that "thick description allows for thick interpretation."[46] Elites in this study seem to prefer a less-detailed route; instead of offering "thick meanings" filled with attributions and judgments, they advance a much more skeletal narrative that merely glosses the history, qualities, and activities of partisan institutions. While this rhetoric may be inspired by the best intentions (i.e., as a way of protecting a loose, decentralized party system), it is likely that these skeletal portrayals may prevent citizens from understanding the party system in complex and sympathetic ways.

And this is ironic since political parties have one of the richest histories of any institution in the United States. According to John Aldrich, parties began to form as early as 1790 in response to the problems of "majority instability" (i.e., the unsteadiness of temporary majority coalitions that dealt with problems on an issue-by-issue basis).[47] Because problem solving was both difficult and unpredictable when new majorities had to be built on an issue-by-issue basis, several founders (e.g., Alexander Hamilton, James Madison, Thomas Jefferson) found it beneficial to "organize their supporters" into teams. Gradually, Aldrich continues, these teams strengthened over time, widened their scope with respect to members and issues, and became "the first political parties of modern democratic form in this or any nation."[48] Given their longevity, their textured past, and the passions surrounding them, one might think that parties would inspire fulsome description from elites. Interestingly, however, my data suggest much the opposite.

The variable *time* examines the extent to which elites place labels in the present, past, and future. As table 3.4 shows, overall party labels are placed in the present 80.2 percent of the time, in the past 18.6 percent of the time, and in the future just 1.2 percent of the time. These data become more descriptive when broken down by genre. Textbook authors—as one would imagine—are most likely to mention the past followed by candidates, legislators, and journalists. Candidates—also as one would expect—are most likely to feature the future, followed by legislators, authors, and journalists.

Table 3.4. Party Labels by *Time* Variable—Overall and by Genre (in percentages)

	Overall	Speeches	News	Debates	Textbooks
In present	80.2	78.4	93.6	86.9	54.4
In past	18.6	16.3	6.3	12.7	45.3
As potential	1.2	4.3	.1	.4	.3

Note: Overall percentages may not add to 100 owing to rounding and/or unequal sample sizes.

Chapter 5 explores the unique aspects of each of these genres, as well as how and why they depend on specific labels. What is interesting here, though, is that if textbooks are ignored, then parties are placed in the past just 11.6 percent of the time and, speeches aside, labels are placed in the future just 9.5 percent of the time. Why do political parties have no past? No future?

From a strategic perspective, there are a few reasons why elites (at least those supportive of parties) might treat party labels presentistically. An obvious one, of course, is that parties cannot be held accountable for their pasts. Mistakes, blunders, corruption, graft, and scandals—all connected with party lineage—remain left out of the conversation (not to mention voters' political memories) when the past goes unmentioned.

Another benefit of ignoring the past is that a rhetoric of the moment is highly efficient for intraparty communication. As V. O. Key has noted, there are often as many disagreements within a party as between the parties. Thus, conversations rooted in the moment can be more careful and grounded as well as less likely to offend various factions of the party. Similarly, ignoring the past can also be beneficial in public communication. While parties know that their best chance of electing their candidates is to mobilize loyal voters, they also know that swing votes often decide elections. In this way, rhetorically sidestepping the past may open up space for new or independent voters to feel comfortable with the party's candidate.

While party strategists and candidates might find presentistic politics advantageous, scholars are typically troubled by it. Aldrich, for one, has written that three forces shape a political party: ambitious politicians, governmental institutions, and political history. History matters because it describes the ideas, values, and technological possibilities available at any given moment, says Aldrich, making a more meaningful understanding of these institutions possible.[49]

To abandon history, though, is to deny the tasks, contributions, emotions, and successes of parties in the past. Vivid memories of famous political speeches had biased my own expectations for the *time* variable, encouraging me to believe that candidates—at least—would discuss the history of party in order to build solidarity among voters. Notice how Senator Ted Kennedy engages in exactly this strategy in his memorable speech delivered to the 1980 Democratic National Convention:

> There were some who said we should be silent about our difference on issues during this convention, but the heritage of the Democratic party has been a history of democracy. We fight hard because we care deeply about our principles and purposes. We did not flee this struggle. We wel-

come the contrast with the empty and expedient spectacle last month in Detroit where no nomination was contested, no question was debated, and no one dared to raise any doubt or dissent.[50]

Kennedy's speech is striking, largely because it serves as an antithesis to many of the patterns found in my data. Kennedy connects the Democrats with the past, something that only 16.3 percent of the candidates did (and it will be interesting to see—after Senator Bob Dole was widely critiqued for heralding the past in the 1996 campaign—if candidates will increase or decrease their reminiscences in future elections). Kennedy also praises spirited political conflict; chapter 6, in contrast, shows how American citizens typically deplore such conflicts and how, as a result, elites refuse to feature them in discourse. Kennedy also offers a thick party narrative, whereas my data show that elites generally hesitate to "expose differences," "fight hard," or "care deeply."

Few of the texts in this data set offer the richness deployed by Kennedy, and—interestingly—those who came closest were Hubert Humphrey and Walter Mondale, liberal Democrats who, like Kennedy, served in the Senate but never had the opportunity to serve as the nation's chief executive (although Humphrey and Mondale did secure the party's nomination). In the following speech, for example, Mondale emphasizes many of the themes that Kennedy does. It may be either a coincidence or a pattern that both of these respected senators wove thick party narratives into their discourse but were never elected to the presidency. In either case, the rhetoric serves as the exception to the rule, thick description in a dataset otherwise composed of thin descriptions:

> We've never had an election with higher stakes and deeper differences than in 1984. This election is not about jellybeans and pen pals. It's about the future of our country.
>
> You have to watch these *Republicans*. They've done a lot of graverobbing this year. Whenever a *Democrat* dies, they suddenly discover they liked him after all. So they honor Franklin Roosevelt. They honor Harry Truman. They even tried to take our Hubert Humphrey from us the other day. Hubert's mad as hell about that.
>
> This president went all over the country saying what a good friend he was of John Kennedy. Minnesota, in case the national press doesn't know it, loved Jack Kennedy, and it was Minnesota that put Jack Kennedy over the top for president of the United States in 1960.
>
> Then it turns out that while I was chairman of Minnesotans for Kennedy, Mr. Reagan was chairman of that thing called *Democrats for*

Nixon. In the same year, he wrote a letter in which he said Kennedy got his ideas from Karl Marx and Adolf Hitler.

That's the difference. I liked Kennedy because he stood for what is best in America. I don't like Ronald Reagan's policies because he's closed the door on opportunity and decency for millions and millions of Americans. And that's the difference. . . . Today I'm asking you to join me in building America's future. You gave me a chance as attorney general, many, many times as senator, and then as vice president, to travel this country more widely than I think any other living American has traveled.[51]

When elites abandon political history, they may also encourage citizens to forget that parties socialized, organized, instructed, and provided for massive numbers of Americans in another place and time. Michael Nelson has noted how parties helped members of his family directly by offering them the opportunity to go to college. He writes, "I know that politics was the vehicle that integrated generations of our immigrant ancestors into the main-stream of American society—the job on the city road crew that my German grandfather got from the Frank Hague machine in Jersey City is the reason that my father and then I were later able to build careers of our own in the private sector."[52] Touching as such narratives are, they are rarely heard among professional politicians themselves.

Thus, presentism exacts a price, since an understanding of the past inevitably informs our understanding of the present. When political labels are stripped of their history, Americans ultimately develop a shallow understanding of parties. As social influence researchers attest, individuals who are only casually involved in an issue are more likely to be persuaded by contrary messages. From this perspective, the finding that parties are stripped of their histories suggests that their meanings are more open to manipulation by both senders and receivers of messages.

Another pattern in the data is a general reluctance of speakers to pass judgment on political parties. Given American ambivalence about parties, one might expect to find a great deal of evaluation or criticism in the discourse examined. Surprisingly, that is not the case. Specifically, two additional variables, *context* and *quality*, reveal a tendency in the texts to offer "unclear" or "balanced" judgments rather than clearly "positive" or "negative" ones. There are two possible interpretations of this trend. One is that these variables were poorly constructed, that they did not measure what they purported to measure. Another is that the measures are valid and that received opinion is simply wrong. But which interpretation is correct and why?

First, consider the variable *context*, which measures the speaker's attribution of the social scene facing the party under discussion (see table 3.5). Overall, a discernible valence was evident for 47.1 percent of the labels (positive condition 23.0 percent; negative condition 24.1 percent). This means that in 52.9 percent of the cases, the context was less certain—either falling into the identity (24.9 percent) or unclear/balanced (28.0 percent) categories.

Table 3.5. Party Labels by *Context* Variable (in percentages)

Unclear	14.5
Identity	24.9
Positive	23.0
Negative	24.1
Balanced	13.5

When creating my content-analytic variables, I had not intended to include an identity condition. Given research exploring the negativity of congressional debates[53] and media coverage[54] and the positive slant to textbooks,[55] I had expected to see many value-based attributions in the texts. In a pretest of my coding scheme, however, I noticed that the "unclear" category held a considerable number of texts. Many of these texts used party labels in the following way: "Bill Clinton, a *Democrat*, is running for president." Because there were so many of these simple references to party labels, I added the identity condition to the coding scheme.

That was a fortuitous decision. Unlike other research that reports overwhelming negativity in political texts, this study finds that elite voices are just as likely to treat party terms as a mere demographic as they are to praise or revile them. Perhaps this trend in discourse lends support to Martin Wattenberg's point that American citizens feel neutral, rather than negative, about political parties.[56] Wattenberg concludes that the distinction between neutrality and negativity is critical, for "if voters are actually discontented with political parties, then the parties' chances for recovery in the near future are doubtful; but if people feel only neutral toward them, then the door remains open for party renewal."[57] By not constituting party labels as overwhelmingly negative, then the elites in this study may help keep this "door of party renewal" open.

The variable *quality*, which examines the party attributes stressed by the speaker, recorded more nonjudgments than judgments (see table 3.6).

Table 3.6.   Party Labels by _Quality_ Variable (in percentages)

	Overall	Speeches	News	Debates	Textbooks
None	50.1	64.7	38.7	47.3	52.2
Action	9.2	1.9	3.2	13.6	19.5
Emotion	13.8	6.8	24.4	14.2	7.3
Unity	22.6	19.5	30.7	23.1	14.8
Clarity	4.3	7.1	3.0	1.8	6.2

Note: Overall percentages may not add to 100 owing to rounding and/or unequal sample sizes.

The most common category for this variable was "none" (50.1 percent), followed by "unity" (22.6 percent), "emotion" (13.8 percent), "action" (9.2 percent), and "clarity" (4.3 percent). In three of the four genres, when attributions were made, "unity" was the top category (speeches, 19.5 percent; news, 30.7 percent; debates, 23.1 percent); textbooks, in contrast, featured "action" as the highest category (19.5 percent).

What, then, does it mean that elites rarely assign qualities (or attributes) to parties? Rhetorical researchers have noted how embellishment, or the heavy use of adjectives, can slow "down a passage by de-emphasizing human and material action."[58] Table 3.6 shows that, rather than modify parties, elites were often efficient when describing them, rarely pausing to adorn them. There could be at least two reasons for this. For one thing, elites can assume that party meanings are already well understood and that such depictions are not necessary. In contrast, they might prefer that party meanings be left nebulous, opting for a less-detailed discourse as a result. In either case, it remains interesting that they refrain from embellishment in their characterizations of party.

Another powerful trend over time is that parties are portrayed largely as campaign organizations. The variable _task_ examines the jobs that parties are said to perform in political life (see table 3.7). I found that 43.3 percent of the labels fall in the campaign condition, followed by 33.0 percent in the governing condition, 9.0 percent in the mobilizing condition, and 14.8 percent in the mixed and not applicable conditions.

Admittedly, these percentages are somewhat skewed due to the texts sampled: both the speeches and the news articles were drawn during campaign periods. Nonetheless, these voices prefer certain tasks to others. For instance, candidates—despite their presence in a campaign—are more likely to mention governing than the news is. For their part, journalists are more likely to mention the mobilizing function of parties (reporting on events,

Table 3.7.   Party Labels by *Task* Variable—Overall and by Genre (in percentages)

	Overall	Speeches	News	Debates	Textbooks
Not applicable	9.9	13.4	5.2	10.5	11.4
Mobilization	9.0	4.4	9.9	5.1	18.2
Campaign	43.3	50.8	72.0	7.5	44.5
Governing	33.0	29.6	9.0	70.5	18.2
Mixed	4.9	1.8	3.8	6.4	7.8

Note: Overall percentages may not add to 100 owing to rounding and/or unequal sample sizes.

discussing the efforts of parties to increase turnout, etc.) than the candidates are (although it is important to note that their overall tendency to do so was limited).

These data suggest that while reporters are writing about the parties, one key theme gets left out of the story: governance. As is seen here, labels are only associated with governing 9.0 percent of the time. This pattern would no doubt disturb political scientist Nelson Polsby, who argued in 1983 that "no newly elected President in the entire history of the republic was less prepared to take office than Jimmy Carter, unless it was Ronald Reagan."[59] Polsby's point was not personal but institutional. In his book *Consequences of Party Reform*, he notes that when the public is allowed to select presidential nominees, they do not often attend to the issues of preparation or political experience. That journalists rarely link parties to governance (especially during campaign periods) underscores Polsby's concern. If the public is not primed by the media to think of parties as governing (as well as campaigning) bodies, then they are likely to be attracted to ersatz candidates with limited governing experience. Indeed, the success of candidates such as Ross Perot, Jesse Ventura, Sonny Bono, and Arnold Schwarzenegger may indicate that such "priming failures" have already exacted their tolls.

In an important book, E. J. Dionne has observed that Americans are cynical because they believe that Democrats and Republicans are offering them false choices. These data suggest that an underemphasis on the governing role of parties during campaigns may offer another type of false choice. Although political scientists are mixed as to whether parties are campaign or governing institutions, most would agree that parties are interested primarily in attaining power and that they emerge organically to organize the disparate interests of a legislature. Yet when parties are framed largely as campaign entities, citizens are unlikely to view them in a more multidimensional way. Such a view has political consequences.

CONCLUSION

Traditionally, scholars have examined what parties are and what they do.[60] This chapter has attempted something different: an analysis of what party labels have meant in political conversations. A first set of conclusions is that elites have used these labels continuously, hierarchically, and skeletally over the past fifty years in the United States. These trends tell us about the meanings of party labels and a bit about the preferences and latent assumptions of political elites who—despite their four unique job descriptions—constitute parties in similar ways. Because party labels have been consistently discussed in these ways, they enjoy a certain type of symbolic capital—over both the elites who construct them and the citizens who are often guided by such constructions.

Political, cultural, and historical perspectives help inform the "cultural collusions" found in this chapter. From the political perspective, Frank Sorauf's work encourages us to see that it is difficult for Americans to think "outside of the two-party system." He asserts that the United States has had a two-party system for over 150 years and that during this time the "inescapable, crucial fact" is that almost all partisan conflict in the United States has been channeled through two major political parties.[61] Because of its political dominance and resilience, the two-party system may simply pattern elites' understandings of parties as well as determine how they discuss them. From a political development perspective, Samuel Huntington has claimed that Americans possess a "traditional" mind-set that encourages them to accept their political world as being predetermined. Here, because Americans have accepted the system as given (and the laws as being preestablished), it stands to reason that they may, too, see parties as an inevitable element of the system.[62] Similarly, Daniel Boorstin has argued that a characteristic of American political thought is the axiom of "givenness"—that politics and ideas are a gift from the past.[63] From his perspective (as well as that of Huntington), the finding that four different sets of elites articulate the same version of partisanship makes sense; having been raised in the American climate, these elites instinctively feel pressured to look to tradition (indeed all the way back to the late 1700s) to understand the present moment.

That elites continue to use party labels, portray them in a hierarchical manner, and discuss them skeletally are somewhat modest findings. Their modesty, however, fades when we consider their consistency and when we reckon with the underlying cultural myths their consistencies reveal. Yet because aggregate data like those reported here often reveal what they also conceal, the following chapters address specific meanings of party related to time, genre, and label. To the effects of time we now turn.

NOTES

1. Thomas Jefferson, letter to Henry Lee, 10 August 1824, in *The Writings of Thomas Jefferson*, vol. 16, ed. Andrew A. Lipscomb and Andrew Ellery Bergh (Washington, D.C.: Thomas Jefferson Memorial Association, 1903–1904), 13.

2. Thomas Jefferson, letter to Francis Hopkinson, 13 March 1789, in *The Writings of Thomas Jefferson*, vol. 16, ed. Andrew A. Lipscomb and Andrew Ellery Bergh (Washington, D.C.: Thomas Jefferson Memorial Association, 1903–1904), 300.

3. John F. Bibby, "In Defense of the Two-Party System," in *Multiparty Politics in America*, ed. Paul S. Herrnson and J. C. Green (Lanham, Md.: Rowman & Littlefield, 1997), 73–74.

4. Jack Dennis, "Trends in Public Support for the American Party System," *British Journal of Political Science* 5 (1975): 230.

5. The density ratios are as follows: 1995 = .151; 1957 = .039; 1964 = .020; 1979 = .017 (density ratio = party labels / all words in sample × 100).

6. House of Representatives, Representative Bill Richardson of New Mexico, 104th Cong., 1st sess., *Congressional Record* 141 (21 March 1995): 3352–98.

7. Adlai Stevenson, "Campaign Speech," Silver Spring, Md. (20 September 1956), Annenberg/Pew Archive of Presidential Discourse, CD-ROM (Philadelphia: Annenberg School for Communication, University of Pennsylvania, 2000).

8. Ronald Reagan, "Campaign Speech," Valley Stream, N.Y. (26 October 1984), Annenberg/Pew Archive of Presidential Discourse, CD-ROM (Philadelphia: Annenberg School for Communication, University of Pennsylvania, 2000).

9. George H. W. Bush, "Campaign Speech," Kingsburg, Calif. (14 September 1988), Annenberg/Pew Archive of Presidential Discourse, CD-ROM (Philadelphia: Annenberg School for Communication, University of Pennsylvania, 2000).

10. George H. W. Bush, "Campaign Speech," Humboldt, S.D. (2 September 1992), Annenberg/Pew Archive of Presidential Discourse, CD-ROM (Philadelphia: Annenberg School for Communication, University of Pennsylvania, 2000).

11. Bob Dole, "Acceptance Address to the Republican National Convention" (16 August 1996), Annenberg/Pew Archive of Presidential Discourse, CD-ROM (Philadelphia: Annenberg School for Communication, University of Pennsylvania, 2000).

12. George W. Bush, "Acceptance Address to the Republican Nominating Convention" (3 August 2000), Campaign Mapping Project database, University of Texas at Austin.

13. See Roderick P. Hart, *Campaign Talk: Why Elections Are Good for Us* (Princeton, N.J.: Princeton University Press, 2000).

14. Marcel Lewinski et al., *Consent of the Governed: A Study of American Government* (Glenview, Ill.: Scott Foresman, 1987), 174.

15. Richard E. Gross and Arnold W. Seibel, *American Citizenship: The Way We Govern* (Englewood Cliffs, N.J.: Prenctice-Hall, 1979), 436.

16. Carl Everett Ladd, *The American Polity: The People and Their Government*, 3rd ed. (New York: Norton, 1985), 437.

17. Michael Dukakis, "A Strong and Secure America," campaign address at Georgetown University, Washington, D.C. (14 September 1988), Annenberg/Pew Archive of Presidential Discourse, CD-ROM (Philadelphia: Annenberg School for Communication, University of Pennsylvania, 2000).

18. George H. W. Bush, "Acceptance Speech at the Republican National Convention," Houston, Texas (20 August 1992), Annenberg/Pew Archive of Presidential Discourse, CD-ROM (Philadelphia: Annenberg School for Communication, University of Pennsylvania, 2000).

19. See Mark L. Knapp, *Social Intercourse: From Greeting to Goodbye* (Boston: Allyn & Bacon 1978); Gerard I. Nierenberg and Henry H. Colero, *Meta-talk* (New York: Simon & Schuster, 1981).

20. Richard Nixon, "Remarks on Accepting the Presidential Nomination of the Republican National Convention" (23 August 1972), Annenberg/Pew Archive of Presidential Discourse, CD-ROM (Philadelphia: Annenberg School for Communication, University of Pennsylvania, 2000).

21. Richard Nixon, "Campaign Speech," Charleston, W.V., Civic Center (27 September 1960), Annenberg/Pew Archive of Presidential Discourse, CD-ROM (Philadelphia: Annenberg School for Communication, University of Pennsylvania, 2000).

22. Richard Nixon, "Campaign Speech," New York City, Columbian Republican League luncheon, Commodore Hotel (5 October 1960), Annenberg/Pew Archive of Presidential Discourse, CD-ROM (Philadelphia: Annenberg School for Communication, University of Pennsylvania, 2000).

23. Kenneth Burke, *A Rhetoric of Motives* (Berkeley: University of California Press, 1969).

24. Roderick P. Hart, *Modern Rhetorical Criticism* (New York: Harper Collins, 1990), 362.

25. House of Representatives, Representative Jennifer Dunn of Washington, 104th Cong., 1st sess., *Congressional Record* 141 (21 March 1995): 3352–98.

26. The bill was eventually vetoed by President Clinton, however.

27. See Richard Fenno, "U. S. House Legislators in Their Constituencies: An Exploration," *American Political Science Review* 71, no. 3 (September 1977): 914.

28. "Stevenson Asks Truth from GOP; Accuses Administration of Withholding Facts from Public on World Situation," Associated Press–United Press International wire, 7 September 1956.

29. James MacGregor Burns, Jack W. Pelatson, and Thomas E. Cronin, *Government by the People*, 11th ed. (Englewood Cliffs, N.J.: Prentice Hall, 1981).

30. See Cornelius Cotter et al., *Party Organizations and American Politics* (New York: Praeger, 1984), 168.

31. See V. O. Key, *Politics, Parties, and Pressure Groups*, 5th ed. (New York: Crowell, 1964); see also, Frank Sorauf and Paul Allen Beck, *Party Politics in America*, 6th ed. (Glenview, Ill.: Scott Foresman, 1988).

32. Gerald Pomper, *Passions and Interests: Political Party Concepts of American Democracy* (Lawrence: University of Kansas Press, 1992), 5.

33. John Aldrich, *Why Parties? The Origin and Transformation of Party Politics in America* (Chicago: University of Chicago Press, 1995), 4.

34. Bartels writes that one account for the revival of partisan voting in the 1990s may be that "increasing partisanship in the electorate represents a response at the mass level to increasing partisanship at the elite level. . . . In an era in which parties in government seem increasingly consequential, the public may increasingly come to develop and apply partisan predispositions of exactly the sort described by the authors of *The American Voter.*" Larry Bartels, "Partisanship and Voting Behavior, 1952–1996," *American Journal of Political Science* 44 (2000): 35–50.

35. The *independent* label deviates from this pattern somewhat, a point discussed in chapter 6.

36. House of Representatives, Representative Jamie Whitten of Mississippi, 88th Cong., 2nd sess., *Congressional Record* 110 (3 February 1995): 1684.

37. Ronald Reagan, "Speech to the Republican National Convention," Detroit, Mich. (17 July 1980), Annenberg/Pew Archive of Presidential Discourse, CD-ROM (Philadelphia: Annenberg School for Communication, University of Pennsylvania, 2000).

38. Kathleen Hall Jamieson, *Eloquence in an Electronic Age* (Oxford: Oxford University Press, 1988), 170.

39. Jamieson, *Eloquence*, 189.

40. Kenneth Burke, *On Symbols and Society* (Chicago: University of Chicago Press, 1989), 69.

41. See Eric Eisenberg and Harold Lloyd Goodall Jr., *Organizational Communication: Balancing Creativity and Constraint* (New York: St. Martin's Press, 1993), 56.

42. Murray Edelman, *The Symbolic Uses of Politics* (Urbana: University of Illinois Press, 1964), 187, 191.

43. Michael Nelson, "Why Americans Hate Politics and Politicians," *PS: Political Science and Politics* 28, no. 1 (1995): 72–78.

44. E. E. Schattschneider, *Party Government* (New York: Holt, Rinehart and Winston, 1942), 129, 132–33.

45. See Clifford Geertz, "Thick Description: Toward an Interpretive Theory of Culture," in *The Interpretation of Cultures: Selected Essays,* ed. Clifford Geertz (New York: Basic Books, 1973), 3–30.

46. Norman K. Denzin, *Interpretive Interactionism* (Newbury Park, Calif.: Sage, 1989).

47. Aldrich, *Why Parties?* 70.

48. Aldrich, *Why Parties?* 69.

49. Aldrich, *Why Parties?* 5.

50. Edward Kennedy, "Address to the Democratic National Convention," New York City (12 August 1980). Accessible via the John F. Kennedy Library and Museum, www.jfklibrary.org/e081280.htm (20 October 1999).

51. Walter Mondale, "Principles, Campaign Address," Mondale rally, Duluth, Minn. (30 October 1984), Annenberg/Pew Archive of Presidential Discourse, CD-ROM (Philadelphia: Annenberg School for Communication, University of Pennsylvania, 2000).

52. Nelson, "Why Americans Hate Politics," 72.

53. Eric Uslaner, *The Decline of Comity in Congress* (Ann Arbor: University of Michigan Press, 1995).

54. Thomas E. Patterson, "Bad News, Period," *PS: Political Science and Politics* 29, no. 1 (1996): 17–21.

55. Thomas J. Cronin, "The Textbook Presidency and Political Science," in *Perspectives on the Presidency*, ed. Stanley Bach and George T. Sulzner (Lexington, Mass.: D. C. Heath, 1974).

56. Specifically, Wattenberg has written that "the growing neutrality toward the parties seems to be that fewer people are translating their likes and dislikes about the candidates and the candidates' stand on specific issues into likes and dislikes about the parties. . . . The reason for party decline has not been that people no longer see any important differences between the parties. Indeed, the trend toward neutrality would have been even sharper if the frequency of comments concerning the general philosophies and group benefits offered by the parties had not remained fairly stable. Rather, the problem the parties face is that they are considered less relevant in solving the most important domestic and foreign policy issues of the day. In the voters' mind, the parties are losing their association with the candidates and the issues the candidates stand for." Martin Wattenberg, *The Decline of American Political Parties, 1952–1996* (Cambridge, Mass.: Harvard University Press, 1998), 88–89.

57. Wattenberg, *Decline*, 51.

58. Roderick P. Hart, *Diction 4.0: The Text Analysis Program* (Thousand Oaks, Calif.: Sage, 1997).

59. Nelson Polsby, *Consequences of Party Reform* (Oxford: Oxford University Press, 1983), 3.

60. S. E. Finer, *The Changing British Party System, 1945–1979* (Washington, D.C.: American Enterprise Institute, 1980), xii.

61. Sorauf and Beck, *Party Politics*, 35.

62. Samuel Huntington, *Political Order in Changing Societies* (New Haven, Conn.: Yale University Press, 1968), 96.

63. See Daniel Boorstin, "The Genius of American Politics," in *The American Polity Reader*, ed. Ann G. Serow, W. Wayne Shannon, and Everett C. Ladd (New York: Norton, 1990), 19–23.

4

THE EVOLVING PARTY

Time was, Democratic and Republican convention acceptance addresses sounded downright partisan. In 1948, for instance, Harry Truman told his audience that "it was time to get together and beat the enemy"; "victory has become a habit of our party"; and

> the reason is that the people know that the *Democratic party* is the people's party, and the *Republican party* is the party of special interest, and it always has been and always will be. The record of the *Democratic party* is written in the accomplishments of the last 16 years. . . . Confidence and security have been brought to the people by the *Democratic party*. Farm income has increased from less than $2 1/2 billion in 1932 to more than $18 billion in 1947. Never in the world were the farmers of any republic or any kingdom or any other country as prosperous as the farmers of the United States; and if they don't do their duty by the *Democratic party*, they are the most ungrateful people in the world!

But Truman was not finished. He continued by noting that "wages and salaries in this country have increased from $29 billion in 1933 to more than $128 billion in 1947. That's labor, and labor never had but one friend in politics, and that is the *Democratic party* and Franklin D. Roosevelt. And I say to labor what I have said to the farmers: they are the most ungrateful people in the world if they pass the *Democratic party* by this year."[1]

Four years later, General Dwight Eisenhower addressed his Republican Nominating Convention with a similar sense of fervor: in his speech, he wanted to win, and he wanted his fellow Republicans to win as well. Like Truman, he framed the contest in militaristic terms, proclaiming, "Today is the first day of this great battle. The road that leads to November 4 is a fighting road. In that fight I will keep nothing in reserve. Before this I stood on the eve of battle. Before every attack it has always been my practice to seek out our men in their camps and on the roads and talk with them face to face about their concerns and discuss with them the great mission to which we were all committed."[2] And, like Truman, Eisenhower employed party labels to rally the troops: "we must have more *Republicans* in our state and local offices; more *Republican* governments in our states; a *Republican* majority in the United States House of Representatives and in the United States Senate; and, of course, a *Republican* in the White House."[3]

Forty-eight years later, the presidential nominees approached their audiences with far less partisan fidelity. Governor George W. Bush, for instance, attempted to position himself as a "uniter not a divider" as he faced his 2000 Republican Nominating Convention. In that speech, he shared that he had "worked with *Republicans* and *Democrats* to get things done," credited Democrats in Texas as being central to his success in the past, and suggested that Republicans and Democrats should work together in the future, specifically "to end the politics of fear and save Social Security together." But he did not stop there; embracing a theme of "togetherness" he went on to salute a friend on the other side of the aisle, saying "a bittersweet part of tonight is that someone is missing, the late Lt. Governor of Texas Bob Bullock. Bob was a *Democrat*, a crusty veteran of Texas politics, and my great friend. He worked by my side, endorsed my re-election, and I know he is with me in spirit in saying to those who would malign our state for political gain. . . . Don't mess with Texas."[4]

For his part, Al Gore avoided the terms *Democrat* and *Republican* entirely in his address to the Democratic Nominating Convention, opting instead to proclaim, "I stand here tonight as my own man."[5] Gore's aversion to party labels sets him apart from all other candidates in this sample (see chapter 5); moreover, as discussed shortly, his hesitation to emphasize partisanship served as a stark contrast to W. Bush (who employed party labels in an optimistic and inclusive way, one that acknowledged the loyalties present in the aforementioned speeches from 1948 and 1952, but one that did so in a less heavy-handed fashion).

While chapter 3 addresses the three dominant themes in party language use, chapter 4 looks underneath them for trends over time. Perhaps not surprisingly, the patterns show linguistic support for the key political theories of these years. After running descriptive statistics and crosstabs by year, decade, and fifteen-year periods, four findings were apparent in the data: party labels were associated with a monolithic time (1948–1960), a liminal time (1961–1979), a fragmented time (1980–1999), and a moment of resurgence (campaign 2000). This chapter describes the meanings of party labels found in these eras, interprets these meanings in light of the prominent political models regnant at the time, and speculates about what these depictions of party labels may mean for the next century.

ERA I—A MONOLITHIC PERIOD (1948–1960)

American democratic thinkers have traditionally embraced two theories of political groups. A first perspective has held that groups cannot be trusted. James Madison voiced this concern in *Federalist #10*, writing that groups were a "necessary evil" and that a government must be created to "control their effects."[6] Over two hundred years later, scholarship by John Hibbing and Elizabeth Theiss Morse shows that American citizens continue to be wary of political groups. They write,

> To put it simply, Americans tend to dislike virtually all of the democratic processes.... They dislike compromise and bargaining, they dislike committees and bureaucracy, they dislike political parties and interest groups, they dislike big salaries and big staffs, they dislike slowness and multiple stages, and they dislike debate and publicly hashing things out, referring to such actions as haggling or bickering.[7]

For the past two hundred years, then, there have been those who have been suspicious of organized political entities.

Another perspective held by pluralist scholars, however, is more optimistic about such groups. Widely popular in the 1950s, pluralist thought posited that competing groups can benefit democracy by exerting influence over its leaders, for as Robert Dahl once put it, "virtually no one, and certainly no group of more than a few individuals, is entirely lacking in influence resources."[8] In reflecting back on that political moment, many have argued that pluralism was a "good fit" for the 1950s largely because those years featured a high degree of consensus, a minimal American state, and a "realist" approach to politics (three underpinnings of the theory).[9] At that time, pluralism was so accepted that scholars John Dryzek and Stephen Leonard suggest that it came closer to uniting the field of political science than any other theoretical construct before or since.[10] Yet empirical realities of the 1960s challenged the golden age of pluralism, specifically because this theoretical model could not account for (1) Vietnam policy (pluralism assumes a small role for the state, but during the Vietnam crisis, the state clearly put its wishes ahead of those objecting to foreign intervention); (2) the thickening of the post–New Deal state (pluralism assumes a minimal state but welfare programs require the government to grow in order to collect and redistribute resources); and, ultimately, (3) why some groups were regarded as being more equal than others (pluralism assumes a level of equality among groups, and it cannot explain why wealthy groups have greater access to the system than less wealthy or minority groups).[11]

Having witnessed these changes to the pluralist model, scholars were tempted in the 1990s to doubt the interpretive power of pluralism and to regard this theoretical approach as being dated or threadbare. Even though history has not been kind to the model, the construct of pluralism is extremely helpful in interpreting the meanings of party labels between the years of 1948 and 1960 because the foundations of pluralist thought (i.e., a faith in groups and in bargaining) are well represented in my data during those years.

One way that the echo of pluralism appears is in simple descriptive statistics. For instance, the *party* label appears most frequently during this time in news coverage and in campaign speeches (see figure 4.1). These figures inspire obvious concerns: How is it that the party label appears more often in Era I? And what can explain its general decrease over time (and reappearance in the news in campaign 2000)?

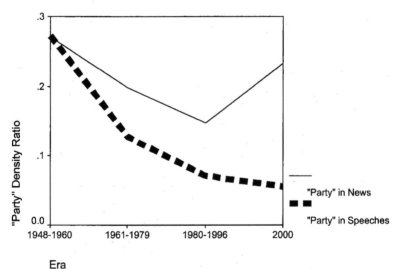

Figure 4.1.   *Party* in Speeches and News, by Era
*Density ratio = *party* / all words in genre × 100

A first answer can be found in the campaign speeches from Era I. Observe how, in the following text from 1960, John F. Kennedy voices confidence in the two-party system and enthusiastically links himself to other Democrats. Notice that there is a naturalness in the appearance of party labels, one that seems strange to contemporary eyes:

> I think what counts are the men that the *political parties* put up, and I think *party* labels mean a great deal. I am not impressed by this leap year progressivism which comes upon the *Republican party* every 4 years, when they support and sustain programs which they fight against year after year in the Congress. The *Democratic party* in this century has produced Wilson and Roosevelt and Truman. There is not any doubt that none of those men would have been nominated by the *Republicans*, and I don't think there is any chance at all that the *Democratic party* in this century would have nominated McKinley or Taft or Coolidge or Harding or Landon or Dewey or Nixon. No *Democrat* ever "Stood pat with McKinley" or "Kept cool with Coolidge" or "Returned to normalcy with Harding," or ran on a program in 1936 of repealing the Social Security Act, which Alf Landon did, or ran like Thomas E. Dewey. Mr. Nixon in Boston the other day said I was another Truman, and I returned the compliment and said he was another Dewey. And he has not said I was another Truman since, but I wish he would. I regard it as a compliment.[12]

Kennedy was rhetorically proud to be a member of the Democratic Party, but his speech should not blind readers to the fact that he was not the first choice of that party in 1960. As Kathleen Hall Jamieson recounts in her historical look at presidential campaigns, Kennedy became the Democratic nominee only after defeating his chief rival Senator Hubert Humphrey in two key primaries and derailing a last-minute bid by Texas senator Lyndon Johnson and Missouri senator Stuart Symington.[13] Despite, or perhaps because of, the challenges facing his candidacy, Kennedy applauds party labels explicitly and party competition implicitly. In doing so, his message supports the "competing group concept" so central to a pluralist approach.

Moreover, if we look at this speech closely, we see that Kennedy also supports the "competing group concept" in his very word choice. In this passage, Kennedy uses the word *party* five times, referring to *political parties*, *party labels*, the *Republican Party*, and the *Democratic Party* twice. Kennedy's practice of referring to *Democratic* and *Republican parties* instead of just to *Democrats* or *Republicans* is a rhetorical characteristic of Era I, as well as a pattern that has decreased over time. While this may appear to be a subtle difference (referring to someone as a member of the Democratic Party as opposed to a simply a Democrat), it is a key finding of this chapter. Because words help individuals understand their environments, both candidates and journalists in Era I encourage citizens to consider the collective in understanding political parties; this emphasis, as figure 4.1 shows, slips out of discourse somewhat as elites move to a more individualistic construction of partisanship in Eras II to IV. What is important here is the conscious (or perhaps unconscious) decision to use collective markers.

Use of the party label also typified congressional debates during Era I. As table 4.1 shows, *party* was the most common label in the 1957 congressional debate, appearing almost twice as often as the *Democratic* and *Republican* labels.[14] Consistent with the pattern in presidential speeches in figures 4.1, table 4.1 displays how congressional debates have experienced a direct linear decrease in the use of *party* labels.[15] An example of the prevalence of the *party* label can be found in the discussion of the Civil Rights Act of 1957. Interestingly, notice how Florida Democratic representative Billy Matthews's use of *party* is as prominent as that of candidate Kennedy:

> Now, Mr. Chairman, I want to point out that although the proponents of this legislation are in both *parties*, that opponents also are in both *parties*. This is a sectional problem. Every member of the Republican *party* from the Deep South, and every member from the Democratic *party* from the Deep South, is opposing this legislation. It is my sincere conviction that there will be no political advantage to be derived from supporting this bill for either party. Yet I am just as convinced as I can be that there will be as many votes cast for this bill because of the belief that it will help get votes (from citizens who were being denied the franchise at the time) in the next election.[16]

An intriguing aspect of the 1957 debate on civil rights is that it features almost as many intraparty conflicts as interparty conflicts, with members from the North largely supporting the act and those from the South

Table 4.1.   Party Labels in Congressional Debates: *Party, Democrat, Republican* (in percentages)

	Party	Democrat	Republican
1957	41.5	24.5	25.4
1964	21.8	30.8	37.6
1995	11.6	27.9	57.0

largely opposing it. In connection with this debate, one cannot be sure whether the high number *party* labels resulted from (1) conflicts within and between the parties (the Democratic Party in Congress split its vote more evenly on this bill than any of the other debates examined); (2) a Congress governed by the norms of reciprocity, courtesy, and institutional regard (the House in the 1950s and 1960s was governed by partisan folkways, summed by Rayburn's maxim "to get along, go along");[17] (3) a rhetorical manifestation of the key tenets of pluralism (pluralism, as an approach, maintains that groups bargain with one another to influence policy); (4) a time when many political elites chose to use these labels (i.e., candidates, journalists, and legislators); or (5) all of these possibilities. What is clear, however, is an emphasis on the collective. In the Matthews's statement, the representative employs the terms *Democratic Party* and *Republican Party* instead of the construction *Democrats* and *Republicans*, which, as we will see, was more popular during Era III. Although these differences could result from mere stylistic fashion, they could also reflect real, philosophical differences in legislators' comparative faith in the very possibility of political interdependence. In either case, the reliance on—and subsequent decrease of—the collective merits attention.

The variable *associations* measures the persons with whom political parties must share space (same party, different party, voters, political interest groups, the media, etc.). As table 4.2 shows, party labels are most likely to interact with "party entities" (their own party or a different party) during Era I, a finding that is especially apparent in news coverage. Media scholars argue that news stories require drama and conflict. My data show that journalists find the story of campaigns existing between parties during Era I rather than between individual candidates (another trend that emerges in Era III). Consider how the following passages paint campaigns as being contests between groups as much as being ones between the ambitious politicians. In this first text, from a 1948 *New York Times* article, notice an emphasis on collective cues, including the size of the crowd; an appreciation of partisan statements;

Table 4.2. Party Labels by *Associations* Variable, by Era (in percentages)

	Same party	Different party	Other	None
Era I: 1948–1960	28.2	37.4	24.7	9.7
Era II: 1961–1979	22.1	36.9	27.5	13.4
Era III: 1980–1996	19.5	35.1	30.6	14.8
Era IV: 2000	36.5	30.8	25.0	7.7

Note: Overall percentages may not add to 100 owing to rounding to the nearest tenth.

and Truman's confidence in voicing his anger at the other party—not the other party's candidate:

> About 25,000 persons gathered in the State Fair Grounds to hear Mr. Truman. They laughed at his gibes at the *Republicans* and they applauded when he said: "I am a home grown American farm product. And I'm proud of the breed. I represent the completely unterrified form of American democracy. I stand for the simple, straightforward, straight line *Democratic party*. That *party* has always stood for government in the interest of the farmer and the workingman and all the people of this country."
>
> He called the *Democratic party* "the great middle of the road party, the party of the farmers and the workers and the small business men and the party of the young people."
>
> Mr. Truman said that he treasured "the right to disagree about ourselves" and he did "not worry too much about the many violent arguments we *Democrats* have." . . . The *Republican party* and its Presidential candidate, he asserted, have "made me fighting mad." He said that the *Republicans* were "spending money in carload lots" and were "buying themselves all kinds of strange bedfellows." He also asserted that "*Republicanism* puts the almighty dollar first and is not above using a little Tidelands oil money to grease the way to power."[18]

A similar emphasis appears in another *New York Times* column, this one from 1952 in which Governor Adlai Stevenson is quoted as telling the South "that its prosperity and political power lay in the *Democratic party* and not 'in following those embittered apostates who proclaim themselves Democrats while supporting the nominee of the *Republican party*.'" Note that the identification is between the Southerners and the Democratic Party (not the Democratic candidate) and that the opposing candidate (General Eisenhower) is never named. The article continues by paraphrasing Stevenson's belief in "the prosperity of the South now, as compared to what it had been in the past under *Republican* administration, and the power of Southern *Democrats* in their *party* and particularly on Capitol Hill."[19] In 1956, an article in the *Washington Post* opens by quoting a question of President Dwight Eisenhower's about parties, not candidates. The lead sentence reads, "Adlai Stevenson said here tonight that he was willing to fight out the 1956 campaign on an issue of President Eisenhower's own choosing: which *party*, *Republican* or *Democratic*, has done most for the American people." The article continues by quoting Eisenhower's question: "Which *party* in these recent years has done more to help all citizens meet the problems of their daily lives? Which *party* has helped more not with words but with deeds?" Then it provides this response from Stevenson:

> "President Eisenhower has defined the issue. And I speak for every Democrat in the country when I say that we accept the issue as he defines it.
>
> I ask every one of you to consider in terms of your own knowledge . . . which *party* has done more to help you meet your problems?
>
> Which *party* brought in the system of social security and old age benefits and which *party* opposed it?
>
> Which *party* established the principle of a national minimum wage and which *party* opposed it?
>
> Which *party* fought for guarantee of collective bargaining and which *party* fought against it?"[20]

In these instances, conflicts and accomplishments are linked to groups through the *party* label, not to individual actors and, curiously, are not claimed by individual candidates. There is a comfort in acknowledging, standing by, and promoting the collective—both in the candidate statements chosen for quotation here and in the news frames surrounding them.

In contrast, consider the following *Washington Post* article, which describes the 2000 primary contest. While the story does not appear in my original data set, it does provide something of an exaggerated example of how journalists have developed a less-deferential tone toward parties as collectives over the years, locating political drama within individual politicians rather than in the party system itself.

> For that matter even the "legitimate" candidates, the ones sanctioned by the national political press, have some of the characteristics of cable creatures. Steve Forbes is so very CNBC. Elizabeth Dole has Lifetime written all over her. Go down the list and you see a bunch of folks—Buchanan, Forbes, Dole, Gary Bauer, Alan Keyes—who believe that when seeking political office the most natural entry-level position is the presidency of the United States. It's possible that they have decided to seek the White House only because the job of Supreme Commander of the Galaxy isn't open.
>
> Meanwhile hyper-credentialed Al Gore has just learned that Daniel Patrick Moynihan endorses Bill Bradley, which could portend a swing of several, perhaps even a dozen, votes among bow-tied Ivy League professors.
>
> The polls show Bradley heavily eroded Gore's early lead, but it's possible that this merely means that people are rooting for Bradley, urging

him on, hoping to generate some excitement. Rooting for someone in September is not quite the same thing as voting for him the next year. Which brings up the thing we really should be talking about today, the Ryder Cup.[21]

In both content and style, journalists have changed how they describe campaigns. Although the links between candidates and parties in Era I may seem trivial at first glance, they are considerably more stark when compared to reportage in Era III. That is, when journalists portray campaigns as contests between competing groups, readers are encouraged to see candidates as being subordinate to parties and the two-party system as a dominating force. When journalists portray campaigns as being responsive to the actions of the media and ambitious individuals, however, readers may well become "primed" to view the parties as being less consequential in politics.

A considerable emphasis is placed on party unity during Era I. The variable *quality* examines the attributes assigned to the party labels (action, emotion, unity, or clarity). The data show that "unity" is stressed more often during Era I than in the next two eras (I = 28.0 percent, II = 25.9 percent, III = 16.3 percent); this *quality* reemerges in campaign 2000 in the speeches and news coverage of George W. Bush, but intriguingly, it takes on a much breezier tone in that campaign. Because parties were strong during Era I (comparatively at least), candidates were not afraid to herald them and remind voters to be true to them. Note how Thomas Dewey takes the first approach by repeating the word *unity* throughout the following speech. While Dewey's lofty tones can be found in almost any political campaign, the confidence and centrality of the *party* label makes it a paradigmatic example of the rhetoric found in Era I: "I come free to join with you in selecting to serve our nation the finest men and women in the country, free to unite our *party* and our country in meeting the grave challenge of our time. United we can match this challenge with the depth of understanding and largeness of spirit."[22]

A similar emphasis on unity appears in an article describing how Governor Earl Warren (of California) views this attribute as a political and cultural asset of his Republican Party—one that would make the party more fit to bring people together, to solve problems, and to perform on the world stage. The article reads,

> Gov. Earl Warren of California formally opened the Republican national campaign here tonight with a national unity appeal embodying an implied promise on behalf of his own party to keep the drive for votes

"vigorous but friendly" and "free from the prejudice of party, class or race." . . . The Republican party, he said, never before had been so united; there was "no left segment to splinter off" and there was "no segment on the right to secede." Republican leaders, he promised, could use party unity to "unite the nation" and attack not only domestic problems but "work with the representatives of both parties for an honorable, lasting world peace not through vacillation or appeasement but through the council table and the United Nations."[23]

Party unity is consistently presented as a cherished prize in politics during Era I, and intriguingly, candidates do not shy away from demanding it from voters nor do journalists portray such demands as being anomalous requests. Consider Truman's words at the Democratic Nominating Convention that open the chapter ("Labor never had but one friend in politics and that is the Democratic party and Franklin D. Roosevelt"). There is a confidence and naturalness in his demands, one that future Democrats (say, Al Gore) have not had the rhetorical guts or instincts to insist from an audience. The ordinariness of demanding and expecting loyalty from voters and members of a party can be seen in news articles from Era I. For instance, in 1948, President Harry Truman's "give 'em hell, smoke 'em out" attacks on the Republican Party were reported as pleasing his own party faithful.[24] In that same year, the *New York Times* detailed how "the hold of *party* traditions and loyalty remains largely intact in Arkansas despite widespread opposition to President Truman's civil rights proposals, and there is every indication that the state's nine electoral votes will be cast for the Presidential nominee of the Democratic *party*. Mr. Truman is not a popular figure in Arkansas, but the principal expression heard here is that because of his *party* label, he represents 'the lesser of two evils.'"[25] In both of these examples, partisan fervor was welcomed, and party labels were revered.

Michael Schudson has written about the political and cultural aspects of unity over time, contending that citizenship has moved from an age of assent (in which citizens defer to elites) to an age of affiliation (in which citizens identify with parties) to an age of informed citizenship (in which citizens, because of political reforms, are responsible for becoming educated on politics) to an age of the rights-bearing citizen (in which politics can seen as saturating public life). While some bemoan this shift, Schudson does not, concluding that the rise of politics in public life has done more to enhance democracy than to endanger it.[26] This study provides additional textual support for Schudson's model and for the movement from a citizenship of affiliation (or interdependence—as revealed by high use of the *party* label and "unity" attributions) to a citizenship of independence (as discussed in the subsequent sections of this chapter).

Schudson places the relationship between citizens and government during the 1950s and 1960s in historical context, critiquing the collectivist spirit of that time. As he reminds us, unity cannot unequivocally be held as a marker of a democracy's health. Schudson eschews a romantic longing for the past, reminding us that a more united time was not necessarily a healthier time:

> As I have suggested, there can be too much trust as well as too little, and the baseline measures of trust from the 1950s and early 1960s surely reflected a moment of unusual consensus in American life held together by Cold War paranoia, middle class complacency, postwar affluence, and the continuing denial of a voice in public life to women and minorities. Some of the skepticism of major institutions today is amply warranted. Skepticism can be healthy. Some of today's skepticism is in a grand old American tradition that distrusts all politics and politicians. Then, again, some of it seems to express a deeper alienation or aimlessness, especially among the young. But in the crude measures we have, there is no distinguishing a healthy inclination to question authority from a depressed withdrawal in which it is impossible to place faith in anyone or anything.[27]

George W. Bush's "uniter not a divider" theme in 2000 seems to respect both the desire for the collective and the skepticism that conjoins one's being forced into a group. The slogan rests on Bush's experiences with a conservative legislature in Texas, where, in his words, he "worked with Democrats, and [had] been endorsed by Democrats. And, through common sense and plain dealing, we have gotten things done."[28] Here, this motto praises the idea of unity and, in a sense, presents Bush as being an embodiment of it. Intriguingly—and perhaps consistent with Schudson's acknowledgment that Americans have become more suspicious about collectives—Bush does not ask citizens to act (e.g., "Farmers stay true to the Democratic party") or to compromise (e.g., "Arkansans stay true to the Democratic label") to achieve unity. All they would have to do is to respect the idea and perhaps have faith in him, and Bush would provide this cherished ideal. In speaking on behalf of himself and his vice presidential candidate (Dick Cheney), Bush states, "We will inspire and unite. We will not appeal to people's darker impulses. We will appeal to their better angels. We are going to prove that politics can be better and higher. . . . If you share these hopes whether you are a Republican, Democrat or Independent we want your help. Together we can begin again."[29] Timely words, these for a country that had just witnessed the impeachment of a Democratic president by a Republican Congress (following a lengthy investigation by a conservative independent counsel).

As Daniel Rodgers has argued, "words legitimize the outward frame of politics; they create those pictures in our heads which make the structures of authority tolerable and understandable."[30] We have seen here that between 1948 and 1960 labels are used to legitimize parties, giving them a monolithic, if not a deterministic, political image. There was an unquestioned hardiness associated with the *party* label in particular that lent party a type of symbolic power over candidates, citizens, journalists, and the political conversation. Given American ambivalence toward parties and given the inevitable fractiousness of professional politicians, the trends noted here are only suggestive. But, as this section has revealed, party dissensus was not the striking feature of Era I, a time when parties were described with calm, political assurance in the United States.

ERA II—A LIMINAL PERIOD (1961–1979)

Critical elections are defined as electoral contests marked by significant shifts in established voting patterns signaling an enduring realignment of the electorate. Scholars who study these moments note that a realignment was due in the late 1960s (marking the end of the New Deal party system), and they have had various ways of describing if, how, or why that realignment did or did not occur. In Walter Dean Burnham's mind, a change did appear, but it was not a "traditional realignment" (one in which a fifth to a third of the voters shifted their partisan allegiances).[31] In 1974, Burnham wrote that "the American electorate is now deep into the most sweeping transformation it has experienced since the Civil War. It is undergoing a critical realignment of a radically different kind from any in American electoral history."[32] To Burnham, this realignment was not fueled by parties but was cutting across older partisan linkages between the rulers and the ruled, taking place within the system, instead of between the parties. A consequence of this realignment, for Burnham, was the "dissolution of the party as an intervener between the voter and the objects of his votes at the polls."[33]

The texts from Era II provide symbolic support for the type of realignment Burnham envisioned. In its ideal form, Burnham tells us, a realignment has several characteristics, including a short-lived but intense disruption of traditional patterns of voting behavior, abnormally high intensity (including contested party conventions, ideological polarizations, heavy voter participation), and a third-party revolt ("which reveals the incapacity of 'politics as usual' to integrate, much less aggregate, emergent political demand").[34] As if to substantiate some of these criteria, the discussions of party labels during Era II display the greatest emphasis on the campaign-related role of parties, the highest level of "mass partisanship," and the highest use of *independent* labels in campaign speeches. While these three rhetorical patterns do not provide indisputable proof for the types of change Burnham saw in the electorate, they are suggestive and help to describe how the concept of party moved from a monolithic place to a liminal place during these highly turbulent years.

One way to preview the destabilization of party meanings found during this period is to begin with a statement by President Nixon during his reelection campaign in 1972. His sentiment—that the country is more important than party—seems to provide rhetorical evidence for Burnham's contention that party had begun to lose its role as an intervener between the voter and the objects of his or her votes. Notice how Nixon's speech contrasts sharply with the confidence in political parties found in Era I:

> I am not going to talk to you in terms of whether you should be *Democrats* or *Republicans*. The future of this country is much more important than what our *party* label is. I am simply talking about your responsibilities and your opportunities as American citizens with the right and the power to vote. In that respect, I think the new generation of American voters is going to be good for this country. You are going to bring enthusiasm to our elective process that is for sure. You are going to bring idealism to it.[35]

Political scientist Samuel Kernell's research in *Going Public: New Strategies of Presidential Leadership* blends well with Burnham's realignment argument to help interpret statements like Nixon's. Kernell writes that in the middle of the last century, presidents (for example, Franklin D. Roosevelt) worked within a system of institutional pluralism (a system "bound together by calculated fealty to a network of protocoalitions and a dense normative system for which bargaining was the prescribed behavior").[36] In Kernell's model, three changes in American politics—the rise of the modern welfare state, advancements in communications and transportation technologies, and the decline of political parties in the candidate-selection process—have replaced institutional pluralism with individual pluralism, a model "constituted of independent members who have few group or institutional loyalties and who are generally less interested in sacrificing short-run, private career goals for the longer-term benefits of bargaining."[37] Kernell has found that politicians in the individualized pluralistic system have incentives to "go public" rather than do their bargaining within the confines of Washington, D.C. That is, instead of focusing their energies inside the beltway, they take their ideas out to the public in their own localities. Although Kernell advances "going public" as a political strategy, doing so has cultural and rhetorical significance, not the least of which is a destabilization in the meanings of party.

It is important to note that parties are not discussed as falling apart in Era II; had they really fallen apart, party labels would have fallen out of discourse completely. Instead, party became a tenuous, not a stable, source of political identity. One shift in meaning, interestingly, is a buoyant one: in general, Era II is the most optimistic period under examination, with slightly higher levels of emotional partisanship (I = 4.0 percent, II = 4.9 percent, III = 3.5 percent, IV = 1.9 percent—variable: *behavior*),[38] with "a positive context" for partisanship (I = 22.9 percent, II = 24.3 percent, III = 22.5 percent, IV = 20.2 percent—variable: *context*),[39] as well as with a lower level of party as "part of the problem" statements as compared to those of Eras I and III only (I = 19.1 percent, II = 16.0 percent, III = 23.1 percent—variable: *role*).[40] Admittedly, the differences here are modest, but while Era I constitutes party as a strong collective, Era II seems more prone to associate party labels with political potential.

Of the four genres in Era II, candidates are most likely to mention the "feeling" and the "positive context" aspects of party labels and are least likely to place them in a "negative context." Given the conditions of the time—the Vietnam conflict, civil rights and women's rights protests, major political assassinations, McGovern–Fraser party reforms, and Watergate (just to name a few)—how could candidates be so positive? One possibility is that they were merely being careful. In the face of a changing electorate, candidates deemphasized the negative aspects of party labels probably because the candidates were uncertain about how the impending realignment would manifest itself and did not want to lose (or offend) valuable supporters along the way. Observe, for example, the positive and emotional language in Jimmy Carter's speech delivered to the Democratic National Convention in 1980:

> And we are going to beat the Republicans in November. We'll win because we are the *party of a great President* who knew how to get reelected—Franklin Delano Roosevelt. And we are the *party of a courageous*

fighter who knew how to give hell, Harry Truman. And as Truman said, he just told the truth and they thought it was hell. And we're the *party of a gallant man of spirit,* John Fitzgerald Kennedy. And we're the *party of a great leader of compassion,* Lyndon Baines Johnson, and the *party of a great man* who should have been President, who would have been one of the greatest Presidents in history, Hubert Horatio Hornblower Humphrey. I have appreciated what this convention has said about Senator Humphrey, a great man who epitomized the *spirit of the Democratic Party.* And I would like to say that we are also the party of Governor Jerry Brown and Senator Edward Kennedy. I'd like to say a personal word to Senator Kennedy. Ted, you're a tough competitor and a superb campaigner, and I can attest to that. Your speech before this convention was a *magnificent statement of what the Democratic party* is and what it means to the people of this country and why a Democratic victory is so important this year.[41]

This speech has been critiqued elsewhere, particularly because of Carter's mistake when pronouncing Hubert Humphrey's name, but it is a fitting example of the almost counterintuitive optimism found during this period. Here, Carter describes Humphrey as being magnificent, but he also assigns each of the other Democrats an admiring word or adjective, including "great," "courageous," "gallant," and "compassion." Why, one wonders, did Carter make such collegial overstatements?

Although Carter's popularity has risen since he left the White House, his tenure in office is remembered as one of curious leadership, gross attention to detail at the expense of vision, and failed international decision making. More immediately, throughout the 1980 primary season, Carter had endured attacks from challenger Senator Edward "Ted" Kennedy (D-MA). Thus, in delivering this speech to the Democratic convention, he had a distinct rhetorical challenge: to unite the party and to inspire their belief in him.

Yet as a politician from Era II, Carter has a rhetorical situation that is not unique. After all, six of the eight presidential candidates during this period had also faced tensions at their conventions (e.g., Barry Goldwater, Hubert Humphrey, Richard Nixon in 1968; George McGovern, Gerald Ford, and Carter); only Lyndon Johnson in 1964 and Ronald Reagan in 1980 escaped these problems. Most of these candidates had to sell themselves to a party convention that had not chosen them directly (they had achieved success in the primary system) and/or had not chosen them enthusiastically (because the primaries had been contentious). By Era III, the system was accustomed to seeing candidates at the convention who had not been handpicked by the parties, but during Era II this was still a novelty. As the primaries began to challenge the party oligarchy in the candidate-selection process, party labels became more positive, almost as if to provide rhetorical compensation for the political turmoil being experienced at the time.

Journalists also placed party labels in a positive context during this era and, like the candidates, did so through the use of adjectives as well as buoyant words that usually do not make it past the copyeditor. Notice, for example, the language surrounding the following party labels ("cheering," "tumultuous," "welcome," "shouting," "jamming") appearing in newspaper coverage of the time:

> In what Mayor Daley called "the greatest salute to a candidate ever given in the City of Chicago," thousands of placard carrying city workers, bands, floats, and fire engines filled the short parade route along Michigan Avenue. A fireworks display greeted Carter . . . a "vivid demonstration of party loyalty."[42]

> Earlier in the day in Cleveland Humphrey, terming himself the "O. J. Simpson of the Democratic party," told cheering supporters that he would lead his party to a come from behind victory in November. The Democratic presidential nominee invoked the example of the University of Southern California football star whose last quarter touchdowns Saturday defeated Humphrey's alma mater, the University of Minnesota.[43]

> His talk followed a tumultuous welcome filled with ticker tape and confetti in downtown Los Angeles as his motorcade followed a twenty block parade route through street crowds estimated by the police at more than 200,000. Thousands of shouting Nixon partisans rushed into the streets, jamming close to the open car. . . . The Los Angeles County Republican organization had promised a "confetti jungle" and it more than kept its word.[44]

These passages are interesting for two reasons: first, because these buoyant descriptors are normally not found in the "usually objective" news text; second, because these texts portray party at the mass level. Both of these patterns contribute to the upbeat spirit of Era II.

The variable *position* determines whether elites link voters to the party (e.g., "*Third-party* supporter, Mr. Jones said . . .") or whether party is viewed as an instrument of elites (e.g., "*Democrats* will vote to override the president's veto"). On this variable, the results show that parties during Era II are less likely to be associated with elites and slightly more likely to be linked to mass notions of partisanship (21.6 percent) than are Eras I (19.1 percent) or III (15.0 percent). All three of the news stories described here portray citizens as finding their meanings in their party affiliations. Perhaps it makes sense that as politicians focus more and more on the public, news coverage would feature such cues as well.

Era II also features the highest use of *independent* statements in campaign speeches. Figure 4.2 displays the total occurrence of the *independent* label in the speeches found in the Campaign Mapping Project. This differential use of the *independent* label can be explained in light of research on Burnham's work on critical elections. As mentioned, third-party activity is common before a critical realignment, and its use here could be a natural precursor to same. In retrospect, it seems curious that the *independent* label appears more in Era II than in Era III (with the latter being a time that features two high-profile independent candidacies—John Anderson in 1980, H. Ross Perot in 1992—a point discussed in chapter 6).

Scholars speak freely about the differences between campaigning and governing (i.e., the types of skills each activity requires, the types of candidates willing to submit to the campaign process, and the types of talented governors who refuse to do so), and perhaps Era II provides rhetorical evidence of the gulf between these activities. During these years, parties were tied to campaign functions more than they were during Era I or III. While the rhetorical characteristics of portraying parties as campaigners have already been detailed (chapter 3), it is important to observe that much of this discourse opened up during Era II.

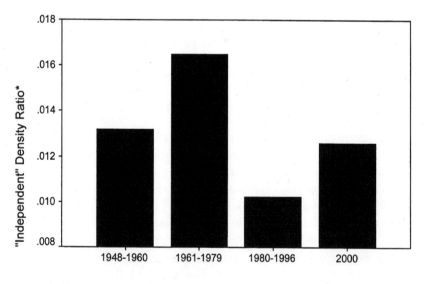

Figure 4.2.   *Independent* in Speeches, by Era
*Density ratio = *independent* / all words in speeches × 100

Overall, Era II seems to be a time of transition: the powerful party structure gave way to a more specialized one, and the monolithic party turned into a more situated coalition. Interpreting this shift in historical perspective, one finds that as the parties begin losing control over the candidate-selection process, elites do not respond by portraying them as being weak or negative. That they hesitate to do so reveals that—even during these tumultuous years—something about parties is seen as worth protecting.

ERA III—A FRAGMENTED PERIOD (1980–1996)

If news coverage during Era I locates drama between competing groups, then much of the drama during Era III involves a set of other actors connected to labels. Observe these newspaper articles from 1988 and 1992, respectively:

> Entering the final week of his long quest for the presidency, Republican nominee George Bush said today he has no regrets about the tone of the campaign he has waged and rejected the suggestion that Americans are disgusted by his focus on such themes as prison furloughs and the Pledge of Allegiance. . . . "I don't consider the way I am campaigning as personal," Bush said, responding to public opinion surveys that show voter disenchantment with the harshness of the campaign. Bush said he had not used "a lot of real flamboyant language. I mean, I've not called him 'pathetic,'" the term Democratic nominee Michael S. Dukakis uses to describe Bush's antidrug effort. Asked if he believes that voters in general approve of his approach, Bush replied, "My supporters sure do."[45]

> Ross Perot was at it again yesterday, teasing the American electorate and bedeviling the two major parties by declaring that he had "made a mistake" when he dropped out of the presidential race last July and by saying he would reconsider his plans over the next week. Typically, Perot made the comments during a television interview. Typically, he could not be pinned down on CBS's "This Morning" about whether he would run for president. And typically, he insisted that the final decision would really be up to his "volunteers."[46]

Instead of emphasizing collective force of political party labels, these columns point to several political realities of Era III, including a new set of forces on the campaign landscape, such as:

- the growth and widespread use of public opinion polling, a development that has helped campaigns target voting blocs and journalists report on who is ahead, behind, and catching up in a campaign;

- a public concern with negative campaigning practices;
- a focus on the campaign audience as a set of markets, with special attention dedicated to the undecided, independent, or swing voter;
- society's willingness to consider wealthy political novices as being viable candidates for high-profile positions; and
- the empirical and reified power of television in the American body politic.

As the tone and content of these news clips suggest, questions that would have been laughable in the earlier periods no longer seem implausible. A Texas billionaire with no experience in government as a candidate for the United States Presidency? Why not? If a candidate possesses the desire, money, and marketing know-how, then anything in Era III appears possible. Even college professors, apt to move more slowly than other segments of the body politic, admit to this. In describing how the presidential selection process has become less dominated by parties and has opened to a new range of ambitious office seekers, John Aldrich writes, "The monopoly has been broken, an alternative means now exists."[47]

Alan Ehrenhalt's *The United States of Ambition: Politicians, Power, and the Pursuit of Office* offers a series of powerful examples detailing this shift. The political system, in Ehrenhalt's mind, has gone professional as "full-time as institutions that once were closed and tightly controlled are now open to virtually anyone with the skill and ambition to manipulate them."[48] Ehrenhalt writes,

> Political careers are open to ambition now in a way that has not been true in America in most of this century. Those with the desire for office and the ability to manipulate the instruments of the system—the fundraising, the personal campaigning, the opportunities to express themselves in public—confront very few limits on their capacity to reach the top. The bosses and party leaders who used to pass judgment on political careers have just about all departed the scene. They are no longer a significant barrier to entry.[49]

The uses of party labels in Era III reflect these concerns. Specifically, party became more particularistic during this time, as revealed by the following trends in my data. Era III sees the lowest levels of

- "same party" references (I = 28.2 percent, II = 22.1 percent, III = 19.5 percent, IV = 36.5 percent—variable: *associations*);

- "unity" statements (I = 28.0 percent, II = 25.9 percent, III = 16.3 percent, IV = 39.4 percent—variable: *quality*); and
- global partisan statements (I = 12.4 percent, II = 11.8 percent, III = 8.0 percent, IV = 15.4 percent—variable: *position*).

Additionally, Era III sees the lowest use of the *party* label (I = 28.0 percent, II = 22.7 percent, III = 17.0 percent, IV = 19.2 percent—variable: *labels*) and the highest use of the word *liberal* (I = 9.7 percent, II = 9.4 percent, III = 14.8 percent, IV = 9.6 percent—variable: *labels*). Taken together, these findings indicate that elites discussed partisanship as an individualistic—as opposed to a collective—endeavor between the years of 1981 and 1996, suggesting that the "narrowing" of the electorate was then being evidenced both in word and deed.

After running crosstabs on these findings, I found that the 1995 welfare reform debate features the lowest level of "same party" references of any genre for this era. As discussed, Congress is the institution that relies on partisanship most heavily; yet, legislators do not evoke the collective during the 1995 welfare reform debate, preferring instead to argue against the *Democrats*, who were being unreasonable, or the *Republicans*, who had created mean-spirited legislation. The question, of course, emerges: why is it that legislators no longer use collectives?

One explanation might be found in the types of legislators who now run for Congress. Alan Ehrenhalt explains how legislators during Era III have become more competitive and less respectful of both the seniority system and their fellow partisans. He points to the career of Phil Gramm (R-TX) in both the Congress and the Senate as an example of this trend. Entering the House as a conservative Democrat (and leaving Texas A&M University as an economics professor), Gramm first announced that he knew more about economics than anyone who had entered Congress in the past thirty years and then ostracized himself by working on his own version of the federal budget.[50] In 1984, Gramm moved to the Senate (having switched to the Republican Party), where he was liked no better than he was in the House. Ehrenhalt details how after Gramm called Senator Patrick Moynihan (D-NY) "weak on defense," the respected former Harvard professor responded, "You're in the Senate one year fella. You don't do that to another Senator."[51] It stands to reason that legislators who do not adhere as strictly to the norms of reciprocity and seniority may use fewer party labels than their predecessors do, preferring to speak in a more self-centered (if not self-serving) fashion.[52]

The finding that labels are increasingly particularistic becomes interesting when interpreted through recent work analyzing parties in light of marketing principles. During Era III, it was not uncommon to hear elites refer to "such and such a market" or a particular demographic (e.g., "Turn out the women's vote," "Target African Americans," "Don't ignore the Latinos," "Mobilize soccer moms"). In the same vein, Neil Collins and Patrick Butler apply a marketing framework from business scholar Philip Kotler to party activities. Specifically, their schema features four positions: *leader* (highest share of market), *challenger* (chosen to depose leader), *follower* (purposeful concentration on target market, imitative rather than innovative), and *nicher* (leader in narrowly defined market, specialist appeal).[53] The distinction between a leader and a nicher in this typology is particularly relevant to the shift of party meanings over time. Collins and Butler describe leaders as being the players with the highest market share, who provide "the acknowledged orientation point for the others. . . . They may not be highly regarded, liked or even respected by competitors, but they are the accepted leaders."[54] In contrast, a nicher opts to control a small, well-defined market. They write, "The key success factor of the niche player is that it specializes in serving the needs of the niche better than other, more casual, competitors."[55]

Their schema also reflects changes that I found in the meaning of party labels over time. In describing the strategy of the leader, Collins and Butler write,

A number of strategic directions are common among market leaders. For the political party, where analysis shows that the player is in the position of market leader, three appropriate types of strategy can be anticipated: expanding the total market, expanding market share further, and defending market share. By virtue of holding the leadership position, the leader is subject to continuous attack. Defensive strategies are therefore of particular importance. The world of commerce is full of stories of market leaders who were successfully beaten into a lesser place or who vanished in a tough competitive environment. It is not feasible in the long run, however, only to defend a position. This would assume that the world is static. Even the most narrowly defined product markets entail some competitive dynamic. So, the leader must also consider expanding the total market, thereby gaining more sales and revenues, or increasing its already dominant share further, even when market size remains constant.[56]

Where parties are concerned, Democrats and Republicans have undoubtedly been "leaders" in the American context. But as Collins and Butler note, a defensive strategy cannot effectively maintain a market, because several challenges to the party system—structural reforms, information technologies (e.g., television), and increased cynicism—have threatened the leaders' control of the system. The language of Era III shows that elites had come to see political party labels through the marketing lens of nichers. This may be an inevitable tendency, for as Walter Dean Burnham's earlier point suggests, parties have shifted in importance for the electorate over time. Nevertheless, when the leaders of a market—Democrats and Republicans— are discussed as nichers, several things may be happening and many of them may be highly consequential.

From a strategic perspective, the natural advantages held by the Democratic and Republican brands become less obvious when party representatives begin to approach politics in the same way as less-traditional politicians do. Indeed, when respected public officials vacate their offices so that they can position themselves as running "outside the system" (e.g., Senator Bob Dole's leaving the Senate after thirty-five years on the Hill to run for president in 1996), it may be to salute a perceived understanding that voters have come to believe that "outsiderness" is as good, or better, than political experience. Clearly, the logic of the nicher erodes part of the traditional party advantage.

From a social perspective, when major parties (as well as minor parties) become engaged in niche marketing, splintered demographics become more important than Americans as a whole, a troubling notion indeed for a nation struggling to find its commonalities. Political scholars have long debated whether parties can ever be more than campaign coalitions, but— rhetorically, at least—these coalitions somehow managed to inspire a greater sense of collectivity in earlier times. When party labels are portrayed as divisive, however, expectations for interdependence will likely disappear; when parties are no longer discussed as groups, it is likely that they will no longer be thought of as groups.

It is also likely that they will not act as groups. As political scientist V. O. Key has noted, one blessing of two-party government is that "two sets of politicians" compete with one another and protect the system from tyranny and corruption. Thus, when parties are portrayed as being composed of individuals who are out for themselves, it becomes hard to discern who is working to challenge the government. An important point this, for as Burnham has written, when parties fail to represent interests in a polity, moneyed interests will undoubtedly fill the void. As he has argued,

> so far as it is known, the blunt alternative to party government is the concentration of political power, locally or nationally, in the hands of

those who already possess concentrated economic power. If no adequate substitute for party as means for mobilizing non-elite influence on the governing process has yet been discovered, the obvious growth of "image" and "personality" voting in recent decades should be a matter of some concern to those who would like to see a more complete restoration of the democratic process in the United States.[57]

Still another instance of fragmentation can be found in the number of voter references witnessed in Era III—a trend that started in the 1980s and continued into the 2000 campaign (I = 15.3 percent, II = 15.3 percent, III = 21.7 percent, IV = 20.4 percent—variable: *associations*). Whereas Era II moved parties closer to the masses, Era III mentioned voters by name. Consider the following news texts from the 1984, 1988, and 1996 campaigns. In these columns, journalists feature the opinions of Monty Clark (a schoolteacher), Marcia Tye (a homemaker), Kathleen Bakalarski (a forty-two-year-old homemaker), and Teri Crie (a forty-four-year-old school librarian). Such reportage dramatizes that, in Era III, parties have to be prepared to respond to the identifiable needs of identifiable individuals:

> Around the room, people nodded agreement. "I noticed that too," said *Monty Clark*, a schoolteacher who is a moderate to conservative Democrat and who has been supporting Reagan. "It was much more pronounced tonight. When Reagan didn't have a script in his mind, he was in much more difficulty. Mondale looked like the standout tonight."[58]

> *Marcia Tye*, a homemaker in Warren, is an independent who expressed no preference before the debate. She voted for Jimmy Carter in 1980 and for Walter Mondale in 1984, but now leans toward Bush because "Dukakis is too liberal." She thinks the problems of the homeless and of available housing are exaggerated. She saw Dukakis as being less prepared and a "little anxious and nervous."[59]

> At an outdoor cafe, the conversation of two San Diego women discussing the two main presidential contenders suggests the reasons. "Every time he speaks, I cringe," said *Kathleen Bakalarski*, a 42-year-old homemaker who hasn't decided how she will vote in the November election but finds little reason to support the Republican. She and her friend, *Teri Crie*, a 44-year-old school librarian, are registered Republicans. Even so, they find Dole's stances have little in common with their own.[60]

Elites also constitute parties as being active during Era III. The *potency* variable assesses whether party labels are depicted as acting or being acted upon. This period sees a higher degree of agency (54.9 percent) than Era I (41.9 percent) or II (43.1 percent)—a sense of agency that would transcend into Era IV (55.0 percent). Era III also saw the least number of instances in which party labels were depicted as "acted against" (24.6 percent) compared to the other years under study (I = 40.0 percent, II = 38.2 percent, IV = 25.0 percent). In these three ways, party labels gained a sense of energy that was not as present in the earlier periods, a pattern that is closely related to the types of verbs associated with parties during Era III. For instance, consider these statements from the 1995 congressional debate in which party labels were often placed adjacent to working verbs: "Republicans are proposing," "Republicans are making," "Both Democrats and Republicans want to end welfare," "The Republican bill micromanages the plans of the states," and "Democrats are strong on work." While this again may appear simply to be a case of stylistic fashion (more verbs per noun in the 1990s than in the 1950s), this trend may also reveal assumptions about the times in which the elites lived. The energy that they placed in the collective during Era I highlights their faith in groups; the movement associated with party labels in Era III, in contrast, reveals a more frenetic understanding of politics.

In retrospect, the *party* label appears to have served a unifying and stabilizing function in Era I that it did not serve in Era III. But why? Perhaps because when parties were described as being teams, political discourse was more orderly (see figure 4.1 for the decrease of the *party* label over time). Although it is foolhardy to celebrate order for order's sake, it is also naïve to believe that a democratic system can work without it. Indeed, as chapter 3 discusses, even though many of the founders of this country passionately argued against political parties, they discovered that governance was unpredictable and unworkable without them. Thus, organized collectives have a much-needed place in a representative democracy, even if that notion is not commonly articulated in the niche-inspired logic of Era III.

Unchecked individualism is not only unhealthy in government but is also a problematic way to study the electorate. In their book *Reading Mixed Signals: Ambivalence in American Public Opinion about Groups*, political scholars Albert Cantril and Susan David Cantril discuss the danger of describing Americans in a particularistic way. Specifically, they discuss survey data on two key matters: citizens' general attitudes toward government and their views about specific government activities.[61] The authors find that they can divide the public into four groups: steady supporters (citizens who support the government, constituting 39 percent of the public), ambivalent supporters (supporters of government in general but not all of its specifics, 12 percent), ambivalent critics (citizens who support programs but do not like government, 20 percent), and steady critics (citizens who do not support government, 18 percent). Cantril and Cantril hold that the most competitive arena of politics consists of ambivalent critics, persons who tend to be ticket splitters and whose votes are up for grabs in most elections.

The authors' analysis is particularly useful in thinking about the niche marketing of Era III. The Cantrils note that although it is easy to categorize voters in simplistic liberal or conservative camps—or to create stereotypes such as "soccer moms" or "angry white males"—doing so conceals more than it reveals.[62] People's attitudes about government are complex, they warn, and trying to force these deeply ambivalent thoughts into unidimensional models sacrifices a richer understanding of how people understand government. So it appears in Era III. Focusing on how parties relate to specific groups may seem like a beneficial election strategy—indeed, targeting certain publics has been successful in recent campaigns and certainly matches the corporatist logic—but ultimately it may be more dangerous than efficient. As Cantril and Cantril conclude, research that pigeonholes individuals' views denies much of what these individuals think about government. The act of chopping up the electorate to win elections may create unnecessary divisions in the public, particularly because there are few attendant political or rhetorical incentives to reunite these groups. While a false notion of community is undesirable (as Michael Schudson's earlier analysis indicates), the manufacturing of artificial divisions in the name of winning elections has problematic long-term effects, too. In a sense, then, the discourse of Era III shows that the spirit of individualism interferes with "combining," a troubling finding for both partisanship and the American political system as traditionally understood.

ERA IV—A MOMENT OF RESURGENCE (CAMPAIGN 2000)

One of the most important players in campaign 2000 was a man whose name was not on the ballot: President Bill Clinton. Clinton's presidency can be remembered for a set of triumphs: eight years of unprecedented economic growth, the first balanced budget (let alone budget surplus) in decades, and aggressive efforts at gaining peace across the world. The nation's first baby boomer president was an artful communicator with an engaging and telegenic presence and was the first Democratic president since Franklin Delano Roosevelt to be elected to a second term. Of course, Clinton's presidency can also be remembered for a set of conflicts. Indeed, while Clinton was the figure head of the Democratic Party, the Republican Party gained control of the House of Representatives for the first time in more than forty years during the 1994 midterm elections; a standoff between the Republican Congress and Clinton White House led to a shutdown of the federal government in 1995; and independent counsel Kenneth Starr's appointment to investigate a failed real estate venture of Clinton in 1994 led to impeachment proceedings against the president. It was in the shadow of Clinton's gifts, indiscretions, and political moments that campaign 2000 was waged. And the campaigns chose two different approaches to emerge from this shadow: Republican governor George W. Bush of Texas employed party labels in a way that was reminiscent of the communal appeals in Era I, while Clinton's vice president, Al Gore, featured a discourse with an almost exaggerated sense of the niche-marketing tactics witnessed in Era III.

Overall, the speeches from campaign 2000, when compared to those of the other periods under investigation, feature higher levels of party labels being "part of the solution" (61.4 percent of all statements—variable: *role*), interaction with the same party (36.5 percent—variable: *associations*), "global" attributions of partisanship (25.0 percent—variable: *position*), action (54.5 percent—variable: *behavior*), and associations with emotion and unity (11.4 percent and 47.7 percent, respectively—variable: *quality*). On these measures, Bush boasts a higher level of "part of the solution" statements (70.4 percent) compared to that of Gore (29.6 percent) and more attributions of unity (61.9 percent) than those of Gore (38.1 percent). For its part, the press seems to follow the sunny Bush lead, depicting party labels as being "part of the solution" more often in campaign 2000 (25 percent—variable: *role*) than during any other era and portraying the labels more often in a positive than in a negative situation (the only era under examination for which this is the case; see variable: *context*).

By praising Democrats and Republicans alike and by encouraging voters to invest in the idea of unity (without demanding that they "do their duty," as did Truman), Bush's use of party labels marks a type of resurgence that fits the sensibilities of a postfragmented era. Bush's brand of compassionate conservatism was positioned at the level of ideas; it asked for faith rather than compromise; it came after the national party conflicts of the 1990s; and it was delivered by an amiable candidate. Accordingly, this strategy may have been newsworthy for at least two reasons: it broke with the past, and it served as a stark contrast to Gore's campaign, which focused more heavily on grounded matters and populist, rather than partisan, appeals (most obviously by not calling on President Clinton to stump for him).

The divergence of the styles and the press's reflection of the optimism and emphasis on the collectives in Bush's speeches can be spotted in the following article, describing this campaign. News such as this underscores the resurgent sense of buoyancy and unity in the Bush camp (as well as the detailed sales pitch of Gore):

> Both men are drawing impressive crowds, all of which stand in place for hours before the candidate arrives. Both have confetti cannons and heart pounding music, but the content of their appearances could not be more different. A Bush rally is reminiscent of an "Up With People" concert, with Bush ticking off his hard differences with Gore on taxation and the size of government but dwelling on his desire to be "a uniter, not a divider," to "raise the spirits of this nation" and "make sure the American dream touches every willing heart." The theme of his campaign tour for the final week is "Bringing America Together."
>
> Gore partisans dismiss this as "cotton candy," but it seems to be tasty. David E. Sohles, 60, publisher of a magazine for Tampa area senior citizens, said Bush has "magical qualities" that will restore awe to the presidency. "I felt good about being alive and being an American," Sohles said as he left a rally last week at the Florida State Fairgrounds, where a poster behind the candidate said "Bush or Bust."
>
> Gore's appearances include a detailed tour of his position papers on education, Social Security and Medicare and a host of other areas where he is promising to fight for middle class families, punctuated with the guttural call to arms, "Are you with me?" Gore is so thorough, however, that sometimes even giddy crowds tend to dwindle as he goes. In Muskegon, Mich., on Sunday night, at the climax of the first day of his "Great Lakes Prosperity Tour," Gore was greeted at the historic train station by a huge crowd of 20,000, Gore said later. The Romanesque station had been lit like a movie set, and while thousands of their neighbors craned their necks to see the Gores on the elevated stage, good old boys at a nearby bar stood on a bench on the back porch, enjoying whiskey and Cokes as they listened. Gore basked in the crowd's adulation bowing, patting his heart, flexing his biceps. But the throng thinned noticeably as he plowed through his pitch. Among those trying to beat the traffic was Rose Justian, 54, an enthusiastic backer who nevertheless said, "He should just let the sheriff give him a T shirt and say goodbye."
>
> Tipper Gore, who is on the road full time and often photographs crowds from the stage, was asked if she had misgivings about carrying the campaign's eat your broccoli approach into the homestretch. She said

voters want a serious, committed person as president. "What people see is what people get," she said. "If it's broccoli, it's broccoli."[63]

The news frame that followed seemed to hold at least two questions: "Will the optimistic uniter be successful?" "Will Gore's more complicated populist approach bore the audience?" Both media frames would ultimately be answered in the affirmative. And Bush's optimistic portayal of party unity, as well as the coverage that it inspired, helped to resuscitate the talk of the party in campaign 2000.

CONCLUSION

A rhetorical examination suggests that party labels have been deployed quite differently over time. In Era I, energy was devoted to uniting members of the party; in Era II, energy was attached to running campaigns and to shifting from the elite level to the mass level of partisanship; in Era III, energy became dissipated, with parties being associated with political tensions and fractures; and in Era IV, the Bush campaign peddled an optimistic unified model of partisanship, and the media followed. Taken together, what do these observations mean?

On one hand, party labels are now more open than they once were. This represents both an opportunity (greater attention to the citizenry) and a cost (less-efficient party decision making, lower levels of respect and power for the party). Political scholar Theodore Lowi has written that the two major parties are now immobilized because they have to promise too many things to too many people.[64] While Lowi describes this as a political problem, it appears to be a symbolic problem as well. As party openness increases, party groupness decreases. Scholars who study the "thickening of the state" argue that once a pattern of growth begins, it is difficult to stop. A similar dynamic is attached to party labels: once party meanings escaped the confines of the monolithic party structure in Era I, it became difficult to rein the meanings in—politically as well as symbolically.

A half century is too short a period to definitively produce cyclical changes in party meanings. It does appear to be the case, however, that identifiable rhetorical shifts have taken place, shifts not wholly dissimilar to previously documented patterns of partisanship. Writing on the breakdown of machine politics, Gerald Pomper claims that "in its stress on coalitional goals, the machine carried the seeds of its own destruction. . . . The greatest defect of the machine was not its corruption; it was most deficient in its training in citizenship. . . . It was inherently unable to teach the broader meaning of citizenship, the involvement of self in a larger social enterprise."[65] In terms of these findings, the focus on the monolithic party in Era I ignored individual citizens and may well have enabled a splintered partisanship in Era III that ignored the collective. In campaign 2000, the Bush team waged a strategy that offered an optimistic and unified message, one created, perhaps, to fill or capitalize on the void created by the messages of Era III.[66]

The meanings of party labels described in this chapter provide at least two sets of expectations for the twenty-first century. In a sense, the changes in partisanship described here parallel the shifts in dominant communications media in the United States (a stronger party during the newspaper era, a liminal party during the early television era, an individualized party during the growth of cable television and the early Internet). Both the Internet and the proliferation of television stations provide greater freedom for citizens to gather their news in diverse ways, and this freedom could affect party meanings in two ways:

- *They could move back to a collectivist meaning.* In the face of this freedom and in the twilight of Bush's successes in campaign 2000, parties may get to the point where they work harder to reconnect with their members; in the face of this freedom, the Internet may—eventually—be dominated by organized interests that have a better chance, and more capital, to attract people who are intimidated by myriad options and who crave a greater sense of communal understanding. Or . . .
- *They could move onward to atomized meaning.* Inspired by the decentralized media, widespread cynicism, and ambitious money-driven candidates, the meanings of parties may become even more decentralized and splintered. While some observers prefer the second route because it ensures individualism, it seems too early to predict the disappearance of parties in the near future (although atomized parties may become a reality, and this reality will certainly change politics as we know it).

Walter Dean Burnham is concerned with exactly this point in his conclusion to *Critical Elections and the Mainsprings of Mass Politics.* There, he claims that popular sovereignty may require an adjustment to the realignment of the late 1960s but that such an adjustment runs counter to politics and culture in the United States. He writes,

The evidence points overwhelmingly to the conclusion that the American polity has entered the most profound turning point in its history. The task confronting it may be no less than the construction of instrumentalities of domestic sovereignty to limit individual freedom in the name of collective necessity, as Lowi implicitly argues. If so, it is difficult indeed to see how this could be possible under auspices which could remotely be called democratic. It would require an entirely new structure of parties and mass behavior, one in which political parties would be the instrumentalities of democratic collective purpose. But this in turn seems inconceivable without a pre-existing revolution in social values. In the present American context such a revolution would only be too likely to be overwhelmed in its early stages by a counterrevolution among those urban and suburban whites whose values and perceived material interests would be placed in the gravest jeopardy. And who proposes to make a democratic revolution against a class which constitutes a majority of the population?[67]

Once again—for better or worse—the best bet when predicting changes in party meanings is to focus on the behavior of elites. As this chapter shows, elites have talked about parties differently over time, but they have never eschewed parties altogether. While the meanings of party have become more specific, they continue to be important institutions in the United States, a point that receives additional support in the next chapter. There, we will observe how some elites (i.e., presidential candidates) gently distance themselves from the party apparatus while others (i.e. journalists) reinforce the centrality of parties in American life. That elites regulate one another's use of party labels is a curious finding and, as we shall see, not an insignificant one.

NOTES

1. Harry Truman, "Acceptance Address to the Democratic Nominating Convention," Philadelphia, Pa. (15 July 1948), Annenberg/Pew Archive of Presidential Discourse, CD-ROM (Philadelphia: Annenberg School for Communication, University of Pennsylvania, 2000).

2. Dwight Eisenhower, "Acceptance Address to the Republican Nominating Convention" (11 July 1952), Annenberg/Pew Archive of Presidential Discourse, CD-ROM (Philadelphia: Annenberg School for Communication, University of Pennsylvania, 2000).

3. Eisenhower, "Acceptance Address" (11 July 1952).

4. George W. Bush, "Acceptance Address to the Republican Nominating Convention," Philadelphia, Pa. (3 August 2000), Campaign Mapping Project database, University of Texas at Austin.

5. Al Gore, "Acceptance Address to the Democratic National Convention," Los Angeles (17 August 2000).

6. See James Madison, *Federalist No. 10*, in *The Federalist Papers*, Alexander Hamilton, John Jay, and James Madison (London: Penguin, 1987).

7. See John R. Hibbing and Elizabeth Theiss Morse, *Congress as Public Enemy: Public Attitudes toward American Political Institutions* (Cambridge: Cambridge University Press, 1995), 18.

8. Robert Dahl, *Who Governs?* (New Haven, Conn.: Yale University Press, 1961).

9. Jon S. Dryzek and Stephen T. Leonard, "History and Discipline in Political Science," *American Political Science Review* 82, no. 4 (1988): 1245–60.

10. Dryzek and Leonard, "History and Discipline."

11. Theodore Lowi, *The End of Liberalism*, 2nd ed. (New York: Norton, 1979); Charles Lindbloom, "The Market as a Prison," *Journal of Politics* 44, no. 2 (May 1982): 324–36.

12. John F. Kennedy, "Campaign Speech," Indianapolis, Ind. (4 October 1960).

13. See Kathleen H. Jamieson, *Packaging the Presidency: A History and Criticism of Presidential Campaign Advertising* (New York: Oxford University Press, 1992), 124.

14. In the 1957 congressional debate on civil rights, I found the following labels: *party* = 41.5 percent, *Democrat* = 24.5 percent, *Republican* = 24.5 percent, *independent* = 0.0 percent, *liberal* = 8.3 percent, and *conservative* = 1.2 percent.

15. Specifically, the data are as follows: Era I party = 41.5 percent of all labels; Era II party = 24.3 percent of all labels; Era III party = 11.6 percent of all labels; Era IV = 18.2 percent of all labels.

16. House of Representatives, Representative D. R. (Billy) Matthews of Florida speaking in the debate on the 1957 Civil Rights Act, *Congressional Record* (11 June 1957): 8844.

17. Eric Uslaner, *The Decline of Comity in Congress* (Ann Arbor: University of Michigan Press, 1993), 5.

18. "Truman Appeals for End of Split in Southern Party," *New York Times*, 20 October 1948, 1A.

19. "Stevenson Assails Party 'Apostates'; Tells South to Guard Economic and Political Gains by Ignoring the Dissidents," *New York Times*, 12 October 1952, 1A.

20. "Adlai Takes Ike's Challenge," *Washington Post*, 3 October 1956, 1A.

21. Joel Achenbach, "The Cable-ized Cabal," *Washington Post*, www.washingtonpost.com/wp-srv/columnists/achenbach/achenbach.htm (24 September 1999).

22. Thomas Dewey, "Acceptance Speech," Republican National Convention (24 June 1948), Annenberg/Pew Archive of Presidential Discourse, CD-ROM (Philadelphia: Annenberg School for Communication, University of Pennsylvania, 2000).

23. "Warren Says GOP Can Bring Unity to Anxious Nation," *New York Times*, 17 September 1948, 1A.

24. "Dewey Held to Net 14 States, Truman 6 by Western Tours," *New York Times*, 4 October 1948, 1A.

25. "Arkansas to Back Truman after All," *New York Times*, 8 October 1948, 3A.

26. Michael Schudson, *The Good Citizen: A History of American Civic Life* (New York: Free Press, 1998), 293.

27. Schudson, *Good Citizen*, 302.

28. George W. Bush, "Campaign Speech" (30 October 2000), Campaign Mapping Project database, University of Texas at Austin.

29. Bush, "Campaign Speech."

30. Daniel T. Rodgers, *Contested Truths: Keywords in American Politics since Independence* (Cambridge, Mass.: Harvard University Press, 1987), 5.

31. Burnham, *Critical Elections*, 6.

32. Walter D. Burnham, *American Politics in the 1970s: Beyond Party?* (New York: Oxford University Press, 1974), 308.

33. Walter Dean Burnham, *Critical Elections and the Mainsprings of American Politics* (New York: Norton, 1970), 355.

34. Burnham, *Critical Elections*, 10.

35. Richard Nixon, "Remarks to the Student Body of Rio Grande High School," Rio Grande City, Tex. (22 September 1972), Annenberg/Pew Archive of Presidential Discourse, CD-ROM (Philadelphia: Annenberg School for Communication, University of Pennsylvania, 2000).

36. Samuel Kernell, *Going Public: New Strategies of Presidential Leadership*, 3rd ed. (Washington, D.C.: Congressional Quarterly Press, 1997), 27.

37. Kernell, *Going Public*, 27–28.

38. Moreover, the percentages for emotional partisanship were even higher in the following categories: in speeches, 7.4 percent; in news, 6.7 percent; with the *independent* label, 7.7 percent; and for the *liberal* label, 13.3 percent.

39. Additionally, the percentages for a positive context for partisanship were even higher in the following categories: in speeches, 33.7 percent; in debates, 27.4 percent; with the *Democratic* label, 29.9 percent; with the *Republican* label, 24.6 percent; and for the *independent* label, 36.4 percent.

40. The percentages for lowest level of "part of the problem" statements were even lower in speeches during Era II in news (10.4 percent) and with the party label during Era II (15.4 percent). Note: The lowest level of "part of a problem" statements appeared in Era IV (7.7 percent) and was influenced by George W. Bush's optimistic campaign strategies.

41. Jimmy Carter, "Acceptance Speech," Democratic National Convention, New York City (14 August 1980), Annenberg/Pew Archive of Presidential Discourse, CD-ROM (Philadelphia: Annenberg School for Communication, University of Pennsylvania, 2000).

42. "Carter Basks in Democrat Glow Here," *Chicago Tribune*, 10 September 1976, 1A.

43. "Humphrey, 'Speaking for Self,' Says Troop Pullout Is Possible," *Los Angeles Times*, 23 September 1968, 20A.

44. "Nixon Advocates Regional Summits to Combat Soviet," *New York Times*, 15 October 1960, 1A.

45. "Bush: No Regrets on Campaign's Tone; Tactics against Opponent Aren't Personal," *Washington Post*, 1 November 1988, 1A.

46. "Perot Reconsiders Withdrawal from Presidential Race," *Washington Post*, 23 September 1992, 12A.

47. John Aldrich, *Why Parties? The Origin and Transformation of Party Politics in America* (Chicago: University of Chicago Press, 1995), 272.

48. Alan Ehrenhalt, *The United States of Ambition: Politicians, Power, and the Pursuit of Office* (New York: Times Books, 1992), 40.

49. Ehrenhalt, *United States of Ambition*, 272–73.

50. Ehrenhalt, *United States of Ambition*, 27

51. Ehrenhalt, *United States of Ambition*, 28.

52. For a discussion of the declining respect for norms of reciprocity and seniority in the House, see Uslaner, *Decline in Comity*.

53. Neil Collins and Paul Butler, "Positioning Political Parties: A Market Analysis," *Journal of Press and Politics* 1, no. 2 (1996): 63–77, 69.

54. Collins and Butler, "Positioning Political Parties," 69.

55. Collins and Butler, "Positioning Political Parties," 74.

56. Collins and Butler, "Positioning Political Parties," 69–70.

57. Walter D. Burnham, "The Changing Shape of the American Political Universe," *American Political Science Review* 59, no. 1 (1965): 7–28.

58. "Group of Viewers Shifts Opinions after TV Debate," *Washington Post*, 9 October 1984, 1A.

59. "Candidates Word Wrestle to a Draw," *Christian Science Monitor*, 27 September 1988, 3A.

60. "California Still Tuning Out Dole; Message Falters in Vote Rich State," *Chicago Tribune*, 29 September 1996, 3A.

61. Albert Cantril and Susan. D. Cantril, *Reading Mixed Signals: Ambivalence in American Public Opinion about Government* (Baltimore, Md.: Johns Hopkins University Press, 1999).

62. David Broder, "Voters of Two Minds," *Washington Post*, 26 September 1999, 7B.

63. "Style Counts, Strategists Say," *Washington Post*, 1 November 2000, 16A.

64. Theodore Lowi, "The Party Crasher," *New York Times Magazine*, 23 August 1992, 28–33.

65. Gerald Pomper, *Passions and Interests: Political Party Concepts of American Democracy* (Lawrence: University of Kansas Press, 1992), 84.

66. With the division surrounding the election of 2000, in which the candidate who won the popular vote did not win the presidency; Bush's first year in office, in which heavy-handed leadership led Republican senator Jim Jeffords to leave the Republican Party, a move that gave the Democratic party control of the U.S. Senate; Bush's third and fourth years in office, in which Bush gained support from

Congress to go to war in Afghanistan and Iraq but lost bipartisan support; and a metaphor of divisiveness in campaign 2004, with journalists discussing "blue," or Democratic, states and "red," or Republican, states, it is uncertain if the confidence surrounding Bush's united bipartisan tone is but a memory for the American body politic.

67. Burnham, *Critical Elections,* 188–89.

5

THE CONFLICTED PARTY

Suppose a legislator, a presidential candidate, a journalist, and a textbook author were to glance at the same painting of the United States Capitol. These four "elites" would undoubtedly walk away from the experience with different interpretations. The legislator might regard the Capitol with ambivalence, recalling moments of unity and victory as well as conflict and compromise. The candidate would look at the Capitol carefully, knowing that he or she must deal delicately with this institution if his or her presidency is to have any hope of success. The journalist might look at the Capitol with different needs, wondering, "How can I break down this group of 535 officials to fit in my column?" And the academic might reflect on how the institution was so important to the founders that it appeared in Article I of the Constitution, as well as how it has given the people a voice in governance and kept the presidency honest for the past two centuries.

In other words, as representatives of their respective groups, do these four individuals see the same thing when looking at the U.S. Capitol? Of course not. Their needs and experiences filter their perceptions of the institution and encourage each observer to notice, appreciate, challenge, and question its several aspects. Naturally, these same biases affect how these groups view political parties. Some elites (legislators speaking in a heated debate) require more of partisanship than do others (authors writing civics textbooks), and these needs encourage these actors to use party labels differently.

This chapter describes how these elites talk about partisanship and how their interpretations range from a highly contested picture of party in congressional debates to a personalized understanding in the news, to a careful depiction in political speeches, to a kind of civics celebration in textbooks.

The data show that elites who are dependent on parties discuss them more critically than do those whose careers are less affected by them. In essence, then, this chapter highlights the relationship between political needs and political depictions, how the former shapes the latter, and how both influence the symbolic capital of party labels.

CONGRESSIONAL MEANINGS

> The political party assumes an obvious, very public form—yet a very shadowy role—in American legislatures. The parties organize majority and minority power in the legislatures, and the legislative leaders and committee chairpersons are usually party oligarchs. Yet despite the appearance and panoply of party power, voting on crucial issues often crosses party lines and violates party pledges and platforms. The party in many forms dominates the American legislatures; yet the effect of party loyalty is often negligible. On this paradox turns much of the scholarly concern and reformist zeal expended on American legislatures.
>
> —Frank Sorauf and Paul Beck[1]

As political scientists Frank Sorauf and Paul Beck write, partisanship is both a dominant and a negligible force in Congress. Although parties organize opinion in the legislature, they cannot guarantee that all members will vote one way or another. This tension, Sorauf and Beck say, guides scholarly understandings of political partisanship. This tension, my data also show, guides how legislators use partisan labels. After closely reading the texts from congressional debates, it appears that legislators use party labels for two purposes: to sharpen partisanship and to mobilize teamwork. Interestingly, both activities require legislators to treat labels rather roughly; indeed, this genre features the most contested meaning of party found in this project.

First, take the variable *role*. Legislators are more likely than other elites to regard party labels as being "part of the problem" (debates = 28.7 percent, speeches = 23.4 percent, news 13.8 percent, books = 10.8 percent). As Sorauf and Beck contend, a key tension in Congress is maintaining loyalty within the party. Theorists from Plato to Kenneth Burke to Newt Gingrich have recognized that an effective way to build solidarity is to create an enemy or an opposite, to build in-group identity through the construction of an out-group. The relatively high number of "part of the problem" statements in congressional debates, then, may be a result of members' seeking a kind of "negative identity."

The severity of the "problem" in these "part of the problem" statements varies considerably, and it depends on the time of the debate and the rhetorical situation. As stated elsewhere, President Eisenhower's Civil Rights Act of 1957 inspired as many tensions within the parties as between them (with Southern Democrats and Republicans opposing the legislation and Northern Democrats and Republicans supporting it). Perhaps because of the social complications of this bill or perhaps because of the norms of an earlier era, there is a sense of gentility in constituting party labels as being part of the problem in those debates, as is the case in the following statement, in which a legislator in the 1957 debate suggests that "both *parties*, in an effort to obtain the votes of these great minority blocks . . . are interested in politics to the point that we would weaken the heritage we have from English jurisprudence which has made this country great."[2] A lofty reference, this was, particularly in its choice of a target ("both parties"), use of the collective ("we"), and reference to the humbling force of history ("English jurisprudence which made this country great").

Other "part of the problem" constructions are not equally restrained. In 1964, another legislator spoke under this rubric but in a more pointed tone than the one in the aforementioned quote, suggesting that "a coalition of *liberals*—*Democrats* and *Republicans*—have the votes and they have refused to accept any amendments which would have improved the legislation. I frankly do not think you could have amended the bill—because even the Ten Commandments would not have been acceptable under these circumstances."[3] In this instance, the *I* statement and the religious reference sharpened the attack. And by 1995, the accusations became more prickly still, with legislators addressing their peers with statements such as the following: "The *Republican* bill is tougher on children than it is on the deadbeat dads who leave them behind. . . . Instead of attacking deadbeats, the *Republican* bill attacks children";[4] and "The *Republican* majority [needs to] stop the war on kids."[5] Of course, there are many ways that these legislators could have used language to oppose one another; what is intriguing is that in these cases, party labels are used and cast as being (increasingly) problematic.

A similar trend appears in the variable *context*. Legislators are more likely than other elites to place party labels in a negative context (debates = 30.7 percent, news = 25.5 percent, speeches = 20.5 percent, books = 17.4 percent). In studying these texts, I noticed that legislators often frame the *party* label and/or the label of their opponent in problematic ways, connecting each to missed opportunities, poor legislation, and dangerous ideas.

Once again, legislators disparage the idea of the collective as well as the out-party in order to increase in-group solidarity.

The trends of placing party labels in a compromised position has increased over time in congressional debates: specifically 22.0 percent of the labels were placed in a negative context in 1957, compared to 26.9 percent in 1964 and 40.7 percent in 1995 (variable: *context*). Specific textual examples illustrate the contestation in debates and echo the shift in tone observed in the previous discussion of the *role* variable. Notice, for instance, the number of words Representative W. Arthur Winsted (D-MS) uses in the 1957 debate before expressing any sort of partisan disgust:

> At the last session of the Congress, when I rose in opposition to the so-called civil rights bill then under consideration, I said that never during my 14 years in the House had I seen a more vindictive, a more unnecessary, a more politically inspired, or a more unconstitutional bill reach this floor for action. I thought it highly improbably that a bill more repugnant to my political philosophy would ever be considered by the House of Representatives. However, members of both *political parties* who are so intent on currying the favor of the Negro and left-wing voters have succeeded in bringing to this floor H.R. 6127, a bill which is even more reprehensible.[6]

Clearly, Representative Winstead is unhappy here; but he places his anger in context, offering a personal narrative before advancing his frustration. Only after taking pains to flatter the institution of Congress itself does he express his disappointment with members of both parties. This rhetorical patience is prevalent in the 1957 and 1964 debates. Even though speakers place labels in negative contexts, they sound somewhat judicious when doing so.

Almost forty years later, Representative John Lewis (D-GA) preferred a more expedient approach. Speaking during the 1995 welfare reform debate, he said, "The American people want firmness. They do not want harshness. And you come across as very harsh, harshly *partisan*, and also harsh on people and soft on work." Then the gloves came off. He continued,

> Mr. Chairman, this *Republican* proposal certainly isn't the Holocaust. But I am concerned, and I must speak up. I urge my colleagues, open your eyes. Read the proposal. Read the small print. Read the *Republican* contract.[7]

Lewis's statement provoked the following response from Representative E. Clay Shaw Jr. (R-FL):

Mr. Chairman, I would like to say to the gentleman on the floor, the gentleman from Georgia. There is no one in this House that I have had more respect for than you. But for you to come on this floor and compare the *Republicans* to the reign of the Nazis is an absolute outrage, and I'm surprised that anybody with your distinguished background would dare to do such a horrible thing.[8]

Because it is so excessive, it is tempting to disregard Representative Lewis's statement as silliness (if not in incredibly bad taste), but doing so would ignore the seriousness of his charge: that the Republican legislation in question was horrific. Shaw noted the gravity of the statement and responded accordingly, further attesting to the hyperbolic tone of the debate in 1995. As evidenced by these statements, the changing climate of the U.S. House has produced a hardened discussion of party labels.

Scholars have attributed this "decline of comity in Congress" to many factors. A popular one has been voiced by political scientist Carll Ladd when he writes that "Congressional Democrats today are much more coherently a liberal party and congressional Republicans more a conservative party than ever before."[9] Indeed, the 104th Congress, elected in 1994 and serving until 1996, was one of the most ideologically polarized Congresses in recent memory and was largely responsible for the 1995 federal government shutdown (a manifestation of the considerable conflict between Speaker Newt Gingrich's Republican House of Representatives and Democratic president Bill Clinton's White House). Perhaps as a result of the shutdown, or simply because of its low public opinion ratings among the citizenry, communication scholar Kathleen Hall Jamieson was commissioned to conduct research on the decline of comity in the 104th Congress.[10]

In her study, Jamieson examined the language found in the *Congressional Record*, conducted interviews with reporters who had covered Congress for a decade or longer, researched press accounts, and incorporated the assessments of members who had served multiple terms. After tracking the language (and the memories of the language) that "disrupted" debate (e.g., demands to take down words, rulings on words, calls for the House to be in order, and calls for a member to suspend), she mapped the tone in Congress over time. In doing so, she found (1) that ten of eleven reporters interviewed had perceived that the level of incivility in Congress was higher than that seen in the past ten years; (2) that actual incivility between the years 1935 and 1995 was higher in the 1935–1951 period than in the 1980–1996 period (while the interim period was relatively quiet); and (3) that although there was less "vulgarity" during the 104th Congress than in earlier moments, this congress was less civil than its recent predecessors were on four measures ("words taken down," "words taken down that go to rulings," "calls for the House to be in order," and "calls for the House to suspend"). The second session of this congress, however, was much more civil than the first; interestingly, during that year both the level of comity as well as legislative productivity increased.

Another factor responsible for the decline of comity in Congress is the rise of the "ambitious" member interested in building power and visibility outside the institution in order to have power within it. In the 1990s, this meant "going public" to attract news coverage. In his analysis of how the media has changed Congress as an institution, Timothy Cook reveals that as recently as forty years ago, members of Congress tried to avoid the media.[11] For instance, Speaker of the House Sam Rayburn preferred to conduct his business inside the institution, without the interference of outside help. Today, the thought of a legislator shirking the media is almost inconceivable. Because legislators have developed such an appetite for media coverage, Cook suggests that their roles have changed from "workhorses" to "showhorses." Although Cook does not attend to the use of party labels in debates, his primary finding can be applied to this analysis: in attempting to garner media coverage—even negative media coverage—many legislators have changed their behavior. Rather than adhere to the old norms of courtesy and reciprocity, many members now adopt a more aggressive public style.

Political scholar Eric Uslaner's analysis provides a nice description of how this metamorphosis has occurred. Noting that Congress was civil not too long ago, he quotes Representative Clem Miller (D-CA), who observed, "One's overwhelming first impression as a member of Congress is the aura of friendliness that surrounds the life of a congressman. . . . The freshman congressman is being constantly made aware of the necessity, even the imperative, of getting along with his fellow congressman."[12] Then, after citing research that party systems tend to be cyclical, Uslaner offers the following statement by Senator Joseph Biden (D-DE):

> There's much less civility than when I came here ten years ago. There aren't as many nice people as there were before. . . . Ten years ago you didn't have people calling each other sons of bitches and vowing to get each other. The first few years, there was only one person who, when he gave me his word, I had to go back down to the office and write it down. Now there's two dozen of them. As you break down the social

amenities one by one, it starts expanding geometrically. Ultimately you don't have any social control. . . . We end up with 100 Proxmires here. One . . . makes a real contribution. All you need is 30 of them to guarantee that the place doesn't work.[13]

Legislators also sharpen partisanship through the use of specific labels, as previewed in chapter 4. Over the past fifty years, there has been a decrease in the use of the word *party* in congressional debates: this label constitutes 41.5 percent of all labels in 1957 but only 21.8 percent in 1964 and 11.6 percent in 1995. Rather than discuss parties as being groups, legislators have become more particularistic with their word choices, preferring the construction "Republicans voted" as opposed to "members of the Republican party vote." This shift may seem subtle, but if one attends to how this substitution alters a sentence, it is clear that the former construction highlights the label's personal agency, ascribing greater responsibility to individuals. The latter construction, in contrast, requires that individuals share agency as members of the Republican group.

In several ways, these data show that legislators use party labels to sharpen partisanship and mobilize teamwork. Specifically, legislators portray party labels as being "part of the problem," place them in a negative context, and increasingly prefer specific party labels (*Democratic* and *Republican*) to the collective term *party*. Most scholars admit that parties in Congress resemble loose coalitions (Frank Sorauf has even referred to them as "exhibiting little more cohesiveness than a 'pick-up team' of playground basketball players").[14] This may be true politically. Rhetorically, however, this study suggests that legislators adhere to a divisive rhetoric that searches for and highlights the differences between the parties (and partisans) in hopes of mobilizing action. To return to the language of chapter 4, when the 435 members of the House are portrayed as belonging to two teams (as they are in Era I), the debate sounds formal, patient, orderly, and polite; forty years later, however, when there seems to be 435 teams in the House, the debate sounds frenetic and negative. Over one hundred years ago, Alexis de Tocqueville noted that the "knowledge of how to combine is the mother of all other forms of knowledge in democratic systems. . . . On its progress depends that of all others. If men are to remain civilized the art of association must develop and improve among them."[15] If the level of comity continues to decrease in Congress, it will be interesting to see if members can find means of association or if—in a more fragmented environment—all party cues will become divisive. Time, of course, will tell this tale and others.

JOURNALISTIC MEANINGS

If legislators heighten partisanship, then what do journalists do? Research on the news coverage of parties provides two expectations. One group of prominent political scientists postulates that coverage of parties, like that of most political institutions, is unflattering. They make their case in varying ways, arguing that media coverage of parties is overwhelmingly negative;[16] maintaining that "reporters have a decidedly low opinion of politics and politicians, and it slants their coverage of Republicans and Democrats alike";[17] and even claiming that when media outlets organize campaigns, journalists "do not have time for parties."[18] On this last point, Martin Wattenberg's content analysis of party labels and candidate names in news coverage from 1952 to 1980 suggests that news has become "candidate-centric" to the expense of party coverage:

> Although the total number of campaign-related stories declined in this period, the actual number of mentions of presidential candidates per year stayed relatively stable. In contrast, the number of instances in which parties were mentioned by name in the stories fell precipitously. More theoretically important than the raw count of mentions, however, is the ratio between coverage of candidates versus that of parties, as this focuses attention squarely on the question of the *relative* degree to which the reading audience was exposed to candidates versus parties. Throughout the whole 1952–1980 period, mentions of candidates outnumbered those of parties, but . . . the ratio increased from about two to one in the 1950s to roughly five to one by 1980. In short, it is clear that subscribers to these newspapers and magazines have over the years been increasingly exposed to a candidate-centered view of presidential campaigns.[19]

While these political scholars voice concerns with how parties have been covered in the news, other observers raise a challenging question: Is dubious coverage better than none at all? Some suggest that it is, indicating that all coverage—despite its tone—matters. For example, journalist Joann Byrd believes that coverage can be equated with power and that the failure of journalists to cover candidates (often of minor parties) violates the press's duty to defend free speech, independent thinking, and the democratic process.[20] Diane Francis reports that after a television station (CFCF) stopped granting the Quality Party (a third party in Canada) media coverage, the party dropped from 6 percent to 1 percent in public opinion polls.[21] And in Australia, Ian Ward found that "media intrusion" has the potential to increase the strength of already frail parties.[22] Naturally, comparative findings cannot easily be generalized to the United States, but they do raise a compelling question: What happens when party labels are covered in the news?

The data here show two things. The findings of this content analysis provide support for the argument that coverage of party labels is largely negative; at the same time, however, they point to a set of journalistic conventions that continue to keep party labels in circulation, a finding of some consequence for political parties. Because party labels are efficient and accessible cues that contribute to the drama of a news story, they continue to appear in newspaper coverage of campaigns and have actually appeared more frequently in the years following Wattenberg's research (intriguingly as the trend of "candidates running away from parties" became a story in its own right). The following examples describe how and why this is the case.

To begin, figure 5.1 provides an update to Wattenberg's content analysis of party mentions in news from 1952 to 1980. The "precipitous" decrease in party mentions spotted by Wattenberg is most severe in the last year of his study; however, if we take a broader look at the use of party labels in news over the years, we see that the decrease has not been linear for this project, as illustrated in figure 5.1—indeed, a gradual increase in label use appears in the 1980s through 2000 (save a decline in the 1992 campaign). At this moment, it seems premature (or dated) to argue that newspapers do not have the time or interest to cover political parties. The small spike in 1996–2000 hints at the opposite. It is too early to tell what this modest increase from 1996 to 2000 means for the future, but at first glance the trend counters the received wisdom that labels are increasingly disappearing from the news.

Figure 5.2 displays a second set of findings that update Wattenberg's content analysis: an examination of the appearances of party labels and candidate names in the news (1952–1980).[23] Similar to his findings, these data show that newspapers have increased their mentions of candidate names over the years. And once again, this figure also reveals two other trends emerging after Wattenberg's analysis: a leveling off in the increase of candidate mentions (occurring alongside an increase in the use of party labels between the 1992 and 2000 elections). While these quantitative trends do not contradict Wattenberg's analysis, they, too, raise new questions, including the following: Do these trends challenge the now-popular myth of candidate-centered campaigns? Why have journalists returned to employ party labels with greater frequency in recent years (with 1992 as an exception)? Will party labels become more salient for American citizens than they were in the 1980s (as the agenda-setting hypothesis might suggest)?

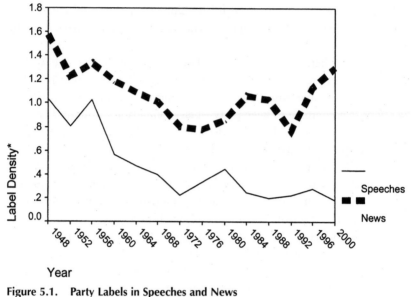

Figure 5.1.   Party Labels in Speeches and News
*Label density = labels / all words in genre × 100

Lance Bennett has argued that the news tends to be dramatized when journalists become preoccupied with finding new and exciting ways to report the events of the day. These data show that journalists may find some excitement in party labels. Note what is discovered, for example, when the variable *context* is used to measure how the journalist's attribution of the social scene affects the party. Of all coded statements, 56.8 percent feature attributions regarding the conditions facing the party (positive, negative, or mixed). Another variable, *quality*, traces the aspects of parties (action, emotion, unity, or clarity) stressed by the journalist. Almost 61.3 percent of the statements in this study feature one of these attributions. And the variable *potency* assesses the journalist's calculation of the force exerted by or upon the party. In over 81.9 percent of these statements, political labels are clearly depicted as causing or responding to action. Taken together, then, these data show that party labels are placed in dramatic situations (*context*), adorned with specific characteristics (*quality*), and given clear attributions of action (*potency*) in the news.[24] These trends suggest that the journalists' view of parties is one of movement and vitality. That is, in routine—and perhaps subconscious—ways, when journalists have chosen to employ party labels over the past half century, they have used them to bring action to their columns.

Another pattern associated with dramatization can be found in the use of the terms *Democrat* and *Republican* in news coverage. After running the fre-

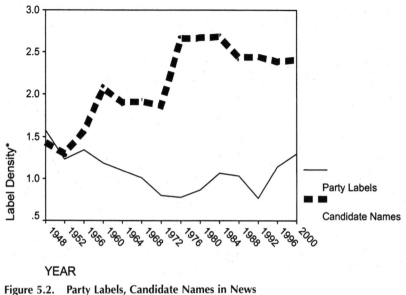

Figure 5.2.   Party Labels, Candidate Names in News
*Label density = labels / all words in genre × 100

quencies of labels by year (for all terms in the Campaign Mapping Project), I saw a surprising trend emerge: in nine of the fourteen elections between 1948 and 2000, journalists have used the label of the losing party more often than that of the winning party (see table 5.1). Specifically, *Republican* was featured more frequently in the news for the years 1948, 1964, and 1996, and *Democrat* was featured more frequently in the years 1956, 1968, 1972, 1984, 1988, and 2000. Moreover, four of the five remaining cases were open-seat contests (1952, 1960, 1976, 1992), with no elected incumbent (the only exception to this trend is the high use of *Republican* in 1980). The causality of this relationship, naturally, is uncertain; it might be the case that losing candidates attract news coverage because of their failing campaigns, or it could be that such overconsideration in the news contributes to their losing efforts. In either case, it appears that, relative to that of the opponent, more news is not necessarily good news for Democratic and Republican nominees.

This pattern does not appear to hold for the *independent* label. Findings from my content analysis show that the terms *Democrat* and *Republican* receive more negative editorial judgments than the term *independent* (variable: *context*). Specifically, 67.1 percent of the *Democratic* labels are placed in a valenced context (23.6 percent of the time positive, 26.4 percent negative, 17.1 percent balanced), as are 60.0 percent of the *Republican* labels (18.6 percent positive, 30.0 percent negative, 11.4 percent balanced).

Table 5.1.   *Democratic* and *Republican* Labels in News

Year	Democrat Density[a]	Republican Density[a]	Winning Party	Received More News
1948	.489	.572	D	R
1952	.492	.522	R	R
1956	.591	.456	R	D
1960	.530	.405 *	D	D
1964	.378	.443	D	R
1968	.376	.280	R	D
1972	.414	.196	R	D
1976	.365	.211	D	D
1980	.251	.281	R	R
1984	.586	.242	R	D
1988	.461	.309	R	D
1992	.332	.251	D	D
1996	.310	.458	D	R
2000	.411	.320	R	D

[a]Density = appearance of label / total word in news coverage × 100

In contrast, the *independent* label is placed in a valenced context just 36.5 percent of the time (18.6 percent positive, 9.3 percent negative, and 8.6 percent balanced). Here, even though the *independent* label is not placed in a positive environment more frequently than the other labels, it is only placed in a negative context one-third as often as the other words. As detailed in chapter 1, many of the early articles in this study constitute the *independent* label as being a mere demographic—a pattern that contributes to a thin description of the label in the 1950s and 1960s. Over time, however, as independent voters began to form the valuable swing vote, the *independent* label began to receive more positive attention in news columns. Perhaps because *the uncertain* independent voters bring mystery to campaigns, particularly in an era of horse-race coverage, they have been treated more generously and with greater fascination than the *more predictable* (and empowered) Democratic or Republican voters.

Another common bias in news discussed by Bennett is the tendency to personalize topics, to concentrate on the "people engaged in political combat" rather than focus on specific issues or notions of power and process."[25] The most obvious marker of this news bias in this project can be found in the variable *associations*, which measures the social entities with which a label must share space (i.e., a party, voters, media, or interest groups). In 31.9 percent of the cases, journalists place a "named partisan" next to a party label, a pattern that is more common in newspapers than in other forms of discourse (see figure 5.3). Consequently, citizens who had

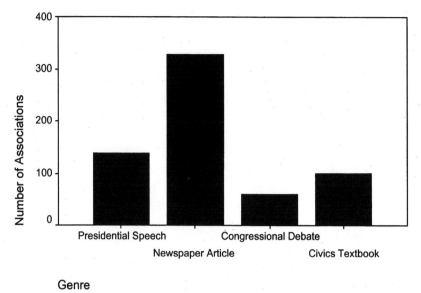

Genre

Figure 5.3. "Named Partisans," by Genre

learned their politics from the news, particularly in the latter years of this study, may have been increasingly primed to think of parties as being "tribal" groups worshipping particular gods, rather than coalitions of like interests working together to get candidates elected and legislation passed.

While focusing on individual partisans, journalists also have commented heavily on the strategies of individual campaigns. One result of this punditry—at least in the 1980s and 1990s—is an emphasis on the "partisan" aspects of campaigns, focusing on such concerns as, Were Democrats campaigning like Democrats, and Republicans as Republicans? Thomas Patterson has observed that journalists now feature the "story behind the story of politics" and unravel that hidden story for news consumers. Notice how the following story, "Clinton Grabs for a Safe Place," provides support for Patterson's contention, especially in unmasking how Bill Clinton is "not acting like a Democrat" in this campaign:

> The last two days, Clinton never mentioned the names Dole or House Speaker Newt Gingrich or, for that matter, the word "Republican"; not until his last stop Friday night, in the Democratic stronghold of Macon, GA., did he use the word "Democrat." Even in a Friday get out the vote conference call with black leaders from 198 cities, he remained resolutely mild, displaying ire only against complacency. "Don't be fooled by the polls," Clinton said. "This turnout question is not an academic

question." Nothing seemed to dent Clinton's determination to present himself as a leader beyond labels, beyond ideology and virtually beyond party.[26]

This excerpt, particularly in its use of data, would be as at home in a scholar's thesis as it is in a news column. Rather than simply trace the steps of Bill Clinton (the candidate visiting Macon, Georgia), this journalist blends a strategic analysis with speculation about the *Democratic* label. In so doing, the journalist carries an entire news story by using the fact that a Democrat omitted the word *Democrat*. Intriguingly, this type of news frame—that of the candidate's running away from the party—may help to interpret two of the patterns in figures 5.1 and 5.2: a trend that journalists are employing more labels even when candidates are reducing their use of them and a trend that candidate names have leveled off in the news (while, again, party labels are experiencing a moderate resurgence). It is possible, too, that this news frame feeds into the relationship seen in figure 5.3; that is, when candidates run against their "party stereotypes," they may call attention to themselves, encourage speculation, and garner news stories like this one, describing Clinton's "determination" to be a leader "beyond party."

Figure 5.4 displays another type of personalization. As with all genres, journalism has come to rely more heavily on the terms *Democrat* and *Re-*

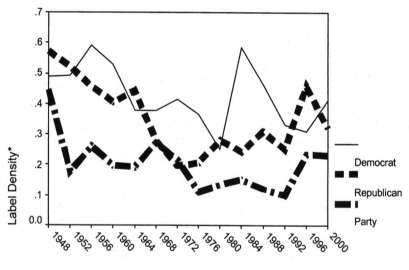

Figure 5.4.   Labels Over Time in News
*Label density = labels / all words in genre × 100

publican than *party* and has done so consistently during the past fifty years. While there could be several explanations for this trend, a basic one might be efficiency; as a rhetorical genre, news writing requires a parsimonious style, and *Democrat* and *Republican* offer more descriptions per unit word than does the *party* label. Over time, though, this practice of highlighting individual partisans becomes problematic when one considers the essence of parties, definitions of which include

- "a *team* of men seeking to control the governing apparatus by gaining office in a duly constituted election";[27]
- "a *group* organized to gain control of government in the name of the group by winning election to public office";[28]
- "a *group* whose members propose to act in concert in the competitive struggle for political power";[29] and
- a "*relatively durable social formation* which seeks offices or power in government, exhibits a structure or organization which links leaders at the centers of government to a significant popular following in the political arena and its local enclaves and generates in-group perspectives or at least symbols of identification or loyalty."[30]

The collective spirit found in these scholarly definitions has been less common over the years in news stories. Instead, readers are confronted with a series of individual partisans and idiosyncratic personalities working with and against the parties. As discussed in chapter 4, a steady diet of such coverage could atomize the publics' understanding of parties and further reward America's individualistic leanings. That is, when readers are "primed" to consider the efficiency of the individual (a strong rhetorical trope and mythic tradition in the United States) rather than the deliberate nature of parties as groups, they are encouraged to accept the image of party as two sets of actors at battle rather than as parts of a system at work.[31]

In sum, party labels continue to be newsworthy and help to propel the campaign narrative, even at a time in which much news is dramatized and personalized. Data such as these complicate the charge that the media do not have time for party labels. Clearly, they do. Even though such labels do not appear as often as named candidates, they have been on the rise for the past twenty years (except during the 1992 election). Admittedly, these points do not counter the charge that party coverage is negative. They do, however, help us realize that focusing on issues of "good or bad" coverage only tells part of the journalists' story about political parties.

Communication scholars often argue that if a thing cannot be spoken, it cannot be imagined. From that perspective, the mere appearance of partisan labels in the news—regardless of their context—can be regarded as being consequential. Such appearances signify a clear interest in parties, however "warped" that intent may become in certain circumstances, and hence can serve as a clear reminder of parties' importance in campaigns. Naturally, for the parties themselves, good coverage is more desirable than bad coverage, but bad coverage seems to be better than none at all. On one hand, party labels are treated roughly in the news, but they also remain central to the political conversation and, hence, central to the political process. All of this suggests that the press may unwittingly inscribe a larger—albeit more subtle and nuanced—role for parties in presidential campaigns than has previously been acknowledged.

SUASORY MEANINGS

Presidential candidates are required to sell many ideas to the American public. Over the past two hundred years, for example, they have tried to get Americans to accept their plans for the future; their records of the past; their personalities, characters, families; and sometimes even their chronological ages. More recently, as campaigns have become increasingly intimate and the body politic more cynical, presidential candidates have also needed to peddle more provocative ideas, including that they have never inhaled, that they will not raise taxes, that they have only lusted in their hearts, that they have been faithful to their wives (despite difficulties in their marriages), and that they speak "good enough" English to be fit to govern. Because citizens hear such appeals so often, they have become mindful of the salesmanship involved in campaigns. But candidates do not just sell themselves to the voter, they also peddle a particular version of partisanship as well.

In 1996, Republican Dick Morris was asked by Democratic president Bill Clinton for help in his reelection bid. History shows that Morris's advice to Clinton was smarter than Morris's own personal conduct; indeed, in 1996, Clinton was reelected, and in that same year Morris was caught in an adulterous affair with a paramour (with whom—if the tabloid media are to believed—he shared state secrets). Morris's public transgressions, however, did not preclude him from writing two books on how future candidates could get elected;[32] in the latter of the two (humbly entitled *The New Prince*, in which Morris is billed as the "modern equivalent of confidante and consigliore to the head of state"), he writes,

If American politicians were truly pragmatic and did what was really in their own best self-interest, our political process would be a lot more clean, positive, nonpartisan, and issue-oriented. It is not practicality which drives the partisanship, negativity, and the never-ending cycle of investigation and recrimination in which we wallow, but a complete misapprehension of what Americans want and what politicians—in their own career self-interest—should offer. If Machiavelli were alive today, he would counsel idealism as the most pragmatic course.[33]

As a campaign consultant, Morris raised a question of interest to both practitioners and theorists: What is in the "best self-interest" of political candidates in the United States? Or, to contextualize the question, What is in the "best self-interest" of candidates in the two-party system? Is it easier to get elected if one distinguishes oneself as a Democrat or a Republican? Or, is it wiser to hide party cues and to run as a centrist candidate? While Morris advised Clinton to do the latter, political theorists contend that there are advantages to both approaches.

First, rational choice scholar Anthony Downs has suggested that there are few incentives in a two-party system for parties to differentiate themselves from one another. In his seminal book *An Economic Theory of Democracy*, Downs observes that to win the crucial middle-of-the-road voters, parties are compelled to "move closer together and become more moderate and less extreme in policy," which causes the distance between Democrats and Republicans to become very small when platforms are being formulated.[34] Specifically, Downs asserts,

1. "a two-party democracy cannot provide stable and effective government unless there is a large measure of ideological consensus among its citizens";
2. "parties in a two-party system deliberately change their platforms so that they resemble one another; whereas parties in a multi-party system try to remain as ideologically distinct from each other as possible"; and
3. "in a two-party system, it is rational for each party to encourage voters to be irrational by making its platform vague and ambiguous."[35]

While these tensions appear in a two-party system, Downs is careful to note that parties in a multiparty system do not feel these pressures; where a voting population is multimodal (or multiparty), Downs predicts that parties will strive to differentiate themselves. This perspective might suggest that there are benefits to elites, in campaigns at least, to downplay the distinctiveness of their party labels.

In contrast, political scholar John Petrocik has suggested that there are benefits to reminding citizens of party strengths and specialties in electoral politics. In his theory of "issue ownership," Petrocik contends that "policy issues originate in the attempt by groups to use government to alter the social and economic status of the group. . . . The policy agenda of a party reflects the demands of the groups which support that party, not the concerns of the party leadership or its candidates."[36] Petrocik uses George H. W. Bush's victory in 1988 to substantiate this theory, contending that Bush's victory resulted, at least in part, from his making conservative issues (i.e., defense, taxes, government spending) salient in the minds of voters. By doing so, Bush was able to capture both the Republican vote and support from traditionally Democratic groups (Southern white Democrats, union households, and Catholics) interested in who could better handle these conservative issues.[37] While Petrocik's theory has not been offered as an exact opposite of Downs—I doubt that Petrocik would advise parties to "own" extreme issues—Petrocik does offer the alternative view that candidates can succeed by differentiating themselves from the other party and by attempting to make their issues salient to voters. This take, then, might contend that reminding voters of party labels would help to prime the electorate to think about the issues that a candidate's party "owns."

Although Downs and Petrocik differ in their predictions, they do share one key assumption that was central to chapter 2: voters have the capacity to distinguish between the two major parties. As detailed there, research conducted by Richard Trilling, Arthur Sanders, Donald Baumer and Harold Gold, and Wendy Rahn and others have found that voters generally believe that the two major parties fit specific, identifiable profiles. While citizens can identify these stereotypes, a curious question presents itself: Do the elites in this study recognize such stereotypical differences when speaking of Democrats and Republicans? Do they, as Dick Morris and Anthony Downs might advise, deliberately imply that the parties have few differences when they use party labels? Or do they, as the Petrocik might expect, emphasize strategic differences between the parties in their label usage?

The current data show that candidates appear to follow both sets of advice: they seem to understand that campaigns are candidate centered, but they also *know better* than to disparage the party system completely. Pulled in these seemingly contradictory directions, candidates adopt a pragmatic strategy: they are very careful with party labels, and when they choose to discuss them, they portray parties as being both useful and systemically desirable.

One way in which speakers treat parties carefully is when they compliment partisanship. This is largely a qualitative distinction in the data, one that may be tied to social psychological research on persuasion, emotions, and attraction. Scholars of social influence know, for example, that when an individual compliments his or her audience, these compliments can increase liking (which leads to persuasion) or distract an audience from the issues (which can also lead to persuasion).[38] Candidates may link parties and emotions intuitively (i.e., they may sense that these appeals are native to campaign oratory) or strategically (i.e., they may sense that emotional appeals are easier to sell than fact-based appeals), or it may be some combination. Whatever the cause, social psychological researchers note that speakers have a much easier time proffering ideas when the mood of an audience has been properly conditioned.[39] Perhaps because candidates are the only elites in this study to present their constructions of party directly to an audience, they work especially hard to flatter partisans, uttering statements like one that Ronald Reagan made in 1980 in Waterbury, Connecticut, "I remember campaigning here when I was running for the *Republican* nomination in the winter of 1980. It was awfully cold then, but your warmth made up for it";[40] or one that Walter Mondale made in 1984 in Merrill, Wisconsin, "To the Speaker and all the good *Democrats* down here let's give them a big hand. . . . This rain makes us grow; it produces *Democrats*. And whether it's hail, or rain, or snow, or clouds, it's all the same: the *Democrats* are going to win in 1984."[41]

Not all candidates were so fluid when complimenting their audiences, but many candidates tried to do so. Indeed, candidates were most likely to place party labels in a positive context (29.9 percent) when compared to textbooks (23.4 percent), debates (22.5 percent), and the news (17.4 percent). This pattern offers an interesting variation on the conventional wisdom that campaigns are becoming more negative or that candidates benefit by distancing themselves from their parties. In speeches at least, candidates appear to believe that they have more to gain by treating parties gingerly than by attacking them.

When noting how gingerly the candidates discuss party, I became curious as to whether or not there was a relationship between label use and candidate victory. To investigate this question, I created a "partisanizer" measure, which simply counts *all* labels that each candidate used and then divides that sum by the total number of words spoken by the candidate. The results of this measure appear in table 5.2. As we see, of the four candidates who used an exceptionally high number of party labels, three lost; of the five candidates who used very few labels, two benefited while three did not. In

Table 5.2.   Partisanizers and Nonpartisanizers: Label Use and Campaign Outcome

	Label use[a]	Outcome
Partisanizer		
Harry Truman (1948)	1.73	Won
Robert Dole (1996)	1.54	Lost
Aldai Stevenson (1952)	1.47	Lost
Aldai Stevenson (1956)	1.44	Lost
Nonpartisanizer		
George H. W. Bush (1988)	0.106	Won
Richard Nixon (1972)	0.123	Won
Al Gore (2000)	0.121	Lost
George H. W. Bush (1992)	0.151	Lost
Walter Mondale (1984)	0.156	Lost

[a]Label use = number of labels used / total number of labels in speeches × 100

analyzing the connection between "partisanizers" and losing, I then examined the largest discrepancies in label use between candidates per year and found that in three of four cases (Harry Truman again being the exception), the candidate who used more labels than his opponent lost the election. Naturally, it would be foolhardy to draw many causal inferences with such a modest analysis, but the relationship appears remarkable: candidates are clearly not rewarded for using more labels than their opponents. Does this mean that candidates begin to sound desperate if they rely too heavily on party labels? Does priming one's own party or excessively discussing the opponent's party turn off an electorate that is nervous about all matters ideological? Is it tempting for losing candidates to turn to party labels as a last-ditch effort to mobilize the base? Any or all of these possibilities may help to inform this pattern.

Parties may have lost control over the presidential-selection process, but that result cannot necessarily be laid at the door of candidate rhetoric. While candidate behavior may not flatter the parties, this analysis of twenty-eight campaigners over fourteen campaigns shows that, in general, the candidates have been careful in their depictions of parties. Thus, an expectation that candidates wage candidate-centered campaigns at the symbolic expense of the parties is not supported here. Even though they do not amplify labels as does the press, when candidates do speak about parties, they attempt to make those attachments palatable to the American public. That they do not always succeed in their quest goes without saying. Their attempts to do so, however, are notable.

PEDAGOGICAL MEANINGS

In 1996, political scientists John Hibbing and Elizabeth Theiss Morse ad-
ministered a beginning-of-the-semester survey to their Introduction to
American Government classes to assess the students' levels of political information. They found:

> Only 5% of the class knew that John Major was the Prime Minister of
> Great Britain; just 5% knew that William Rehnquist was Chief Justice of
> the Supreme Court; 10% could correctly identify the Speaker of the
> House of Representatives; 10% knew the correct length of a term for
> U.S. Senators and for U.S. Representatives; 24% knew there were nine
> justices on the Supreme Court; and 13% of the class did not know that
> Al Gore was vice-president of the United States. Skills in tracking down
> information, critical thinking and expression, alas, were not much better
> than students' knowledge base.[42]

In describing the results to this quiz, Hibbing and Theiss Morse were
disturbed by two findings: the low levels of knowledge displayed by their
students, and the lack of attention that educators allocated to these defi-
ciencies in civic knowledge. In the years since this article was published,
universities, foundations, and media outlets have attended to these issues but
admit that they have not yet been resolved. The general consensus seems to
be that the civics curriculum is not making the grade in the United States.

This assertion is advanced in at least two ways. Some suggest that American citizens are in the midst of a civics deficit simply because educators have
not put the energy into teaching civics correctly. *Washington Post* columnist
E. J. Dionne reports how Terry Pickeral of the Denver-based Education
Commission of the States believes that, even though more than a quarter of
the states now require civics education, "schools, in many ways, have lost their
civic souls" and are not making the effort to teach civics adequately.[43] A dis-
concerting problem, this, for a study conducted by the National Assessment
of Educational Progress released in November 1999 found that one-third of
high school seniors lacked a basic grasp of the principles of American government, and fully three-quarters were not proficient in civics.[44] To these results, Dionne comments, "Civic education feeds a more civically engaged culture. But a culture of civic disengagement gets the education it deserves."[45]

Others claim that current efforts in civic education are misguided, and
studies analyzing civics textbooks underscore this argument. For instance, in
1974, political scholar Thomas Cronin examined representations of U.S.

presidents in textbooks and found that textbooks painted an unrealistic picture of presidents, overemphasizing the capacities of the office and overstating the president's role in regard to policy change. In his conclusion, Cronin worried that these portrayals would lead to unrealistic expectations of presidential behavior.[46] Eight years later, Douglas Hoekstra conducted a follow-up study of the "textbook presidency" and found that textbooks continued to create unrealistic expectations of the presidency, particularly by stressing the many "roles" the chief executive is expected to play.[47] Hoekstra concluded that by depicting such an ambitious assortment of duties for the president to perform, the books were condemning all future presidents to "inescapable failure." J. M. Sanchez's studies of civics textbooks has similarly located a complicated appraisal of the men who have worked in the Oval Office, as 38.5 percent of all presidents received positive evaluations, and just 33 percent of the modern presidents received positive evaluations.[48] These findings trouble him, for "such a lack of objectivity is particularly damaging when it is manifest in introductory texts explicitly tailored for an unsophisticated audience. A distorted accounting of events may be dismissed or challenged by readers who are aware of contradictory interpretations, but, regrettably, most college students are not discriminating consumers of the information dispensed to them in political science textbooks."[49]

One of Cronin's conclusions seems particularly important in interpreting the meaning of these unrealistic expectations of presidents in textbooks. He argued that "we might promote both a more accurate political science and a more resilient civic culture if we make our values more explicit and entertain a more sophisticated recognition of the varying and shifting response to national institutions."[50] While textbooks must meet the needs of publishers and school boards, Cronin's call for honesty is appealing.

Knowing that textbooks tend to overestimate the office of the presidency, how do they portray political parties? Like the aforementioned studies, I found that the portrayals tend to be both positive and inflated. It has been written that civics textbooks are written with two goals: to instruct students and to train citizens.[51] As the following paragraphs attest, authors seem to be doing their part to preserve and protect the concept of party affiliation for American students, even if it sometimes means overstating the efficacy of parties.

To begin, parties are heavily constituted as campaign entities, as revealed in table 5.3. This construction is not unduly emphasized in textbooks—indeed, the percentages in news (72.0 percent) and speeches (50.8 percent) are higher. But this finding becomes more remarkable when we recall that the speeches and news articles were drawn directly from campaign

Table 5.3.   Party Labels by Genre by *Task* Variable (in percentages)

Task	Books	Speeches	News	Debates
Not applicable	11.4	13.4	5.2	10.5
Mobilization	18.2	4.4	9.9	5.1
Campaign	44.5	52.8	72.0	7.5
Governing	18.2	27.7	9.0	70.4
Mixed	7.8	1.8	3.8	6.4

Note: Percentages may not add to 100 owing to rounding to the nearest tenth.

periods, whereas textbooks were drawn randomly across the fifty-year sample. Also featured in this table is the finding that candidates are more likely to link parties to governance (26.9 percent) than textbooks are (18.2 percent). Here, authors are 2.4 times more likely to associate parties with campaigns than with mobilizing or governing activities. What type of message does this send to high school and college students?

Textual examples illustrate the types of parties that students encounter in their school books. Depending on the level of the text (high school or college) and varying a bit by authorial perspective, students read how parties organize political life and make democracy possible. Consider the following two statements from two of the textbooks:

- "*Political parties* take the large number of people who want to run for office and narrow the field down to one candidate."[52]
- "*Political parties* are the only organizations that select and offer candidates for public office. They do this through the nomination process."[53]

Clearly, these authors are constituting parties as being campaign entities and are praising them for providing that service to the country. Returning to the *role* variable, textbook authors are the second-most likely group to suggest that parties are "part of the solution" (37.8 percent, compared to speeches = 38.5 percent, debates = 31.1 percent, and news = 22.3 percent) and least likely to portray them as "part of the problem" (10.8 percent, compared to speeches = 23.4 percent, debates = 28.7 percent, and news = 13.8 percent). Notice also how parties are regarded as being part of the solution in the following statements in that they provide shortcuts for individuals and offer a check on government on behalf of the citizenry:

- "People choose the *party* with which they generally agree, so that they do not have to concern themselves with every issue that comes along."[54]

- "Most Americans believe that *party* competition contributes to the health of the democratic process. Certainly, we are more than just a bit suspicious of those nations that claim to be ruled by their people but do not tolerate the existence of opposing *parties*."[55]

The textbooks have also become even more positive over time, as those published in the 1990s are much more likely than their predecessors to praise the electoral role of parties. This finding is particularly interesting given the concern in the scholarly literature that parties are losing control over the candidate-selection process. The increased praise given to parties over time, then, could result from authors attempting to defend the party system (in light of the parties' decreased role in the candidate-selection process) or from authors attempting to defend the past and/or potential role of parties in the system. Either of these interpretations is possible.

In addition to featuring the campaign-based role of parties, textbook authors portray parties as being more active than the parties described by the other elites in this study. As mentioned, Cronin writes that such authors typically give students an unrealistic understanding of the presidency because the texts overestimate the chief executive's responsibilities and options to exercise power. In this study, textbooks are found to describe parties as being composed of elites interacting with other elites; these descriptions are far more active than those in any other genre, making the "strong party model" particularly apparent in the textbooks.

The authors' attempts to connect parties with activity emerge from several variables. First, the variable *behavior* measures whether parties are depicted as acting, feeling, or thinking entities. In textbooks, parties are described as an acting body 37.0 percent of the time, a thinking body 8.4 percent of the time, a feeling body 2.1 percent of the time, and unclear 52.5 percent of the time. The variable *quality*, on the other hand, assesses the *attributes* associated with parties. When parties are given an attribute, they are most likely to be described in the textbooks as being engaged in action (19.5 percent), unity (14.9 percent), ideological clarity (6.2 percent), and unclear (52.2 percent). Thus, impressionable students are invited to think of the parties as both potent (i.e., active) and distant (i.e., not interacting with citizens). Finally, the variable *position* measures whether parties are constituted at the elite or mass level. In textbooks, parties are constituted as elites 68.8 percent of the time, as masses 17.1 percent of the time, and in a global/undifferentiated sense 14.1 percent of the time (see table 5.4). Moreover, labels are portrayed as directly interacting with citizens just 7.6 percent of the time in books (variable: *associations*). Studies such as the National As-

Table 5.4.   Party Labels by Genre by *Position* Variable (in percentages)

	Books	Speeches	News	Debates
Elite	68.8	68.6	57.1	89.2
Mass	17.1	19.5	31.9	3.9
Global/ undifferentiated	14.1	11.9	11.0	7.0

Note: Percentages may not add to 100 owing to rounding to the nearest tenth.

sessment of Educational Progress often reveal that students possess low levels of knowledge of, and have little interest in, government. This opinion may, in part, stem from the depictions of parties shown here. Textbooks portray parties as being powerful and distanced from citizens, and students are taught—in a sense—that their lives will probably not be touched by the parties and, hence, that parties can be safely deferred to or ignored.

When we consider that textbooks also feature solution-based statements, this last finding may be seen as overstating party activity and success. Additionally, when students are primed to think of parties as being active, they may lose sight of, or fail to be taught to appreciate, the less-dynamic—but important—traits of bargaining, negotiating, and compromise. Textbooks, that is, may be encouraging students to think positively of frenetic campaigns or active but uncritical congresses. But even a moment's reflection shows that active campaigns are not necessarily better campaigns and that more legislation does not necessarily spell a healthier body politic. Indeed, government need not do something at every moment to govern well (a point that rarely appears in the textbooks).

If we consider the otherwise positive portrayals in textbooks and compare them to some of the other meanings advanced in this chapter, students may well become confused by the disconnect between what they read in their civics books and what they see on television or read in newspapers. For instance, in textbooks, students learn that parties "take the large number of people who want to run for office and narrow the field down to one candidate." Yet the personalization biases in news reports seem to imply that ambitious Democrats and Republicans may more obviously play this function.

While the facts appearing in civics textbooks are empirically true, they may not prepare students for the realities of political life. In thinking about how textbooks "could" present parties in order to better prepare students for their roles as citizens, some have called for a "desanitizing" of the civics curriculum. Among the ideas that they would like to see in curriculum are the notions that debate is not a bad word, that the ability to compromise is essential in democratic government, that the democratic process takes time, and that conflict is not the end of the world (indeed, it may be a democratic reality).[56] These suggestions, of course, would have to be negotiated to meet the demands of textbook publishers and educators. But it seems that they would have at least two benefits: offering a more realistic view of politics and providing a richer understanding of political parties. Both are fine ideas.

CONCLUSION

This chapter shows that the meanings of party labels shift somewhat depending on who is discussing them. Legislators need to pass legislation; accordingly, they use partisan labels to sharpen partisanship and mobilize teamwork. Journalists need to write compelling narratives, and so they rely on labels to efficiently advance personalized and dramatic stories. Candidates need to sell themselves to the public and thus constitute partisanship with great care, depicting it as a necessary and useful entity. And textbook authors are responsible for training the next generation of citizens. To meet this end, they celebrate and inflate the meanings of party. Here, it appears that the needs of elites affect their perceptions of parties as well as the ways in which they talk about them.

In a sense, the meanings of party labels are largely managed by elite voices in the United States, but we may well ask if one or another of these voices is becoming dominant. In 2004, at least, it appears that the meaning of partisanship featured in news coverage—largely conflictual—most closely resembles public sentiment toward the parties, thereby overshadowing the cautious or celebratory meanings found among the candidates or the textbooks. As political scholar Thomas Patterson has written, political scientists do not understand why citizens do not like parties. Perhaps the reason is that political scientists feed on a richer diet of party meanings (i.e., moments when they are strong in addition to moments when they are shallow) than do citizens. Accordingly, political scientists have an easier time resisting the media's shallow narratives of party. Most citizens, in contrast, understand the party system largely through the meanings they see in the news that they read or watch.

While it is tempting to blame the media for the public's disillusionment with parties, this chapter shows that this is too simplistic a charge. As figure 5.1 displays, journalists continue to use party labels and to use them more than presidential candidates do. Moreover, as the qualitative examples have illustrated, the media have made candidate-centered campaigns a news story, critiquing candidates who do not embrace partisanship or employ traditional party appeals. In these ways, journalists preserve party labels, a practice that lends itself to at least two interpretations. Pessimists might cite the media research on "priming" or the "second level" of agenda setting and suggest that the dramatized and personalized cues in the news encourage citizens to view the parties negatively.[57] To be sure, this has become a popular charge. On the other hand, optimists might point to traditional agenda-setting research and claim that as long as parties continue to appear in the news (as powerful decision-making elites), they will continue to be on the minds of American citizens—a better place to be than "off the agenda."[58] In either event, this chapter updates research conducted in the 1980s that contends with how the media do not have time for parties. For better or worse, as my data show, they still do and that, at least, seems to be a good thing.

NOTES

1. Frank Sorauf and Paul Allen Beck, *Party Politics in America*, 6th ed. (Glenview, Ill.: Scott Foresman, 1988), 396.

2. House of Representatives, Representative Jamie Whitten of Mississippi, 85th Cong., 1st sess., *Congressional Record* 103 (11 June 1957): 9954.

3. House of Representatives, Representative James Haley of Florida, 88th Cong., 2nd sess., *Congressional Record* 110 (10 February 1964): 2724.

4. House of Representatives, Representative Steny Hoyer, 104th Cong., 1st sess., *Congressional Record* 141 (21 March 1995): 3352–98.

5. House of Representatives, Representative Rosa DeLauro, 104th Cong., 1st sess., *Congressional Record* 141 (21 March 1995): 3352–98.

6. House of Representatives, Representative W. Arthur Winsted of Mississippi, 85th Cong., 1st sess., *Congressional Record* 103 (6 June 1957): 8502.

7. House of Representatives, Representative John Lewis of Georgia, 104th Cong., 1st sess., *Congressional Record* 141 (21 March 1995): 3352–98.

8. House of Representatives, Representative E. Clay Shaw Jr. of Florida, 104th Cong., 1st sess., *Congressional Record* 141 (21 March 1995): 3352–98.

9. Carl Everett Ladd, "Of Political Parties Great and Strong: A Dissent," *American Enterprise* 5, no. 4 (1994): 60–70, 70.

10. Kathleen Hall Jamieson and Erica Falk, "Civility in the House of Representatives: The 105th Congress," report 26 from the Annenberg Public Policy Center, http://appcpenn.org/appc/reports/rep26.pdf (March 1999).

11. Timothy E. Cook, *Making Laws and Making News: Media Strategies in the U.S. House of Representatives* (Washington, D.C.: Brookings, 1989).

12. Eric Uslaner, *The Decline of Comity in Congress* (Ann Arbor: University of Michigan Press, 1993), 4.

13. Alan Ehrenhalt, "In the Senate of the 1980s, Team Spirit Has Given Way to the Rule of Individuals," *Congressional Quarterly Weekly Report* (4 September 1982): 2175–82, cited in Uslaner, *Decline of Comity*, 24–25.

14. Sorauf and Beck, *Party Politics,* 391.

15. Alexis de Tocqueville, *Democracy in America*, ed. J. P. Mayer (1848; New York: Harper & Row, 1969), 517.

16. Michael Robinson and Margaret Sheehan, *Over the Wire and on TV: CBS and UPI in Campaign '80* (New York: Russell Sage Foundation, 1983).

17. Thomas E. Patterson, "Bad News, Period," *PS: Political Science and Politics* 29, no. 1 (1996): 17–21, 17.

18. Patterson, "Bad News."

19. Martin P. Wattenberg, *The Decline of American Political Parties, 1952–1996* (Cambridge, Mass.: Harvard University Press, 1998), 93.

20. Joan Byrd, "Giving People What They Deserve: Why Cover Minor Political Parties?" *Media Studies Journal* 12, no. 2 (1998): 26–30.

21. Diane Francis, "Muzzling the Minority Voice in Quebec," *Macleans* 109, no. 9 (1996): 13.

22. Ian Ward, "Media Intrusion and the Changing Nature of Political Parties in Australia and Canada," *Canadian Journal of Political Science* 26, no. 3 (1993): 478–508.

23. Wattenberg, *Decline*.

24. In greater detail, labels were 1.5 times more likely to be part of the solution than part of the problem (variable: *role*), 1.53 times more likely to be actors than recipients of action (variable: *potency*), and involved in campaigns 71 percent of the time (variable: *task*).

25. W. Lance Bennett, *News: The Politics of Illusion*, 2nd ed. (New York: Macmillan, 1988), 23.

26. "Clinton Grabs for Prizes at Safe Pace; Politics," *Los Angeles Times*, 26 October 1996, 10A.

27. Anthony Downs, *An Economic Theory of Democracy* (New York: Harper, 1957), 25.

28. Joseph A. Schlesinger, "The New American Political Party," *American Political Science Review* 79 (1985): 1152–69, 1153.

29. Joseph A. Schumpeter, *Capitalism, Socialism, and Democracy* (New York: Harper and Row, 1942), 283.

30. William N. Chambers and Walter Dean Burnham, *The American Party Systems: Stages of Political Development* (New York: Oxford University Press, 1975), 5.

31. John R. Hibbing and Elizabeth Theiss-Morse, *Congress as Public Enemy: Public Attitudes toward American Political Institutions* (Cambridge: Cambridge University Press, 1995).

32. Dick Morris, *Behind the Oval Office: Winning the Presidency in the Nineties* (New York: Random House, 1997); Morris, *The New Prince* (Los Angeles: Renaissance Books, 1999).

33. Morris, *New Prince*, xv.

34. Anthony Downs, *An Economic Theory of Democracy* (New York: Harper, 1957), 116–17.

35. Downs, *Economic Theory,* 114–15.

36. John Petrocik, "Issues and Agendas: Electoral Coalitions of the 1988 Election," paper presented to the annual American Political Science Association meeting, Atlanta, Ga., 31 August–3 September 1989, 3.

37. Petrocik concludes, "The post–New Deal party system, although tilted in favor of the Democrats, will elect Republican presidents whenever the campaign can be focused upon conservative issues (crime, traditional morals and values) and problems" (Petrocik, "Issues and Agendas," 25).

38. Robert Cialdini, *Influence: The Psychology of Persuasion* (New York: Quill, 1993).

39. George E. Belch, Michael A. Belch, and Angelina Villareal, "Effects of Advertising Communications: Review of Research," *Research in Marketing* 9 (1987): 59–117; Rebecca H. Holman, "Advertising and Emotionality," in *The Role of Affect in Consumer Behavior*, ed. Robert A. Peterson, Wayne D. Hoyer, and William R. Wilson (Lexington, Mass.: Lexington Books, 1986), 119–40.

40. Ronald Reagan, "Campaign Speech Delivered to Reagan Bush Rally," Waterbury, Conn. (19 September 1984), Annenberg/Pew Archive of Presidential Discourse, CD-ROM (Philadelphia: Annenberg School for Communication, University of Pennsylvania, 2000).

41. Walter Mondale, "What Kind of People Are We," remarks at Merrill, Wisc. (3 September 1984), Annenberg/Pew Archive of Presidential Discourse, CD-ROM (Philadelphia: Annenberg School Communication, University of Pennsylvania, 2000).

42. John Hibbing and Elizabeth Theiss Morse, "Civics Is Not Enough: Teaching Barbarics in K-12," *PS: Political Science and Politics* 29, no. 1 (1996): 57–62, 57.

43. E. J. Dionne, "The Civics Deficit," *Washington Post*, 20 November 1999, 29A.

44. Dionne, "Civics Deficit."

45. Dionne, "Civics Deficit."

46. Thomas J. Cronin, "The Textbook Presidency and Political Science," in *Perspectives on the Presidency*, ed. Stanley Bach and George T. Sulzner (Lexington, Mass.: D. C. Heath, 1974), 54.

47. D. J. Hoesktra, "The 'Textbook Presidency' Revisited," *Presidential Studies Quarterly* 12 (1982): 159–67.

48. J. M. Sanchez, "Old habits Die Hard: The Textbook Presidency Is Alive and Well," *PS: Political Science and Politics* 29, no. 1 (1996): 63–67.

49. J. M. Sanchez, "Awaiting Rehabilitation: The Carter Presidency in Political Science Textbooks," *Presidential Studies Quarterly* 27, no. 2 (1997): 284–97.

50. Cronin, "Textbook Presidency," 74.

51. Cronin, "Textbook Presidency," 63.

52. Richard Remy, *United States Government: Democracy in Action* (New York: Glencoe, 1993), 184.

53. Theodore Lowi and Benjamin Ginsberg, *American Government: Freedom and Power*, 4th ed. (New York: Norton, 1996), 453.

54. Remy, *United States Government*, 274.

55. Lowi and Ginsberg, *American Government*, 453.

56. Hibbing and Theiss-Morse, "Civics Is Not Enough."

57. See Shanto Iyengar, *Is Anyone Responsible? How Television Frames Political Issues* (Chicago: University of Chicago Press, 1991); see Selma Ghanem, "Filling in the Tapestry: The Second Level of Agenda Setting," in *Communication and Democracy: Exploring the Intellectual Frontiers in Agenda-Setting Theory*, ed. Maxwell McCombs, Donald L. Shaw, and David Weaver (Mawhah, N.J.: Lawrence Erlbaum, 1997).

58. Maxwell McCombs and Donald Shaw, "The Agenda-Setting Function of Mass Media," *Public Opinion Quarterly* 36 (1972): 176–85.

6

THE TWO MAJOR PARTIES AND EVERYONE ELSE

During the second televised 2004 presidential debate, President George W. Bush told his immediate and television audiences, "The *National Journal* named Senator Kennedy the most *liberal* senator of all. And that's saying something in that bunch. You might say that took a lot of hard work." In this statement, the president was most likely referring to his opponent Senator John Kerry (and not Ted Kennedy, the senior senator from Massachusetts—although the linkage is a curious one given the label Bush chose to attach to his opponent). Bush continued, "He's going to tax everyone here to fund his programs. . . . That's what *liberals* do. They create government-sponsored health care. Maybe you think that makes sense. I don't."

For his response, Kerry sidestepped the Kennedy reference entirely. He did bite on the label use, though, and responded this way:

> The president is just trying to scare everybody here with throwing labels around. I mean, *compassionate conservative*, what does that mean? Cutting 500,000 kids from after-school programs, cutting 365,000 kids from health care, running up the biggest deficits in American history. Mr. President, you're batting 0 for 2. I mean, seriously—labels don't mean anything. What means something is: Do you have a plan? And I want to talk about my plan some more—I hope we can.

This exchange opens a set of questions for campaign 2004, including the following: What is a *liberal*? What does it mean to call your opponent one? What is a *compassionate conservative*? Why would a candidate such as George W. Bush choose this as a campaign theme? Do labels have meaning? Do they, as Kerry seems to suggest, confuse our ability to attend to weightier matters such as "plans"? This chapter focuses directly on these concerns to gain a better understanding of the meaning of the individual labels in this study. Specifically, a set of questions are examined here—namely, What meanings do elites assign to the labels in this project? Do the elites in this study praise some aspects of parties and partisanship and disparage others? Can political priorities be read from the ways in which they use party labels? And, if so, what can these portrayals tells us about politics in the United States over the past half century?

After studying the terms in the project individually, I found that elites protect the *Democratic* and *Republican* labels, praise the *independent* label, vilify the *liberal* label, and largely ignore the *conservative* one (save a campaign theme of George W. Bush, "compassionate conservative," as mentioned by John Kerry). Conceptually, these patterns display a penchant for stable government, a passion for populism, and an aversion to extremism. One of my expected conclusions of this content analysis was that the demise of the term *liberal* would be a key finding of this chapter and one of the book as well. While that pattern is certainly notable and it is one of the more public examples of why attending to party labels merits attention, the subtle stability of the *Democratic* and *Republican* labels, as well as the increasing cultural purchase of the *independent* label, is a powerful story as well. In a sense, then, this chapter details the types of partisanship that elites value as well as three powerful truths about the American system.

ELITES PREFER A STABLE GOVERNMENT

The previous chapters assess how labels are used en masse, over time, and by profession. The next concern, of course, is how do such usages influence the individual meanings of the labels? Chapters 3 and 4 preview the first finding, and it is one that regards the *party* label: although this term is used less frequently over time, all voices in this project treat it with deference, semantically empowering it so that it may endure. The exact patterns of the *party* label are reported in another book examining the role of language in American political culture (*Political Keywords: Using Language That Uses Us*) and is not reported in depth here, other than to say that *when* speakers use this term, they do so with caution.[1]

A second concern addresses the terms *Democrat* and *Republican*. How do the previously reported trends influence the meanings of these labels? Do these voices prefer one party label to the other? Or are the major labels treated similarly? To test this question, I ran descriptive- and nominal-level statistics on my content analytic data. Intriguingly, I found some evidence for both predictions: the results of chi-square analyses reveal four statistical differences and five nonsignificant differences between the use of the *Democratic* and *Republican* labels.[2] In making sense of these patterns, I found compelling differences on variables measuring evaluations of the parties and nonsignificant differences on variables measuring the structural responsibilities of parties. Here, it appears that elites display preferences between the parties, often favoring *Democrats* over *Republicans*, but ultimately describe both of them as performing similar roles in the body politic. In other words, elites advance a theory that Democrats are slightly preferable to their more conservative peers (especially from 1948 to 1980) but that both Democrats and Republicans are essential to American democracy.

First, consider the evaluative differences between the *Democratic* and *Republican* labels. The findings show that elites are more likely to place Democrats in a positive situation (variable: *context*), a pattern that holds in the campaign texts as well as the governing texts. Simple examples of the "positive context" can be found in the following phrases from newspaper articles from 1952, 1964, 1968, 1980, and 1992, respectively: "It was another good *Democrat*, Senator William Fulbright of Arkansas, who probed the Reconstruction Finance Corp";[3] "Humphrey is a favorite of local *Democrats*";[4] "Mayor Daley told newsmen, 'It will be a great day for the *Democrats*. We'll carry Illinois by a substantial amount'";[5] "the state's three-to-one majority of registered *Democrats* over *Republicans*";[6] and "the Tennessee *Democrat* had sounded articulate and informed."[7]

The *Republican* label is not always treated as generously, a finding that holds across all four genres but is particularly compelling in news coverage during the first two eras of this study (news coverage of the *Republican* label is somewhat more optimistic in responding to the upbeat candidacies of Ronald Reagan in 1980 and 1984 and George W. Bush in 2000). The *context* variable was created not to measure "media bias" but to unpack the sentence in order to assess whether a label is placed in a positive, negative, or balanced condition. By attending to this variable, I discovered that over the years, journalists often place the *Republican* label in adverse situations—not by directly damning the term but by introducing anti-Republican sentiment into articles through the selective use of sources. Intriguingly, when one looks carefully, the "journalist's voice" does not appear biased, but the resulting stories may seem so to readers. Notice how in the following examples, from the *Chicago Tribune* and wire reports, journalists use the words of two Democrats—Aldai Stevenson and John Sparkman—to place the *Republican* label in a compromised position:

- "Stevenson's target—what he calls a divided, quarreling, and disunited *Republican* party—has replaced the straw man 80th Congress that President Truman used effectively in his 'give 'em hell' campaign of 1948, without much defense offered by the Republican opponent, then or now."[8]
- "Senator John Sparkman declared tonight the *Republicans* are waging a 'phony crusade' based on 'the philosophy of fear—the fear of old-thinking men who have no vision of their country's future.'"[9]

Discussions of the *Republican* label become more nuanced over time, and the negativity seen in the years 1948–1980 becomes much more subtle—and sometimes balanced—in the reporting made on the upbeat campaigns of Ronald Reagan (1980, 1984) and George W. Bush (2000). Note two elements of the following *Los Angeles Times* article, from September 21, 1980. In this instance, the reporter quotes a source to discuss the Republican nominee, yet the hypothetical "if" softens the sting resonating from the idea of a lesser candidate's beating the said nominee:

> Some political operatives, however, believe Reagan underestimates the risk involved. Reagan's former campaign manager, John Sears, recently said that if Anderson, "a lesser candidate," is perceived as beating the *Republican* nominee in the debate, "it will do terrible things to Reagan's image."[10]

In 1984, an article in the *New York Times* notes how Democrats were hoping to constrain Republican successes, but it also observes the personal appeal of the Republican presidential nominee: "Most Democratic party officials were avoiding such predictions about the Presidential results. Instead, they worked to limit *Republican* gains in the House of Representatives in the hope of denying Mr. Reagan a sweeping policy mandate to go along with the personal victory many ranking Democratic officials privately said was inevitable."[11] Although it has been tempting for academics and those on the Left to regard George H. W. Bush's indictment of the "liberal media" in 1992 as being a self-serving ploy, these data provide some evidence that *Republican* labels are cast in a more contentious light by the press (directly in campaigns 1948–1980, more subtly thereafter).

Meanwhile, the *Democratic* label has been credited in news reporting for embracing broader concerns and publics than those associated with the

Republican label (variables: *goals* and *position*). This coverage may stem from the types of things that Democratic candidates say on the campaign trail. Observe, for instance, the number of persons Harry Truman intends to help as articulated in the following speech from 1948:

> The Democrats have believed always that the welfare of the whole people should come first, and that means that the farmers, labor, small businessmen, and everybody else in the country should have a fair share of the prosperity that goes around. We have placed the farmers in the best position they have ever been in the history of the world. We have placed labor in its best position it has ever been in the history of the world. And we have been against monopoly from the start. Now, when farmers are prosperous, and when labor gets good wages, business is bound to be good. And that is the reason the national income is higher in this country than it has ever been before in the history of the world.[12]

Stylistically, Democratic candidates have a rich history of including a variety of groups in their campaign speeches. In 1968, for instance, Hubert Humphrey spoke of "an American family," "where people of all races, creeds and colors can work together," "go to school together," "play together," "live together," and "work for this democracy together."[13] In 1972, George McGovern talked about "the oil workers, the steelworkers, the machinists, the teachers and millions of other Americans";[14] and "the women who are seeking a more fulfilling role in American society," "the young who are in a hurry for change, and to the black or brown or red who can wait no longer for change."[15] And in pledging to fight for "the people, not the powerful," Al Gore discussed running with "working families," "firefighters," "the police," "working men and women," "office workers," "construction workers," and "factory workers."[16] In such ways, these candidates link their label directly and indirectly to a desire to use government to help a variety of groups.

In contrast, the *Republican* label is presented as having more pointed goals and as being located at the elite level. This term is generally coupled with a specific philosophy of governance (e.g., smaller is better), with individual policies (e.g., tax cuts), or with moral concerns (e.g., God and faith). While moral stands certainly contribute to the nation's well-being, knowing that a GOP candidate loves God does not offer the same type of tangible help as that viewed in Truman's speech (although it certainly can nurture a coalition craving such a connection). Perhaps because they sense a Republican reluctance to speak for the entire nation, journalists comment on the comparatively pointed goals of Republicans when covering them.

Indeed, in interpreting the Republican goals, journalists even find a story in the constituents left out of their campaign discourse. Examples include an article from 1952, when Harry Truman attracted coverage for accusing the "old guard" Republicans of "trying to pull the wool over farmers' eyes on price supports";[17] another one from 1980, when John Anderson was quoted as saying, "The platform of Ronald Reagan and the *Republican party* repudiates four decades of support for equal rights for women";[18] and still another one from 1992, when a journalist wrote that the Republican convention "rang with repeated attacks on homosexuals and efforts to portray Clinton as anti-family."[19] While no organized group can stand up for everyone, that the Republican party does not make overtures to as many groups as the Democrats (e.g., farmers, women, and gays and lesbians) adds drama to news coverage of GOP campaigns. In campaign 2000, the Bush team worked to couple its candidate and the *Republican* label with the former Texas governor's efforts to "unite" and not "divide" and his working with Democrats in his home state's legislature. His efforts did shift the news frame for that contest, and they served as a contrast to how the *Republican* label was largely treated over the years. Time will tell if the close 2000 contest, the polarization heading into campaign 2004, and the divided outcome of that election will increase or decrease the likelihood that Republicans will garner more generous treatment in the news in the future.

The *goals* variable was inspired by Gerald Pomper's contention that a society cannot exist if its members pursue self-interests exclusively. In this study, however, it seems that this variable captures not just goals but something else: a description of the groups that anchor the respective parties. The *Democratic* label—portrayed as serving more heterogeneous interests—is discussed as being more inclusive, whereas the *Republican* label, representing more homogenous interests, is depicted as having more narrow foci. Journalistically and rhetorically, the former is a happier place to be in news coverage.

Elites are also more likely to regard Democrats (versus Republicans) as being "part of the solution" (variable: *role*). The solution:problem ratios for these variables are 2:1 for Democrats and 1:1 for Republicans (another trend that is somewhat less prevalent during the optimistic candidacies of Ronald Reagan and George W. Bush). Journalists and political candidates seem particularly eager to portray Democrats as being part of the solution. In the news, this emphasis often appears in the use of adjectives, such as those appearing in 1956 and 1976, respectively: "The 5th District will return its able Congressman, another attractive, vigorous, young *Democrat*, Richard Lankford";[20] or "California Gov. Edmund G. Brown Jr., who portrayed the *Democratic* presidential candidate as a choice of 'the future, of possibility, of openness.'"[21]

Candidates, too, depict Democrats as being part of the solution, and such couplings are particularly vivid during the first and second eras of this study. Observe how John Kennedy links his party label to problem solving in 1960:

> Now, the fact of the matter is that I don't say this is Mr. Nixon's fault, but I say we are concerned about it. I say the *Democrats* want to do something about it. I say these are not statistics to us; these are people who need help, and in a country that has more surplus than any other, we can do better. . . . I think we can do better. As long as there are 15 million American families who live in substandard housing, as long as the average wage for laundrywomen in the five largest cities of this country is 65 cents for a 48 hour week, as long as there are nearly 17 million Americans who are not even covered by the dollar minimum wage, as long as 17 million Americans who are over 65 live on an average social security check of less than $78 a month, as long as there is unfinished business before our country, I think there is need for our *party*.[22]

Without doubt, Republicans also use such universalistic appeals at times, but the Democrats' "big tent" philosophy lends itself far better to a "big tent" rhetoric.

George McGovern, too, calls attention to the "people" and the "groups of people" associated with the *Democratic* label. While Kennedy uses specific data to advance his claims, McGovern sounds far more speculative in the following passage. He begins by defining the parties and their missions, and he concludes by showing how Democrats work for honest citizens who honestly need them:

> No political party can serve two masters: the people and the privileged. By heritage and by choice, this is the fundamental difference between the *Democratic party* and the *Republican party*. The *Democratic party* is the party of the people. The *Republican party* is the party of the privileged. And this election is the renewal of a struggle as old as the Great Depression, and as recent as the economic black magic invented by Richard Nixon when he gave us recession and inflation at the same time. . . . The *Republicans* are welcome to Mr. Connally and his exclusive club of oil millionaires. I want the oil workers, the steelworkers, the machinists, the teachers, and millions of other Americans who live on the wages of their work instead of tax loopholes.[23]

In this content analysis, the tendency of Democratic candidates to couple their label with desires to use government to help people gives this party label the edge on the *goals* variable.

A similar pattern appears in the governing condition, where the *Republican* label is more likely to be constituted as being "part of the problem" when analyzed in congressional debates than in any other genre (variable: *role*). As mentioned in chapter 5, the 1995 debate is the most contentious one focused on in this study. In the following two statements, Representative Robert Matsui (D-CA) and Representative Benjamin Cardin (D-MD) argue that Republicans—in their minds, at least—make a habit of frustrating the passage of good legislation. By not wanting to provide for citizens, by failing to view government as being a benevolent force, the Democrats portray the *Republican* label as being purely obstructionist:

> Well, how are you going to get people to work? We all know that in order to create jobs, in order to create people in the workforce, you have to provide job training, you have to provide education, you have to provide day care and transportation, because most of these people on welfare do not have cars. So you have to provide bus labels. The *Republican* bill does not provide any of that.[24]

> The *Republican* bill does not provide the resources to the local governments. Even though H.R. 5 did, there was a change made. The *Republicans* all of a sudden needed some money for a tax cut. So they cut the program even though they knew it was needed. The Democratic bill provides the resources so the States can provide the programs to get people back to work. That is, day care, health care benefits so that welfare people can work. The *Republican* bill dumps the problems on local governments.[25]

All of these examples point to a similar finding: elites treat the *Democratic* label as inhabiting a more positive environment (*context*), as being more interested in a broader group of people (*goals*), and as being devoted to using government to help citizens (*role*). These patterns that have contributed to a more positive evaluative treatment of the *Democratic* label may be related to the Democratic Party's approach to government. That is, elites may be inclined to speak more kindly of the party that has faith in traditional, structural solutions to political and civic problems. As Gerald Pomper has argued,

> The basic Democratic philosophy, from Thomas Jefferson to William Jefferson Clinton, has stressed the value of equality more than liberty, par-

ticularly on matters of economic policy. There is a consistent thread in the party's programs to protect the farmers and small capitalists in the nineteenth century, to support bank depositors and industrial workers and aged pensioners in the New Deal, to support racial minorities in the Great Society, and to aid women and gays in the 1990s. . . . Democrats cannot always admit it, but the fact is they like government. They are policy wonks, career politicians, builders of bureaucracy. That philosophical bent can sometimes lead them into the morass of multicultural education, but it can also lead them to the decencies of universal old age insurance.[26]

Alan Ehrenhalt has advanced a similar point in *The Politics of Ambition*, contending that the Democrats are the natural governing party because they are "not embarrassed to govern."[27] He writes, "The Democratic party is the party of government in the United States, or more precisely the party that believes in government and communicates that belief to nearly everyone who follows politics."[28] Accordingly, Ehrenhalt asserts that Republicans sometimes create problems when fixing them, whereas Democrats sometimes create opportunities by finding problems. In his mind, when Republicans espouse antigovernment rhetoric or claim publicly that they have solved problems (such as when Ronald Reagan "fixed big government" or when George H. W. Bush "ended the Cold War"), there remain few reasons to vote for them. Democrats, in contrast, have no such problem. Their optimistic view of government continues to find difficulties that must be remedied. Symbolically, then, a more generous portrait of the *Democratic* label has been painted in the texts of 1948–2000. It is important to note, nonetheless, that the buoyant campaigns of Ronald Reagan (1980, 1984) and George W. Bush (2000) departed from such trends, and it appears that these candidates were successful in garnering their party's label more munificent coverage in those years.

While the variables discussed here point to three evaluative distinctions between the parties, elites portray Democrats and Republicans as having considerable structural similarities. That is, Democrats and Republicans are depicted as having equal amounts of agency in the system (variable: *potency*), as working within the same time constraints (variable: *time*), as interacting with similar entities (variable: *associations*), as engaging in the same sets of actions (variable: *behavior*), and as possessing the same types of organizational attributes (variable: *quality*). Given that elites seem to approve of Democrats more than Republicans, what can account for these likenesses? What explains the finding that the chi-square tests located no differences between the ways in which the party labels are discussed?

Several understandings are possible, and the most likely ones underscore the inevitability addressed in chapter 3, which can be unpacked from several vantage points. A historical interpretation of these patterns might argue that, once again, American elites have come to regard the parties as given, as established. As a result, it may be thought unnecessary for elites to distinguish between the structural roles of Democrats and Republicans. A similar but socioeconomic explanation might be found in Walter Dean Burnham's contention that the parties work within the same structural conditions in order to protect the system (as well as their place in that system). As Burnham has written, a characteristic of party politics is a "profound incapacity of established political leadership to adapt itself sequentially—or even incrementally—to emergent political demand generated by the losers in our stormy socio-economic transformations." In his mind, "it follows from this that once successful routines are established or reestablished for winning office, there is no motivation among party leaders to disturb the rules of the game."[29]

A rhetorical explanation for cross-party similarities could be that elites are naturally attracted to a sanctioned, generic discourse when describing parties. Roderick Hart has noted that a *genre* is a class of messages having important structural and content similarities that possess the following characteristics: they necessarily develop; they reveal societal truths; they are largely implicit; they stabilize social life; and they affect subsequent perceptions.[30] Because of elites' position and stake in government, they may (consciously or subconsciously) subscribe to and reproduce a standard way of discussing partisanship, thereby ensuring perpetuation of the symbolic (and political) status quo.

There are implications, of course, associated with such generic trappings. As Murray Edelman states, "In politics, as in religion, whatever is ceremonial or banal strengthens reassuring beliefs regardless of their validity and discourages skeptical inquiry about disturbing issues."[31] Time and time again, scholars have shown that Americans somehow find ways to displace their specific dissatisfactions with the political system in order to applaud the overall functioning of the U.S. government. Perhaps this is a trend in the elite's talk of the party as well, rewarding Democrats who are proud to govern, being more abrupt with Republicans who question statist solutions, but ultimately portraying both of these groups as being central to American politics. Although this discourse reveals a preference for the *Democratic* label, it cements the necessity of both parties in the political system and stands in stark contrast to the portrayals of *independents* and *liberals*, as detailed in the following section.

ELITES ACKNOWLEDGE THE POPULIST SPIRIT

Those in power in the American polity have long been confused about what to do with independents. Consider, for instance, how the elite media treated independent candidate Ross Perot's candidacy in 1992. After Perot announced that he would consider running for the presidency on February 20, 1992 (or, more accurately, after this assertion was extracted from him by television interviewer Larry King), Perot received favorable news coverage from March 1992 to June 1992. Perot's positive treatment ended in June, however, for as political scholar John Zaller points out, it was then that Perot became the leading candidate (ahead of both George H. W. Bush and Bill Clinton in public opinion polls).[32] Research from the University of Arizona offered support for Zaller's claim, finding that changes in the tone of news coverage could even be found in the nonverbal treatment accorded Perot by the network news anchors (e.g., Tom Brokaw of NBC, Peter Jennings of ABC, and Dan Rather of CBS).[33] When Perot was a novelty, he received positive attention from network television; when he became a contender, he received the same sort of critical treatment afforded to viable candidates, the type that political scholar Thomas Patterson finds troubling (discussed in chapter 5).

Independent voters have puzzled political scholars, too. Much of their work has been guided by assumptions based on the inevitability of the two-party system in the United States, and, accordingly, they have asked questions such as, Why do such citizens make their lives difficult by not adhering to the tenets of the major parties? One somewhat sympathetic response to this type of question has been outlined by scholars Steven Rosenstone, Roy Behr, and Edward Lazarus, who comment,

> To support a third party challenger, a voter must awaken from the political slumber in which he ordinarily lies, actively seek out information on a contest whose outcome he cannot affect, reject the socialization of his political system, ignore the ridicule and abuse of his friends and neighbors, and accept the fact that when the ballots are counted, his vote will never be in the winner's column.[34]

These authors elaborate that third-party candidates (and voters) face several major obstacles in a two-party system, including constitutional, legal, and administrative provisions; fewer resources and poorer media coverage than that of major party candidates; and a lower standard of respect than that afforded to candidates affiliated with the major parties.

Less-sympathetic accounts of independents can be found in *The Myth of the Independent Voter* and *The American Voter*. In the former book, Bruce Keith and colleagues argue that independents do not really exist, for when these individuals are measured mathematically, they are largely similar to Democratic and Republican voters.[35] In the latter work, Angus Campbell and colleagues demystify the "populist" assumption that independents are more active than the followers of major parties. They state,

> The ideal of the independent citizen, attentive to politics, concerned with the course of government, who weighs the rival appeals of a campaign and reaches a judgment that is unswayed by partisan prejudice, has had such a vigorous history in the tradition of political reform—and has such a hold on civic institution today—that one could easily suppose that the habitual partisan has the more limited interest and concern with politics. But if the usual image of the independent voter is more than a normative ideal, it fits poorly the characteristics of independents in our samples. Far from being more attentive, interested and informed, independents tend as a group to be somewhat less involved in politics. They have somewhat poorer knowledge of the issues, their image of the candidates is fainter, their interest in the campaign is less, their concern over the outcome is relatively slight, and their choice between competing candidates, although it is indeed made later in the campaign, seems much less to spring from discoverable evaluations of the elements of national politics.[36]

While it is tempting for elite journalists and scholars to dismiss independents, they must do so in a culture that loves what independents represent: an air of populism. *Populism* is defined as a set of assumptions that elevates "common people" over power structures and has the following rhetorical markers: references to a "golden age" (one that cannot be retained); conspiracy arguments (in which elites engineer unnatural conditions to the detriment of the common people); clashes between good and evil (in which the "producers"—the oppressed masses who cherish democracy—are pitted against the "nonproducers"—the moneyed elites who ride on the backs of the working poor); recurrent key assumptions (the need for an active citizenry, the recognition of individual values and rights); and an egalitarian spirit (often Christian in nature that stresses a brotherhood of the "common people").[37]

Communication scholar Gary Woodward finds that such a style appeals to self-interest rather than the national interest. As such, the populist style talks about the system by talking against the system, glorifying the common at the expense of institutional elites. Indeed, Woodward notes that Ronald Reagan found the populist style effective, constantly using it to flatter the wisdom and faith of the American electorate.[38]

Given that elites tend to look down at independents but are still attracted to the populist spirit, how have they portrayed the *independent* label? The data show that they have done so deftly, heralding the independent instinct but not the independent actors; elites have used this term to reinvite voters back to the two-party system and have largely eschewed using it to acknowledge candidates who run outside of the two major parties. In a sense, then, elites use the label to navigate between an approval of populism without a parallel legitimization for the actions of populist politicians.

Table 6.1 displays simple frequencies of the *independent* label (drawn from the Campaign Mapping Project). As this table illustrates, the high point for the *independent* label in speeches occurred in 1968 and in news reports in 1980. Thus, while some might assume that independents enjoy greater political currency in the 1990s than in the recent past (e.g., Ross Perot, the Reform Party), the Campaign Mapping Project data do not validate that assumption. Consider also the party identification data listed in table 6.1, which shows that the high point for supporting a third party occurred in 1976, a datum that is as easily explained by disgust with the two-party system after the Watergate scandal as by any sort of genuine support for a new political ideology.[39]

Table 6.1.   *Independent* Label in Speeches and News

	Candidate Speeches n (ratio)[a]	News Reports n (ratio)[a]	Party ID[b]
1948	4 (.013)	3 (.017)	6
1952	4 (.015)	7 (.021)	9
1956	15 (.048)	51 (.013)	10
1960	14 (.029)	47 (.014)	8
1964	5 (.012)	7 (.013)	11
1968	24 (.065)	115 (.036)	13
1972	8 (.022)	2 (.019)	13
1976	7 (.033)	25 (.030)	15
1980	3 (.009)	21 (.114)	13
1984	4 (.010)	5 (.024)	11
1988	4 (.018)	12 (.022)	11
1992	11 (.038)	196 (.038)	12
1996	33 (.026)	186 (.037)	9
2000	16 (.002)	235 (.035)	12

[a]All ratios rely on frequency data from the Campaign Mapping Project and were calculated with the following formula: *independent* label / total word of genre × 100.
[b]From the National Election Studies (1948–2000), www.umich.edu/~nes.

Additionally, there are noteworthy differences in the frequencies found in news and speeches. Although journalists were intrigued by independents in 1980, neither Ronald Reagan nor Jimmy Carter discussed them a great deal. To sum, then, table 6.1 presents several curiosities about independents: the use of the *independent* label has not increased steadily over time; party identification for independents has not increased either; and candidates do not suddenly stress "independence" just because an independent candidate was in the race (while the appearance of George Wallace in the 1968 campaign is met with the highest use of independent labels, John Anderson's candidacy in 1980 is met with the lowest use of such markers).

Qualitative findings add to these quantitative trends. More so than the other party labels, *independents* were placed in a positive context (31.1 percent of the time, with a positive:negative ratio of 3:1—variable: *context*) and were popularly regarded as being part of the solution (variable: *role*). The ratio of solution:problem statements for independents was 14:1, compared to 2:1 for *Democrats* and 1:1 for *Republicans*. Given elites' temptation to look down on independents, what can account for these patterns?

One explanation can be found in the *position* variable, which examines whether parties are constituted at the elite level (in government) or mass level (through voters). As table 6.2 illustrates, the *independent* label is the only one to be consistently framed at the mass level. The ratios of elite:mass statements for the labels include *Democrat* 5:1, *Republican* 10.5:1.0, *independent* 0.5:1.0, *liberal* 3:1, *conservative* 2.5:1.0, and *party* 10:1. Thus, it seems that elites rarely refer to independents "in government"; instead, they used the term to refer to citizens themselves. In 1980, for instance, Jimmy Carter did not use the *independent* label to take on candidate John Anderson, and Ronald Reagan used it only three times (and never to refer to Anderson, either).

In reading the speeches from other campaigns, I found that most major party candidates also refrain from discussing (or marginalizing) indepen-

Table 6.2.   Labels by *Position* Variable (in percentages)

	Elite	Mass	Global/Undifferentiated
Democrat	77.4	15.7	6.9
Republican	87.1	8.3	4.5
Independent	28.8	59.9	11.2
Liberal	65.8	21.9	12.2
Conservative	61.1	24.8	14.1
Party	72.9	7.4	19.7

Note: Overall percentages may not add to 100 owing to rounding to the nearest tenth.

dent candidates, probably because (1) major party candidates do not want to give independents the benefit of being taken seriously (indeed, many independent candidates never get the free media attention that John Anderson and Ross Perot received; consequently, they have a much harder time than traditional candidates do in capturing attention in the two-party system); (2) major party candidates do not want to appear weak by critiquing a lesser candidacy; or (3) they do not want to offend citizens who support independent candidates but who may later think about supporting a major party candidate in the general election. Even though these strategies benefit the major parties politically, they also help the *independent* label rhetorically. That is, because major party candidates do not critique independent candidates, citizens may begin to implicitly assume that "independence" will remain a viable cultural commodity.

When compared to the other labels, *independents* are also portrayed as being most likely to embrace broad goals (13.1 percent) and, consequently, least likely to embrace narrow goals (23.7 percent, variable: *goals*). This is a curious finding, for, as explained earlier, independents are most often linked to the electorate. But how can voters possess broad goals? In reading the texts, I found that it became clear, particularly in the speeches, that elites flatter independents, portraying them as being societally concerned and protective of the nation. Independent citizens, in this way, are not partisan (i.e., preferring one political group to another) but open-minded and autonomous and, hence, quite respectable indeed.

The tendency for candidates (and consequently journalists) to paint independent voters as being desirable may be empowering for antiparty citizens who otherwise feel ignored in American politics. Three years after Perot's 1992 bid, John Kenneth White wrote,

> Most voters do not like political parties. *And they are right not to like them.* They want compelling ideas and candidates whose stories resonate with their own experiences and aspirations. Parties are currently failing miserably in these tasks, and Ross Perot's prominence symbolizes their failure. . . . Moreover, since January 1993 more citizens have contributed money to United We Stand America (Perot's organization) than have given to the Democratic and Republican parties combined! More Americans feel a sense of empowerment by giving fifteen hard-earned dollars to a billionaire than to the major parties.[40]

Researchers who study third-party movements suggest that charismatic leaders are essential to a movement's success. Maybe so, but the political climate of the 1990s (a climate that included increased cynicism and hyper-individualism) seemed unusually receptive to Perot's candidacy. Many of the texts collected in the Campaign Mapping Project underscore why citizens found the independent cause empowering. Witness, for example, the passionate sentiments found in the following letters to the editor, written in 1992 by voters in Salinas, California, and Westport, Massachusetts, respectively:

> There is a saying, "I'm not going to throw my vote away on a third-party candidate who doesn't stand a chance of winning." That type of bovine excrement is going to kill this great country. This is the year that we the "little people" have a chance to make a real difference. . . . Let's give the new kid a try. Vote *Independent*: Vote Ross Perot.[41]

> I address the question, "Is it safe to vote for Ross Perot?" I am one who seeks real change from 12 years of Bush-Reagan build-up of a $4 trillion national debt, a devastated economy but not as bad as that left by the late Soviet Union, of coddling the extremely wealthy whose trickle-down investments were more profitable producing jobs outside the U.S. rather than in it. . . . I think it not only safe but necessary to vote for Ross Perot.[42]

In examining the rhetoric of citizens who supported independent candidates, I found that they had three priorities: a passion for spreading the word about the independent candidacy, a willingness to warn the public that the political edifice was on the brink of collapse, and a preference for the third-party process rather than a third-party platform—that is, independent supporters appear more interested in procedural matters (getting heard, encouraging change) than in substantive ones (repeating a policy platform distinct from those of Democrats and Republicans). Interestingly, in reading letters written about independent candidates, I found that very few Democratic or Republican voters wrote to critique independent candidates. Thus, Democratic and Republican voters, like their candidates, seemed unwilling to disparage the *independent* label.

The tendency to portray independent voters as being a desirable constituency may have underdiscussed constitutive effects, especially for citizens who receive most of their political socialization from the media than from partisan families, communities, or organizations. As these examples illustrate, independent voters are viewed as being essential for success; if politics is a game, that is, then the independent vote is a precious commodity. Consider, for example, how independent voters have been portrayed as being important in the news, particularly in recent tight elections: in 1980, "Ronald Reagan has been winning the competition for *independent* voters";[43] in 1988, "*Independent* voters . . . constitute a healthy portion of the swing vote";[44] and in 1992, "ABC attributed Clinton's growing lead to *independent* voters siding with Clinton after having wavered between voting for Clinton and remaining undecided."[45] And in the closest of recent elections, 2000, the independent voter is praised even more aggressively: "After all, this is the era of *independent* voters."[46] "To be sure, *independent* voters still matter greatly and may tip the election."[47] "[Gore] appealed to *independent* voters, vital to the Democrats' chances of retaining the White House this fall."[48] For citizens who were not raised with a psychological connection to one of the major parties, this sense of worth and value may be attractive.

Many scholars bemoan horse-race news coverage because it displaces substantive issues with strategy. This project suggests why partisans may also dislike it: horse-race coverage heralds independent voters and may even create independent voters out of otherwise Democratic or Republican ones (who do not receive this flattering treatment in news). For, when independent voters are portrayed as being integral to electorate success—as they are in this study—identifying oneself as an independent may offer symbolic empowerment to citizens who are otherwise turned off to politics. It is important to note that this is a type of *symbolic empowerment*, of course, because independent voters cannot vote in many primary elections and it is often the case that many elections do not even feature a non–major party candidate for whom to vote.

While news coverage may court sympathy for the independent enterprise, such candidates nonetheless face many political challenges in the system. For instance, even though H. Ross Perot captured 19 percent of the vote in 1992, the most since Teddy Roosevelt in 1912, his supporters had a hard time staying organized, a point predicted by Gerald Pomper, who contends that third parties require discipline. It might well be the case that the passions that bring independent supporters into politics expires when they must organize and work within a system. Scholars and politicians alike have noticed that when third-party issues become important, major parties often co-opt them, a tendency that prompts Richard Hofstadter to write, "Third parties are like bees: once they have stung, they die."[49]

Hofstadter's choice of words, here, are critical, for they call attention to another pattern in the data: important semantic differences between the *independent* and *third party* labels. In a close reading of the texts, I noticed that the former term works to signify a fight against the system, whereas the latter is inherently seen as being subordinate to the major parties. This discussion may seem to be a minor semantic issue, yet the symbolic purchase of the terms is significant. In scholarly research and in public opinion polling, we must be careful in our word choice—for even if independents (culturally attractive) and third parties (politically subsumed) are both "outside of the two-party system," then the terms are imbued with different meanings in campaign discourse. A respondent to a political poll, for instance, may be far more likely to think positively about the term *independent* than *third party* in survey items. At least they have been primed to do so, given the analysis here.

Political scholars argue that when a large number of independent voters enter the system, the system becomes politically unstable.[50] While this may be true politically, due regard for the *independent* label may be a rhetorical asset for a country. Researchers who study partisan voting trends over time have observed that "critical realignments" may be the chief tension-management device in a nonrevolutionary country such as the United States.[51] It is entirely possible that the *independent* label serves as another type of tension-reduction tool, offering citizens a symbolic alternative to the two-party system, but an alternative that does not, in the main, threaten that system.

Why do American elites talk about independents so respectfully and yet attempt to marginalize them? Perhaps they do so both to honor the electorate's need to think outside the lines and to refresh their political spirits, but not in a way that endangers the status quo or their dominant place in the system. Of course, talk (particularly talk over time) is a necessary ingredient for turning ideas into action. But given the vaunted political inertia so prevalent in the United States, political change—at least at the national level—may continue to be a symbolic reality rather than a policy-related reality for some time.[52] Speaking kindly of independents may be but another way for elites to preserve the power they have historically enjoyed. Or so it seems from the data gathered here.

ELITES ARE AFRAID OF EXCESS

In *The Language of Oppression*, Haig Bosmajian details how names, labels, definitions, and stereotypes have been used to degrade, dehumanize, and suppress individuals. As he has argued, "our identities, who and what we are, how others see us, are greatly affected by the names we are called and the words with which we are labeled. The names, labels, and phrases employed to 'identify' a people may in the end determine their survival."[53]

Every language reflects the prejudices of the society in which it evolved, and it serves to feed future prejudices. While the previous sections of this chapter detail how elites protect the *Democratic* and *Republican* labels and applaud the *independent* label, this section describes how they disparage the *liberal* label and, save efforts of George W. Bush, leave the *conservative* term almost entirely alone. An initial goal of this study was to uncover how *liberal* became a dirty word in American politics. After analyzing the data, I found that the answer was almost too easy to discover: the term *liberal* is drenched in ideology by the Republicans and left undefended by the Democrats. As the following paragraphs illustrate, the *liberal* label is constituted as being heavily ideological and is seen as being synonymous with moral weakness and excess. While its demise in electoral politics is unquestionable (most Americans living at the dawn of the twenty-first century know that the *L* word has been stigmatized), the method of its demise shows what can happen when an organized group takes on a word and the term's natural defenders abandon it.

Of course, this is not the first work to examine the history of the word *liberal*. Raymond Williams includes this term in his text *Keywords*, and in his analysis of the term, he writes,

> *Liberal* has at first sight so clear a political meaning that some of its further associations are puzzling. Yet the political meaning is comparatively modern, and much of the interesting history of the word is earlier. It began in a specific social distinction, to refer to a class of men as distinct from others who were not free. . . . In the established party-political sense, liberal is now clear enough. But liberal as a term of political discourse is complex. It has been under regular and heavy attack from conservative positions, where the sense of lack of restraint and lack of discipline have been brought to bear, and also the sense of a (weak and sentimental) generosity. The sense of a lack of rigor has also been drawn on in intellectual disputes. Against this kind of attack, *liberal* has often been a group term for PROGRESSIVE OR RADICAL opinions, and is still clear in this sense, notably in the USA.[54]

The findings in this project are consistent with Williams's contention that *liberal* is associated with a lack of restraint and an excessive generosity. Interestingly, however, Williams's understanding of the term includes a group of liberals (agents) who defend its use against Marxists—from the Left—and conservatives—from the Right. In this study, I found that elites have stopped defending liberalism altogether, and so its construction as an ideologically undisciplined label has gone unprotected, a potentially dangerous finding in a state such as the United States, which has historically championed pluralism.

A problem, this, for Americans have a rich aversion to political ideology. Several scholars have written on this score, and a key work is E. J. Dionne's important book *Why Americans Hate Politics*.[55] There, Dionne contends that America's distaste for politics stems from their listening to the spokespersons of the major political parties who are often extreme in their views and out of step with the majority of centrist Americans. Dionne notes that the present ideological and party apparatus in the United States contributes to negative campaigning, artificially dichotomous choices, and unnecessary polarization. With both the Left and the Right busy fighting internecine battles, the public feels continually left out. This sense of alienation also appears in arguments advanced by Morris Fiorina. In *Divided Government*, he argues that people often feel frustrated by the need to decide between "San Francisco Democrats" (who many perceive to be "the party of minorities, gay rights activists, radical feminists and peaceniks") and "Reagan Republicans" (the party of "fundamentalists, bigots, and pro-life activists").[56] Writing in 2004, he has also observed a troubling divide for citizens. Following the close 2000 presidential contest, it has become fashionable to talk about the "blue states" (the coastal states that supported Democratic nominee Al Gore) and the "red states" (the heartland and Southern states that supported George W. Bush) and issues of polarization. Fiorina has also spotted such polarization but has observed a nuance as well: the division is far sharper among elites than among the citizenry. As in Dionne's argument, Fiorina locates another grating marker of partisan ideology: redistricted safe seats drawn by legislators who wish to protect their incumbencies or party advantage. Redistricting is a move that can allow increasingly partisan candidates to win safe seats, thereby creating districts with representatives who have opportunities to march out of step to the Left or the Right of many of their constituents.[57]

Polarized representatives—or the perception of them—contributes to John Hibbing and Elizabeth Theiss Morse's observations on why Americans had such little faith in the U.S. Congress in the 1980s and 1990s. One of their key conclusions is that Americans, as a conflict-averse people, overestimate the amount of consensus in the polity and are reluctant to admit that genuine conflict exists (as opposed to unnecessary political posturing). Hibbing and Theiss Morse write,

> Americans dislike compromise and bargaining, they dislike committees and bureaucracy, they dislike political parties and interest groups, they

dislike big salaries and big staffs, they dislike slowness and multiple stages, and they dislike debate and publicly hashing things out, referring to such actions as haggling or bickering. Americans want both procedural efficiency and procedural equity. The "haggling and bickering" so frequently decried by the people could very easily be termed informed discussion. And while eliminating interest groups and political parties might alleviate the sense that equity has been trashed by special interests, it would be impossible for democratic procedures to work in our kind of society without something like them. We need these groups to link the people and governmental structures unless we want to try direct democracy (and the people do not).[58]

The ideological saturation of the *liberal* label in this project can be viewed (in part) in table 6.3. Consider the quantitative trends in speeches, particularly how this label has increased over the years and has been increasingly used by Republican candidates. This second trend is highlighted in bold. Whereas Democrats use the term *liberal* in the 1948, 1952, and 1956 campaigns (and Republicans do not), Republicans use it in the 1980–1996 campaigns (with Bill Clinton using it only three times in 1992—instances that are discussed in the following paragraphs). Not surprisingly, the word has changed as a result.

Both Aldai Stevenson and Bill Clinton use the term three times in the samples gathered here. It is illustrative to attend to the differences between their usages. Take Stevenson. In his comments, as follows, he associates the word with youth and creativity in his first speech; with forward-thinking Republicans in his second speech; and with an everlasting battle against ignorance, poverty, misery, and war in the third:

> Bob Meyner is typical of the new leadership in the Democratic Party: young, *liberal*, creative. It's the kind of leadership that is going to carry the Democratic Party to victory in November.[59]

> In the early part of this century men came to think for the first time about preserving our great natural inheritance. They began to think more and more of keeping our land and our streams and our forests for our children and their children's children, and the leadership in this movement came from two *liberal* Republicans, Theodore Roosevelt and Gilford Pinchot.[60]

> Now I bid you goodnight, with a full heart and a fervent prayer that we will meet often again in the *liberals'* everlasting battle against ignorance, poverty, misery and war.[61]

Table 6.3. The *Liberal* and *Conservative* Labels Over Time in Speeches, News, and Feeling Thermometer Ratings

	Liberal						Conservative					
	Speeches			News			Speeches			News		
	n	Dem	GOP	n	ratio	Feeling therm.[b]	n	Dem	GOP	n	ratio	Feeling therm.
1948	2	2	0	171	.046		2	1	0	18	.005	
1952	1	1	0	33	.008		1	1	0	16	.004	
1956	3	3	0	41	.010		0	0	0	25	.006	
1960	1	1	0	76	.023		8	8	0	66	.020	
1964	6	1	5	89	.024	53	4	2	2	164	.044	57
1968	0	0	0	73	.023	51	1	1	0	68	.021	57
1972	0	0	0	83	.020	54	5	4	1	87	.021	61
1976	5	5	0	161	.039	52	5	5	0	165	.039	59
1980	1	0	1	164	.044	52	10	10	0	134	.036	62
1984	7	0	7	88	.022	56	0	0	0	163	.041	60
1988	15	0	15	366	.070	52	2	0	2	238	.046	61
1992	13	3	10	77	.015	51	5	5	0	153	.030	56
1996	86	0	86[a]	257	.051	52	28	9	19	185	.036	60
2000	0	0	0	176	.026	54	10	1	9	292	.043	59

Note: For the terms *liberal* and *conservative* in speeches, the second and third columns (Dem, GOP) display the raw counts of the liberal and conservative labels as used by Democratic and Republican candidates. For news coverage, the ratios correspond to labels / total words in news × 100.

[a]A ratio was not conducted for speeches, because until 1996, these terms were used sparingly. It is important to note that the Campaign Mapping Project features a larger sample of texts for 1996 than for the other years under examination.

[b]The data for the feeling thermometer column comes from the National Election Studies (1948–2000), www.umich.edu/~nes.

Now, compare those usages of the term—particularly the third—to how Clinton used the word in 1992. In that year, he used the term twice in his acceptance speech at the Democratic National Convention; but even when speaking to the party faithful, he did not use it in a glamorous way. Instead, he used it as a marker of false division. In the first example, Clinton's ideas are framed as neither conservative or liberal; in the second, he argues that the country should go beyond its demographics (with *liberal* being associated with such downtrodden groups as minorities, the poor, the homeless, and gays):

The choice we offer is not conservative or *liberal*; in many ways it's not even Republican or Democratic. It's different. It's new. And it will work.[62]

And so we must say to every American: Look beyond the stereotypes that blind us. We need each other. All of us, we need each other. We don't have a person to waste. And yet for too long politicians have told the most of us that are doing all right that what's really wrong with America is the rest of us. Them. Them, the minorities. Them, the *liberals*. Them, the poor. Them, the homeless. Them, the people with disabilities. Them, the gays. We've gotten to where we've nearly themed ourselves to death. Them and them and them. But this is America. There is no them; there's only us. One nation, under God, indivisible, with liberty, and justice, for all. That is our Pledge of Allegiance, and that's what the New Covenant is all about.[63]

Clinton's third use of the term, as follows, resembles a phrase from his convention speech. Again, he notes that his ideas are neither conservative nor liberal but both. It becomes clear that Clinton's theme of the "New Democrat" does not involve resuscitating the term that Stevenson heralded:

This is not a conservative or a *liberal* idea. It's both. It's different. And the people who have lived with the present system know it will work if we invest what we ought to.[64]

Compare these positive and distanced usages of the term by Democrats to the downright aggressive ways in which Republicans began to douse it with notions of moral weakness and excess in the 1980s and 1990s. An example of the first trend appears in the following statement by Bob Dole, where he questions the moral implications of "*liberal* wink-and-nod policies." Notice how he implies that liberals are responsible for opening up the drug pipeline, making narcotics available to teenagers (whose use of drugs, Dole advises, is "skyrocketing"), and working against the good of the polity.

In this instance, President Clinton is not fighting evil forces but contributing to the moral decay of youth:

> From 1979 to 1992, overall drug use in America dropped 50 percent—50 percent. But President Clinton has opened the crime pipeline up again. And thanks to the *liberal* wink-and-nod policies of this administration, drug use among teenagers has not just started up again; it's skyrocketing upward as former drug czar Bill Bennett can confirm.... The fact is that the country is reaping the bitter harvest of what this administration's liberal policies have sowed.[65]

Republicans also associate liberals with elitism and excess—with caring more about ideas and government than about their constituents. In arguing that limited government is good for the United States, Republicans often portray liberals as being policy happy, interested in developing expensive, unnecessary programs that would increase taxes. The recurrent theme, of course, is that the country should not approve of these extraneous policies advocated by liberals. George H. W. Bush uses this approach in the following passage, associating liberals with a desire to introduce needless change and then—in a clever turn of a phrase—associating this change with the spending habits of liberals:

> He talks about change, change, change. The last time we got that kind of change we had interest rates at 21 percent; we had inflation at 15 percent; we wiped out every family budget. We do not need a *liberal* Democrat in the White House with this spendthrift Congress we got. He talks about change. He talks about change. That's all you'll have left in your pocket if his program goes in, believe me.[66]

Bob Dole, too, accuses liberals of liking policies over ordinary people, and for his part he positions *liberals* and their excessive needs as being out of step with average Americans. But that is not all. Notice how, in the following example, he positions the indulgent liberal (and the indulgent liberal's "constituencies" and "interest groups") far away from "our families," "needs," and "parents," suggesting that liberal alternatives and liberal big government have enslaved America's Moms and Dads:

> So when it comes to a choice between the needs of our families and the needs of his *liberal* constituencies demanding ever and ever and more expensive government, Bill Clinton does what he always does. He takes care of the *liberal* special interest groups, the *liberal* alternatives, more taxes

and more government. But we come at it from a different direction. We want to reduce the middle class family's tax bill so the parents will no longer be wage slaves to *liberal* big government.[67]

In these examples H. W. Bush and Dole tie liberals to entities that Americans find distasteful—most notably weakness, elitist concerns, and extremism. In many ways, liberals are framed as being too ideological to relate to the common-sense needs of "Americans," too excessive to consider straightforward solutions to existing problems.[68] But Republicans are not simply satisfied with drenching the term with negative associations; sometimes, they simply repeat it for effect. Because they had made the term so distasteful by the beginning of the 1996 campaign, the term *liberal* became an efficient devil-like term for them. Consider how Bob Dole uses *liberal* as a term of opprobrium without amplification, as he does in this speech in Macon, Georgia:

> This is the real candidate Clinton, not the candidate who's out there now talking like a conservative. Keep this in mind. He's never changed. He's a *liberal*. He's a *liberal*. He's a *liberal*. Don't let him forget it. And with your help, and God willing, we're going to make it on November 5. Thank you.[69]

As table 6.3 shows, Dole's treatment of the word *liberal* in 1996 made news, perhaps because he used it with such regularity. A close read of the instances of *liberal* in the news shows that a majority of such appearances relates to Dole's disparagement of the word. Fewer articles focus on how Clinton can bounce back from Dole's charges—but even these mentions appear in the frame that *liberals* are morally compromised and excessive. While it is unscientific to generalize from these instances to all news coverage, the trend is nonetheless suggestive: Republicans managed the meaning of *liberal* in 1996, and it appears that the media were complicit in reproducing these managings for the masses. That they were so becomes more compelling when we recall that Republicans have been the only ones using the term since 1980 (save the three Clinton examples cited here).

Intriguingly, George W. Bush broke away from this pattern in 2000, possibly to follow the "uniter not a divider" theme, or maybe to follow the linguistic strategies of Frank Luntz in the year 2000. At the time, Luntz suggested that Republicans should use softer approaches, respect citizens' aversion to the acerbic rhetoric of former Speaker of the House Newt Gingrich, avoid calling attention to their frustration borne of an overzealous tone in the impeachment of President Clinton (in which Clinton's public opinion actually increased, perhaps as a boomerang to partisan efforts on the Right), and be in step with the general prosperity that the country was enjoying. Specifically, Luntz advised critiquing opponents through open-ended rhetorical questions ("Can you name one single thing that Hillary Clinton has ever done for New York?") and admonished Republican candidates to remember that "calling your opponent a *liberal* is over, too, although you may call him a politician, or, better yet, a Washington politician."[70] Bush held off employing the *liberal* label in 2000, but as the 2004 campaign became tight in September and October against Massachusetts senator John Kerry, Bush returned to the term that his father had used to mar another candidate from Massachusetts. As the debate transcript that begins this chapter shows, W. Bush, too, cast his opponent with the brush of excess and ideology—he called him the *L* word.

To sum, table 6.3 shows that not only have the media been complicit in Republican efforts to make *liberal* a pejorative word but the Democrats have failed to defend it. This finding would strike Michael Pfau and Henry Kenski as being strategically unwise, since, as they contend, the golden rule in attack politics is "Once attacked—attack back."[71] Allowing accusations to go unanswered in a campaign is, in their eyes, the equivalent of admitting that said accusations are true. And, as the table shows, the Democrats have let such charges go for over twenty years—significant years, too, for they represent the growth of the Republican information infrastructure as detailed in chapter 1. Even though discourse from talk radio, Republican websites, and nonfiction books are not analyzed here, it stands to reason that the present patterns, or more polarized ones, appear there as well.

Scholars and activists have considered a set of tactics to rally around *liberal* and "bring back the word." One type of resuscitation effort includes reframing the label and then flooding the political system with these new usages. In her history of campaign advertising, Kathleen Hall Jamieson provides advice regarding how Barry Goldwater—the ideological Republican candidate in 1964 who frightened voters with the phrase "Extremism in the defense of liberty is no vice"—could have softened his image with voters. She writes,

> To define himself as the sort of "extremist" we might tolerate in the White House, Goldwater needed first to redefine the meaning of the word, then lodge that new meaning deep in our vocabulary by illustrating it in ways we would welcome. "If it is extreme to stand for a solvent Social Security System," he might have said, "if it is extreme to maintain

Eisenhower's policy of permitting the NATO commander to control the use of low-yield nuclear weapons, if it is extreme to demand that a U.S. Senator spurn expensive gifts from the Bobby Bakers of the world, then Eisenhower was an extremist, most Americans are extremists, and I am an extremist." Instead, Goldwater permitted us to read our own pejorative definition into the word "extremism" and to hear him endorse something we abhorred in the name of defense of liberty.[72]

Similar efforts have been discussed by linguist George Lakoff. To reframe the word *liberal*, Lakoff instructs Democrats to be mindful of three truths: that all ideas need supporting ideas, that framing takes time (and that the Right has been working on establishing its frames for the past thirty years), and that framing efforts should be proactive.[73]

Yet another approach for liberal-leaning candidates and citizens would be to encourage surrogates (individuals not running for office in a given campaign) to stand with the label. Such actions would not necessarily be foolhardy. Many public intellectuals seem to think that the future is open for the Left. E. J. Dionne, for one, contends that the Left enjoys an opportunity that did not exist during the Cold War, for many domestic issues (education, health care, and Social Security) fixture more prominently on the public agenda than they have in the recent past.[74]

Dionne couples these political concerns with symbolic strategies in his 2004 book *Stand Up, Fight Back: Republican Toughs, Democratic Wimps, and the Politics of Revenge*.[75] There he advances a list of ten arguments that Democrats need to stop having with each other and an equal set of arguments that they need to start making. The "right stuff," in his mind, includes questions such as "Whose side is government on?" to break Democrats out of the Republican frames of "big government vs. small government" and "pro-business vs. anti-business." Dionne details data showing support for traditionally "liberal" programs and ideas and contends that "the party that once galvanized a nation by saying that we have nothing to fear but fear itself" has itself become afraid. For the Left to reframe and take back its language, Dionne advises its members to engage in approaches that have served the Right well: invest in think tanks, media outlets, and pundits favorable to the Left's agenda, as well as allocate more resources to message reframing.

Robert Reich, secretary of labor under the Clinton administration, has advanced a similar case.[76] For his part, though, he encourages liberals to fight to redefine the subject (rather than try to change it). Reich contends that Republicans have too long battered Democrats with moral issues (e.g., sex outside of marriage, abortion, children out of wedlock, divorce and gay rights) and advises, "Liberals should be screaming from the rooftops about the real decline of public morality, about the real abuses: fraudulent accounting and stock manipulation, insider trading, tax evasion, exorbitant pay of top executives, financial conflicts of interest, bribery of public officials." Like others who have written on this subject, he maintains that the Left needs to attend to its message, work to fund an information infrastructure that counters that on the Right, and build a "ground troops" of "grassroots moral activism." A key contribution of his book for the current purposes, though, is his inclusion of an appendix featuring polling data that support his contention that citizens are politically sympathetic to traditionally liberal causes, just not when the *liberal* label is affixed to such policies. Thus, efforts by a liberal advocate to champion the term could conceivably be successful.

Table 6.3 also presents the frequency data of the term *conservative* in the campaign speeches and news reports in the Campaign Mapping Project as well as the feeling thermometer ratings for this term. The uses of the *conservative* label serve as a stark contrast to the uses of *liberal*. Table 6.3 shows that while several Republican candidates in this project have worked to sully the *liberal* label, Democratic candidates have not responded by increasing their use of the *conservative* label. There has been a gradual increase in the use of *conservative* in press reports, but this increase has not been met with the sharpening found in the word *liberal*. Chi-square analyses between these words reveal significant differences between them on the two key evaluative variables: *role* and *context*. Not surprisingly, the output in both instances favors the *conservative* label.[77] Consider these patterns. The *liberal* label is more likely to be "part of the problem" (36.7 percent) than "part of the solution" (12.9 percent) in campaign conversations; these patterns are the opposite for the *conservative* term (which is portrayed as being "part of the solution" 30.3 percent of the time and "part of the problem" 14.4 percent of the time— variable: *role*). Similarly, the *liberal* label is placed in a negative condition 38.3 percent of the time and a positive condition 8.9 percent of the time; once again, the patterns are switched for the *conservative* label, which is placed in a negative condition 21.2 percent of the time and a positive situation 18.3 percent of the time (variable: *context*).

Conservative appeared on the national conversation in the 2000 campaign when George W. Bush coupled the term with *compassion*. Notice how Bush introduces his campaign theme in his acceptance address to the Republican National Convention: "But the alternative to bureaucracy is not indifference. It is to put *conservative* values and *conservative* ideas into the thick of the fight for justice and opportunity. This is what I mean by *compassion-*

ate conservatism. And on this ground we will govern our nation."[78] A month later, he linked his *compassionate conservative* mantra more directly to citizens: "For over a year, we have been applying creative, *conservative* ideas to the job of helping real people. That is the meaning of *compassionate conservatism*. That is the message of my campaign. That is a cause worth waging, and a cause we will win together."[79]

For his part, Al Gore did not challenge W. Bush's campaign theme. As table 6.3 shows, he only uses the word once in the Campaign Mapping Project textbase, and in that instance he does not even allude to his opponent's optimistic construction. As seen in the following passage, Gore's use of the term has less to do with the GOP's campaign 2000 adornments than with traditional notions of economic responsibility:

> And over the last eight years, we have seen the benefits of doing two things simultaneously. Number one, balancing the budget, not because that's, you know, some *conservative* symbol, but because when you demonstrate that we can get our act together, then the marketplace, the investors, the world market, they start having a lot of respect for our ability to get our act together, and that keeps our interest rates low, and that in itself gets more money in circulation in our economy.[80]

Although *compassionate conservative* is a recent arrival on the semantic campaign terrain, there has yet to be an organized, systematic political campaign to challenge it (at least in the texts from the Campaign Mapping Project textbase). It is important to note that, should groups desire to reposition this term, they will face something of an uphill battle, especially given the cultural attractiveness of the term *conservative* in the United States and its relative attractiveness to the term *liberal* (a term that resides in the country's mind as the evil twin of *conservatism*). Repositioning Bush's brand of *conservatism*, however, might be an easier place to start. Should other candidates in the future adopt his mantra, Democrats might launch efforts that parallel the moves Republicans have made on the term *liberal*: linking the word to negative terms and repeating it with abandon. That is, if Democrats want to move the brand of *compassionate conservatism*, they have to take a more aggressive approach than that of the reference to "*conservative* symbol[s]" in Gore's comments or the question of "*Compassionate conservative*, what does that mean?" which appears in John Kerry's debate statement at the opening of this chapter; to really move the brand, they would have to engage in the types of symbolic assaults that the Republicans in this sample have waged on the *L* word.

CONCLUSION

No one in power ever wants to lose it. Perhaps it is not surprising, then, that the elites in this study paint an establishmentarian picture of politics, protecting the *party*, *Democratic*, and *Republican* labels; praising the populist spirit of the *independent* label; and ridiculing the ideology attached to *liberals*. In a sense, by describing political parties, elites also describe themselves: they like the structure that empowers them; they are sympathetic to populism; they find extreme ideology distasteful. This chapter, then, produces two sets of findings: an understanding of party politics as well as one of the American system writ large.

As vivid as the decline of the word *liberal* has been, the penchant for discussing the two-party system (*Democrats* and *Republicans*) and the challengers to the system (*independents*) in different ways seems to be the real contribution of this chapter. Interestingly, these patterns fit with Edelman's observation of what is and is not off-limits in politics. He writes,

> Whenever a political issues threatens to produce conflict or an impasse or a result unacceptable to elites, some will define and perceive it as inappropriate to politics: as calling for specialized expertise rather than political negotiation and compromise. There is always a good deal of receptivity throughout the population to this way of defining a difficult issue, for it allows people who are worried but baffled by a problem to believe that those who know best will deal with it.[81]

Time, of course, will change the meanings described here and, consequently, the understandings that citizens will develop about parties. What will those trajectories be? It is uncertain if the *independent* label will continue to receive such praise, particularly should independent candidates become successful in attaining office, influencing policy, or drawing a considerable amount of the vote from the two major parties. If independents gain increased momentum, members of the two-party system may well reassert their dominance by either (1) referring to independent candidates as "third-party" candidates (as journalists began to do after Ross Perot's popularity surpassed that of Bill Clinton and George Bush in the 1992 campaign), or (2) simply ignoring them (as Jimmy Carter and Ronald Reagan did John Anderson's candidacy in 1980). Indeed, both of these strategies appear in the rhetoric of Era II, 1961–1980, the time that featured the highest number of *independent* labels in this study.

The future of the *liberal* label is also uncertain. If Democrats organize and find someone to serve as an advocate for this term, it might become a popular referent for the politics that millions of Americans already support. If the economy were to decline, for example, the chances for restoring the label might well increase. While the meanings of *independent* and *liberal* may change, substantial modification in the *Democratic* and *Republican* labels is unlikely (at least as long as elite voices help to guide the talk of the party in the United States). Some adaptations may occur, but I expect that they will continue to be protected by a structurally protective system. Too many careers, at this point, depend on it.

NOTES

1. Roderick P. Hart et al., *Political Keywords: Using Language That Uses Us* (New York: Oxford, 2005).

2. I conducted chi-square analyses on nine variables of interest. The results of the tests are as follows: *role*, $\chi^2(3) = 36.39$, $p = .000$; *position*, $\chi^2(2) = 24.56$, $p = .000$; *goals*, $\chi^2(3) = 11.13$, $p = .011$; *context*, $\chi^2(4) = 10.41$, $p = .034$; *behavior*, $\chi^2(3) = 6.70$, $p = .082$; *time*, $\chi^2(2) = 4.40$, $p = .111$; *potency*, $\chi^2(3) = 4.73$, $p = .193$; *quality*, $\chi^2(4) = 4.29$, $p = .368$; *associations*, $\chi^2(10) = 9.64$, $p = .473$.

3. "Sparkman Rips McCarthyism," Associated Press–United Press International wire, 10 September 1952, 19A.

4. "Humphrey Has 70-30 Margin over Miller," *Washington Post*, 5 September 1964, 2A.

5. "U.S. Electorate Deeply Divided," *Chicago Tribune*, 5 November 1968, 1A.

6. "Voter Turnout of 60% to 78% Expected in Area," *Washington Post,* 4 November 1980, 1A.

7. "Clash May Point Way for Campaign's Final Weeks; Republican Relies on Negativism, Democrat Parties and Independent Is Clearly Outsider," *Washington Post*, 14 October 1992, 1 A.

8. "Gov. Stevenson Eases into Role of Aggressor; Takes Each Issue as Personal Challenge," *Chicago Tribune*, 8 September 1952, 5A.

9. "Sparkman Charges GOP Uses Fear Philosophy; Old Thinking Men Have No Vision of Their Country's Future," United Press International wire, 19 October 1952.

10. "Reagan, Anderson to Aim at Each Other in Debate, Not Carter," *Los Angeles Times*, 21 September 1980, 4A.

11. "GOP Seeks Shift in Party Loyalty in Election Today," *New York Times*, 6 November, 1984, 1A.

12. Harry Truman, "Campaign Speech," St. Louis, Mo. (30 October 1948), Annenberg/Pew Archive of Presidential Discourse, CD-ROM (Philadelphia: Annenberg School for Communication, University of Pennsylvania, 2000).

13. Hubert Humphrey, "Campaign Speech," San Antonio, Tex. (23 October 1968), Annenberg/Pew Archive of Presidential Discourse, CD-ROM (Philadelphia: Annenberg School for Communication, University of Pennsylvania, 2000).

14. George McGovern, "Campaign Speech," Alameda County, Calif. (4 September 1972), Annenberg/Pew Archive of Presidential Discourse, CD-ROM (Philadelphia: Annenberg School for Communication, University of Pennsylvania, 2000).

15. George McGovern, "Campaign Speech," St. Louis, Mo. (7 October 1972), Annenberg/Pew Archive of Presidential Discourse, CD-ROM (Philadelphia: Annenberg School for Communication, University of Pennsylvania, 2000).

16. Al Gore, "Campaign Address," Chicago (4 September 2000), Campaign Mapping Project database, University of Texas at Austin.

17. "Truman Ridicules Eisenhower Plans; President Charges General Takes Superman Pose on Korea Proposals," Associated Press–United Press International wire, 10 October 1952.

18. "Reagan's Age Muddles His Thinking; Anderson," *Chicago Tribune*, 16 September 1980, 6A.

19. "Clinton Having Success in Neutralizing 'Values' Issue," *Los Angeles Times*, 8 September 1992, 1A.

20. "Nominee Raps Tactics; Lauds Maryland Slate," *Washington Post*, 21 September 1956, 1A.

21. "Ford Not Inspiring, Carter Tells Crowd," *Atlanta Journal-Constitution*, 5 November 1976, 1A.

22. John F. Kennedy, "Speech," Buffalo, N.Y. (28 September 1960), Annenberg/Pew Archive of Presidential Discourse, CD-ROM (Philadelphia: Annenberg School for Communication, University of Pennsylvania, 2000).

23. George McGovern, "Campaign Speech," Alameda County, Calif. (4 September 1972), Annenberg/Pew Archive of Presidential Discourse, CD-ROM (Philadelphia: Annenberg School for Communication, University of Pennsylvania, 2000).

24. House of Representatives, Representative Robert Matsui of California, 104th Cong., 1st sess., *Congressional Record* 141 (21 March 1995): 3352–98.

25. House of Representatives, Representative Benjamin Cardin of Maryland, 104th Cong., 1st sess., *Congressional Record* 141 (21 March 1995): 3352–98.

26. Gerald Pomper, "Comments by Practitioners and Scholars," in *The Politics of Ideas: Intellectual Challenges to the Party after 1992,* ed. John Kenneth White and John Clifford Green (Lanham, Md.: Rowman & Littlefield, 1995), 101–2.

27. Alan Ehrenhalt, *The United States of Ambition* (New York: Time Books, 1992).

28. Ehrenhalt, *United States of Ambition*, 224.

29. Walter Dean Burnham, *Critical Elections and the Mainsprings of Politics* (New York: Harper, 1970), 183.

30. Roderick P. Hart, *Modern Rhetorical Criticism* (New York: Harper Collins, 1990), 183.

31. Murray Edelman, *Political Language: Words That Succeed and Policies That Fail* (New York: Academic Press, 1977), 3.

32. See John Zaller, "The Rise and Fall of Candidate Perot: Unmediated Versus Mediated Politics (Part I)," *Political Communication* 11, no. 4 (1994): 357–91; John Zaller, "The Rise and Fall of Candidate Perot: The Outsider Versus the Political System (Part II)," *Political Communication* 12, no. 1 (1995): 97–124.

33. Henry C. Kenski et al., "Perot: Media Framing," paper presented to the Speech Communication Association, New Orleans, La. (November 1994).

34. Steven Rosenstone, Roy Behr, and Edward Lazarus, *Third Parties in America: Citizen Response to Major Party Failure* (Princeton, N.J.: Princeton University Press, 1984), 46–47.

35. Bruce E. Keith et al., *The Myth of the Independent Voter* (Berkeley: University of California Press, 1992).

36. Angus Campbell et al., *The American Voter* (New York: Wiley, 1960), 143.

37. See Howard S. Ehrlich, "Populist Rhetoric Reassessed: A Paradox," *Quarterly Journal of Speech* 63 (1977): 143–51.

38. Gary Woodward, "Reagan as Roosevelt: The Elasticity of Pseduo-Populist Appeals," *Central States Speech Journal* 34 (1983): 44–58.

39. See Campbell et al., *American Voter*.

40. John K. White, "Reviving the Parties: What Must be Done?" in *The Politics of Ideas: Intellectual Challenges to the Party after 1992*, ed. John Kenneth White and John Clifford Green (Lanham, Md.: Rowman & Littlefield, 1995), 4–27, 13–14.

41. R. Matus, "Vote for Perot: He Addresses Issues," *Salinas Californian*, 10 October 1992, 6A.

42. H. Stevens, "Perot Vote Necessary," *Fall River Herald News*, 26 October 1992, 4A.

43. "Polls Show Shifts Aiding Reagan," *New York Times*, 1 October 1980, 1A.

44. "Both Sides Woo Reagan Democrats," *Atlanta Journal-Constitution*, 19 September 1988, 1A.

45. "Clinton Regains Huge Lead, New Poll Reveals," *Chicago Tribune*, 1 September 1992, 4A.

46. "Parties Reign, in Independent Age Voters Increasingly Register 'Independent,' but Two Parties Buoyed by Money and Fired Up Voters," *Christian Science Monitor*, 1 August 2000, 1A.

47. "Parties Reign."

48. "Lieberman Castigates GOP; Gore's Appearance with Daughter Provides an Emotional Spark," *Chicago Tribune*, 17 August 2000, 1A.

49. Richard Hofstadter, *The Age of Reform* (New York: Vintage Books, 1955).

50. V. Lance Tarrance, Walter DeVries, and Donna L. Mosher, *Checked and Balanced: How Ticket Splitters Are Shaping the New Balance of Power in American Politics* (Grand Rapids, Mich.: Wm. B. Eerdmans, 1998).

51. Burnham, *Critical Elections*, 181.

52. Burnham, *Critical Elections*, 189.

53. Haij Bosmajian, *The Language of Oppression* (Lanham, Md.: University Press of America, 1983), 9.

54. Raymond Williams, *Keywords: A Vocabulary of Culture and Society* (New York: Oxford, 1976), 181.

55. E. J. Dionne, *Why Americans Hate Politics* (New York: Simon & Schuster, 1991).

56. Morris Fiorina, *Divided Government* (New York: Macmillan, 1992), 74.

57. Morris Fiorina, "What Culture Wars?" *Wall Street Journal,* 14 July 2004, 14A.

58. John R. Hibbing and Elizabeth Theiss-Morse, *Congress as Public Enemy* (Cambridge: Cambridge University Press, 1995), 18.

59. Aldai Stevenson, "Campaign Speech," Palisades Park, N.J. (9 September 1956), Annenberg/Pew Archive of Presidential Discourse, CD-ROM (Philadelphia: Annenberg School for Communication, University of Pennsylvania, 2000).

60. Aldai Stevenson, "Campaign Speech," Elkins, W.V. (4 October 1956), Annenberg/Pew Archive of Presidential Discourse, CD-ROM (Philadelphia: Annenberg School for Communication, University of Pennsylvania, 2000).

61. Aldai Stevenson, "Concession Statement" (6 November 1956), Annenberg/Pew Archive of Presidential Discourse, CD-ROM (Philadelphia: Annenberg School for Communication, University of Pennsylvania, 2000).

62. Bill Clinton, "Acceptance Speech," Democratic National Convention, New York City, N.Y. (16 July 1992), Annenberg/Pew Archive of Presidential Discourse, CD-ROM (Philadelphia: Annenberg School for Communication, University of Pennsylvania, 2000).

63. Clinton, "Acceptance Speech."

64. Bill Clinton, "Welfare Reform Speech: A Second Chance," delivered to the Clayton County Office of Family and Children's Services, Jonesboro, Ga. (9 September 1992), Annenberg/Pew Archive of Presidential Discourse, CD-ROM (Philadelphia: Annenberg School for Communication, University of Pennsylvania, 2000).

65. Robert Dole, "Campaign Speech," Villanova University (16 September 1996), Annenberg/Pew Archive of Presidential Discourse, CD-ROM (Philadelphia: Annenberg School for Communication, University of Pennsylvania, 2000).

66. George H. W. Bush, "Remarks to the Community," Gastonia, N.C. (21 October 1992), Annenberg/Pew Archive of Presidential Discourse, CD-ROM (Philadelphia: Annenberg School for Communication, University of Pennsylvania, 2000).

67. Robert Dole, "Remarks," Elizabethtown College (2 October 1996), Annenberg/Pew Archive of Presidential Discourse, CD-ROM (Philadelphia: Annenberg School for Communication, University of Pennsylvania, 2000).

68. Dionne, *Why Americans Hate Politics.*

69. Robert Dole, "Campaign Address," Macon, Ga. (23 October 1996), Annenberg/Pew Archive of Presidential Discourse, CD-ROM (Philadelphia: Annenberg School for Communication, University of Pensylvania, 2000).

70. Nicholas Lemann, "The Word Lab: The Mad Scientist behind What the Candidates Say," *New Yorker,* 16 October 2000, 100.

71. Michael Pfau and Hank Kenski, *Attack Politics: Strategy and Defense* (New York: Praeger, 1990).

72. Kathleen Hall Jamieson, *Packaging the Presidency*, 2nd ed. (Oxford: Oxford University Press, 1992), 183.

73. George Lakoff's advice on taking a word back, in "Interview with George Lakoff" posted 15 January 2004, *Alternet.org*, www.alternet.org/story/17574.

74. E. J. Dionne, "Need a Map? The Left," *Washington Post*, 31 October 1999, 16A.

75. E. J. Dionne, *Stand Up, Fight Back: Republican Toughs, Democratic Wimps, and the Politics of Revenge* (New York: Simon and Schuster, 2004).

76. Robert Reich, *Why Liberals Win Will the Battle for America* (New York: Knopf, 2004).

77. *Role*, $\chi^2(3)$ = 36.26, p = .000; *context*, $\chi^2(4)$ = 26.45, p = .000.

78. George W. Bush, "Republican National Convention Acceptance Speech," Philadelphia, Pa. (3 August 2000), Campaign Mapping Project database, University of Texas at Austin.

79. George W. Bush, "Speech to California Republican Party Convention via Satellite," Austin, Tex. (16 September 2000), Campaign Mapping Project database, University of Texas at Austin.

80. Al Gore, "Speech to Howard University," Washington, D.C. (15 September 2000), Campaign Mapping Project database, University of Texas at Austin.

81. Edelman, *Political Language*, 136–37.

7

BRAND DOMINANCE:
CONSISTENCY PREVAILS

> Political parties created democracy, and . . . democracy is un-
> thinkable save in terms of parties.
>
> —E. E. Schattschneider, *Party Government*[1]

One wonders if political scientist E. E. Schattschneider had any idea that this sentence would become one of the most cited phrases in political party research. Indeed, these thirteen words appear in thousands of books, articles, chapters, conference papers, doctoral dissertations, master's theses, term papers, and even class syllabi on the topic of political parties. So widely quoted is the phrase that one might be tempted to ask what it is about it that demands repetition. Several initial responses, of course, are possible. This sentence is direct. This sentence is dramatic. This sentence appears in a seminal work. This sentence serves as a type of historical artifact in political science, possessing a sense of ecological validity in 1942, when initially written, that it may never have again (or at least in the same way) in American politics. All of these answers may be at least partially true, and yet all of them only partly account for a truly intriguing aspect of this heavily quoted line: that it appears in works that argue for as well as against the "strong parties thesis." Conduct a search on these words and you will notice that scholars have quoted this phrase to set up studies that claim that parties are powerful, to serve as a straw man in projects that question the strength of parties, and even to be postulated as a hypothesis in works that show uncertain support for party strength.

Although political scientists have long attended to this sentence for its relationship to the political capital of parties, the job of this book is to uncover another type of worth: the symbolic capital of party labels. Thus, this

book is most interested in how phrases such as this one affect our understandings of, if, and how parties can get work done in the polity. And so,
Schattschneider's thirteen words have special meaning here. Whether one
looks to academics such as Kenneth Burke (who has argued that individuals are constrained in thought by the words available to them in discourse)
or lay theorists such as Reggie Jackson (whose keen awareness of "the
power of attention" opens this book) to make sense of the fascination with
Schattschneider's sentiment, the outcome is the same: this phrase, repeated
as it is, cements the power of parties—symbolically, at least—in the imagi-
nation of the very academic community directly responsible for guiding our
understanding of these institutions. It does so deftly, though. And therein lies
its power.

The primary goal of this book is to make sense of what party labels
have come to mean in 2004 by tracing how different sets of voices have discussed them in the past. Key assumptions are that most Americans come to
know politics through language, that label meanings are largely managed by
political elites, that labels serve as efficient and powerful shortcuts in modern life, and that patterns of label stability and change are often quite subtle. This said, a main contribution of this book can be phrased quite simply:
the party system has underestimated symbolic capital in the United States
because most of the time American discourse does not allow us to think
outside of it. While citizens, elected officials, journalists, and scholars alike
have been passionately ambivalent about parties for the past two hundred
years, few have taken a step back from these activities to analyze the contours, motivations, and effects of the discourse this sentiment produces. Intriguingly, as citizens wring their hands over them and as researchers continue to conduct a "deathwatch" over them, an overriding matter of
practical significance is elided. The very fact that scholars and citizens continue to critique parties suggests that many have been captivated by them,
and the very practice of comparing today's institution to yesterday's is an act
of submission, symbolically at least, to this construct.

THE TALK OF THE PARTY

Language is big business at the dawn of the twenty-first century. In the year
that this book is written, branding is omnipresent, and terms such as *brand
management* and *brand warfare* are almost clichés. Given the number of messages in play in an information age, corporations are acknowledging the
need to manage their labels as best that any entity can in the cluttered mes-

sage environment. As such, companies are spending billions of dollars hiring public relations firms to concoct new message properties and compelling placement strategies for their brands. But this is not all. Even organizations that one might imagine to be "above" branding have gotten into the act. Examples here include the *New York Times* and its conducting self-studies to assess how one journalist's indiscretions affected its brand as the "newspaper of record," governmental agencies and their hiring marketing professionals to oversee their "branding" practices, and special interest groups with their working to get celebrities (such as actresses Julia Roberts and Meryl Streep and puppet Kermit the Frog) to testify before Congress to attract a positive visual brand in the minds of the public. The ubiquity of branding, however, should not imply that it is an easy process nor that products or groups who reluctantly engage in it are viewed with any sympathy. In today's overcommunicated society, unrefined messages (such as advertisements with low production values or websites with modest technological enhancements) are viewed alongside sophisticated and artful branding techniques; it is less common for individuals to applaud unpolished brands for "getting into" the message marketplace than to wonder why a person or group is publicizing an unfinished message in the first place. This reality creates a problem for parties; as discussed in chapter 1, contemporary marketing practices have hailed a public that feels much more warmly about Clorox bleach than either the Democratic or Republican parties.

A key theme throughout this book is that labels and brands are discussed in a dynamic message environment that is littered with connotations of the past, of the present, and from the opposition. Brand associations and identification cannot be dictated from public relations or a political campaign, no matter how clever or well funded the tactics are. These are realities of an information age. This book has attempted to look back to look ahead, to begin to understand the strength of the parties in 2004 by navigating the symbolic strengths and strains evident in the ways in which four sets of elites have discussed them over a fifty-year period. And several strengths and strains have been located. The following paragraphs first detail these characteristics and then combine them to make sense of such patterns through the lens of branding practices.

For instance, chapter 3 presents a discussion of consistent meanings about party labels by addressing variables from this content analysis that did *not* appear to vary across genre, time, or label. The data reveal that elites used party labels continuously (having employed them throughout the past fifty years), hierarchically (using labels to describe partisans as being elites), and skeletally (focusing on loose party coalitions, thereby describing "thin" versus "thick" partisanship). In these ways, party labels have not been for-saken (as data sets ending in 1980 might suggest); have not had their priv-ileged positions challenged; and yet, surprisingly, have not been discussed in detailed ways. The third pattern here is notable, for en masse the lan-guage of partisanship has not been adorned in ways that would lead the bedrock terms—*party, Democrat, Republican*—to pick up or drop meanings in public life. These key words, then, have not been prepared for symbolic change in ways that the terms *independent* and *liberal* have been. The se-mantic security of the key terms rests in part in their not being modified excessively or saddled with symbolic opportunities or compromises. Such skeletal discussions help to explain their steadiness.

If skeletal treatments have contributed to the status quo and thus un-derscore symbolic might, then the second finding regarding consistent elite constructions may help to pinpoint one reason why citizens have become so frustrated with the party system, especially at a time when so many for-profit brands work to target citizens directly. In detailing how party labels, considered together, have largely been constituted as a group of elites, chap-ter 3 addresses one remarkable departure from this pattern: Ronald Reagan's efforts to name specific citizens in his speeches and connect them to party labels. That chapter describes how such efforts may have invited citizens to imagine themselves as being part of the party (or, for millions of voters, to feel at home in Reagan's party, or at least not to counterargue considering voting for Reagan's party had they voted for Democrats in the past). The chapter also notes how such efforts may have built good will or, in Kath-leen Hall Jamieson's words, inspired "affection preventing him from attack." While Reagan was the first to do this, George W. Bush displayed a similar penchant for linking citizens to party labels—although Reagan's efforts here are more notable if only that he was the first to do so.

Such invitations, tucked in a shower of elite messages, may be alluring for a set of reasons. First, such overtures, rare as they are in the macropat-terns in which parties are discussed, may be warmly received. Studies fo-cusing on attitudes about government reveal that a key source of citizen dis-appointment is that Americans feel "shut out" of the process by "Washington insiders, careerist politicians, and special interests who now seem to control the political system itself" and that, rather than feel "op-posed to government, citizens feel estranged from it."[2] Even if such citizens do not want to actually get involved in the bargaining, conflict, and com-promise central to government, they want to know that such opportunities exist. Language such as Reagan's, even modest rhetorical linkages between citizens and the parties, may symbolically close the gap between citizens and the party system (at least in the imaginations of those listening to such discussions).

Second, it is notable that this space is much more likely to be closed on the campaign trail than during a moment of governance. A goal of this project has been to trace how four sets of voices have discussed these labels, and a reason for having done so is that their meanings sit in the crosstalk of such conversations. That such activities take place on the campaign trail follows observations made by others that the campaign trail "opens up politics" and demands a type of rhetorical inclusion not heard when political elites are speaking in Washington, D.C.[3]

A lesson can be drawn from the popular participation inspired in the Reagan texts: in a democratic state, citizens like to be, and should be, "tapped." While chapter 3 shows that parties are largely constituted as elites, chapter 6 shows that portrayals of the *independent* label break from that trend. From a practical standpoint, this pattern makes sense simply because independents have not held the offices that members of the two major parties have held. But from a symbolic perspective—one that Ronald Reagan natively understood—reminding citizens that they, too, are part of a party may be a wise rhetorical strategy. While experienced politicians may find it beneath them to take a lesson from third-party challengers, it seems that discussing parties as being entities comprising both elites and citizens would be a savvy campaign tactic as well as a way to improve the democratic health of the polity by rhetorically reengaging the electorate.

Another trend in the data is that elites have constituted partisanship in at least four ways over the past fifty years and that these portrayals adhere closely to the political models relevant during those times. Indeed, between the years 1948 and 1960, parties are portrayed as being collectives (as the pluralist theorists might predict); between 1961 and 1979, they are described as moving into a liminal space (as critical realignment scholars might expect); and between 1980 and 1999 parties are associated with frenetic action and a splintered body politic (as contemporary understandings of party would presume). One intriguing aspect of the partisanship featured in Era III is that party labels are depicted via the marketing strategy of "nichers," a strategy that may have short-term benefits but negative long-term implications for the parties. When prominent Democrats and Republicans begin to approach politics in the same way as less-traditional politicians, or when they vacate their offices so that they can position themselves as running "outside the system" (e.g., Senator Bob Dole's leaving the Senate after thirty-five years on the Hill to run for president in 1996), voters may come to believe that "outsiderness" is as good, or better, than political experience.

While candidates may regard this strategy as being savvy in capturing the votes of specific groups (reflecting the particularistic sensibilities of the years 1980–1999), this strategy may function to erode the traditional party advantage in campaigns and fracture a public that is already struggling to find its commonalities.

This function may have also fed into patterns that appeared in campaign 2000 and questions that emerged surrounding the 2004 campaign. First, consider campaign 2000. As detailed in chapter 4, Al Gore's speeches appeared as an exaggerated version of the niche-marketing tactics of Era III, whereas George W. Bush's language hearkened back to an earlier, collective tone. Even though there were many complications facing Gore in that campaign (perhaps the largest of which were uncertainties as to how to run in the shadow of an impeached president Bill Clinton), it is intriguing that his niche-marketing approach featured the lowest number of party references of any candidate in this study. In a campaign in which Gore downplayed his connection to a charismatic president, he similarly did so with his party. As a result, voters may have felt forsaken on two counts: they were not encouraged to project their relationship with Clinton to Gore, nor were they primed to think of their psychological connection to the Democratic cause.

Members of the W. Bush team ran a completely different campaign in that year, when they had their candidate emphasize his ability to reach across the partisan aisle and build coalitions in Texas state government. In making this case, W. Bush emphasized his willingness to work with both "Democrats" and "Republicans," suggesting that many "Democrats" were for him "because he didn't disappoint." His return to party labels, particularly in such generous ways, primed a familiar and attractive sense of belonging (reminiscent of the pluralist tone in Era I) but did not emphasize the sharper, more partisan aspects of party labels (as was present in the pluralist Era I). His return to party labels and sense of collective may have benefited from the growing information infrastructure on the Right (which provided him an audience receptive to a the idea of a conservative collective); it may have served as cues to convince Republican elites that this relative newcomer to politics could honor the partisan powers and processes in place; and it may have reached out to Democratic voters who may have been disappointed with President Clinton's behaviors, may have been underwhelmed by Gore's candidacy, or may have simply been intrigued by the self-proclaimed "uniter not a divider" from Texas.

Political scholar Gerald Pomper has offered an insightful account of how party systems have changed over time, and he notes how when earlier systems mastered certain techniques (e.g., coalitional goals under party machines) they overlooked others (e.g., teaching the meaning of involvement and cultivating loyal followers).[4] In the current data, the focus on the monolithic party in Era I may have left individual citizens feeling ignored and, consequently, may well have spawned the splintered partisanship in Era III, which in turn ignored the collective. In campaign 2000, a sense of union was resuscitated by W. Bush and repeated in media reports, but events following that campaign leave many questioning whether Bush's "uniter not a divider" appeals can be believed. Such events include that of U.S. senator Jim Jeffords and his leaving the Republican Party in the spring of 2001 to protest against heavy-handed leadership, conflicts surrounding faith-based initiative programs and the second Gulf War (during W. Bush's first term), and discussions surrounding the president's support of a constitutional amendment to define marriage as being that "between a man and a woman." These developments may have made issues of partisanship more salient to citizens under this "uniter's" watch and as the country headed into the 2004 election.

In putting these four patterns in chapter 4 together, one wonders where labels will move in the future. Will they move forward to a more atomized meaning (following advances in communications technology, the niche-marketing tactics of Era III)? Will they gravitate back to a more collectivist meaning (following communal or preferred meanings in spite of new technologies)? In answering these questions, we may be safest to watch the language of elites. No one else's livelihood depends so directly on the continuance of political parties as do these actors.

The four sets of elites in this study have differing needs for political parties, and chapter 5 presents their idiosyncratic perspectives on partisanship. There we learn that legislators use party labels to sharpen partisanship and mobilize teamwork, that journalists use them in personalized and dramatic ways, that candidates prefer a careful and useful constitution of parties, and that textbook authors celebrate and inflate the meanings of party. In recent years, these four voices have intersected in interesting ways: first, candidates who did not emphasize party labels (e.g., Bill Clinton in 1992 and 1996, Al Gore in 2000) became newsworthy for journalists, who critiqued their "candidate-centered" strategies; and, second, in nine of the fourteen elections between 1948 and 2000, the party label mentioned most frequently in the news during the general election campaign lost on election day. Ostensibly, that is, it behooves candidates to attend to parties (and to avoid negative party-based news coverage) but not to fixate on such matters and thereby alienate the voters.

In essence, chapter 5 displays how the meanings of partisanship range from contested ones (found in debates and the media) to more supportive ones (appearing in speeches and textbooks). In wondering what effects, if any, these constitutions have on the polity, it would be interesting to see if one voice is most clearly responsible for the public's feelings about parties. That is, do we see a spiral of publicity in the United States such that citizens are encouraged to believe the negative meanings in the news? Or do we see a spiral of silence in that the positive meanings featured in campaign speeches and civics textbooks fail to command widespread attention? In other words, are citizens convinced to think negatively about partisanship, or are they just not encouraged to think about it positively? Martin Wattenberg's observation that citizens feel disconnected from parties may have summed public sentiment in the 1980s and 1990s. As some of the terms related to partisanship have shifted (namely, *liberal* and *independent*), it may be fruitful to rerun such tests on public opinion data, particularly data that have been collected in an open-ended fashion to get a sense of how citizens' talk mirrors or departs from the elite patterns described here.

Chapter 6 shows that elites prefer some aspects of partisanship to others, protecting the stability of *Democrats, Republicans,* and *parties*; praising the populism associated with the *independent* label; and condemning the ideology connected with the *liberal* label. In the early stages of this research, I had expected that a key finding of this project would explain how and why *liberal* became a dirty word. In retrospect, that explanation is relatively simple: Republicans began infusing the term with negative connotations as early as 1964 and more aggressively in the 1980s and 1990s, and Democrats did nothing to protect it (indeed, in this sample Bill Clinton is the only Democrat to use the term since 1980, and he does not use it in supportive ways). More impressive and less obvious are the ways in which elites preserve the strength of the *Democrat* and *Republican* labels and flatter *independent* citizens but not *independent* candidates.

While the themes explored in this study answer many questions about parties, they also raise others. Surprisingly, one particular set of topics is rarely coupled with parties. Because such concerns are left out of the conversation and, in a sense, are negated in discourse, it is curious to attend to what was left out of the talk of the party.

A first item that is conspicuous by its absence in discussions of parties is money. In 1952, presidential candidates spent approximately a combined $16 million on the campaign. By 1996, this amount increased to an estimated $120 million and by 2000 an estimated $300 million.[5] Campaign 2004 is believed to be the most expensive ever, with President George W.

Bush, Senator John Kerry, and their political parties and allied groups hav-ing spent more than $600 million on television and radio commercials—triple the amount that was spent on such items in 2000.[6] And, even with the McCain–Feingold campaign finance reforms of 2002 limiting the po-litical parties' ability to raise unlimited soft money contributions, the Dem-ocratic and Republican parties are believed to have raised more than $1 bil-lion in contributions through mid-October 2004, beating their total raised during the same period in the 2000 election, when they could still accept much larger individual donations.[7] Despite the amount of money spent on campaigns and despite the amounts raised by the parties, very few texts in this study associate the parties with money or interest groups (only 1.1 per-cent of all labels made such associations).

How could something as vital as money to a capitalist system escape mention? Naturally, such topics may appear in American discourse but may have just failed to have been captured in this analysis (e.g., such discussions may reside in business columns or specialty publications but not in main-stream campaign coverage). Alternatively, money could be something that citizens understand to be important but are uncomfortable discussing. In ei-ther case, the absence of such discussions is not just an interesting question but a vital one: if elites do not talk about money, do people really realize how important it is to democratic governance in general and to campaign-ing in particular? Do they consider how parties, as organized groups, can work to protect citizens from moneyed elites? Walter Dean Burnham re-minds us of this important role of parties, when he writes,

> Political parties, with all their well-known human and structural short-comings, are the only devices thus far invented by the wit of Western man that can, with some effectiveness, generate countervailing collective power on behalf of the many individually powerless against the relatively few who are individually or organizationally powerful. Their disappear-ance as active intermediaries, if not as preliminary screening devices, would only entail the unchallenged ascendancy of the already powerful, unless new structures of collective power were somehow developed to replace them, and unless conditions in America's social structure and po-litical culture came to be such that they could be effectively used.[8]

Therefore, if money and interest groups are left out of the mainstream cam-paign conversation, citizens may fail to appreciate how parties as organized groups can serve to protect citizens from the already powerful. Traditionally, elected officials have hesitated to discuss finances. Only vivid examples (e.g., Richard Nixon's "Checkers" speech) serve as exceptions to this powerful rule.

A second entity missing from this study is an articulation of political time. As discussed in chapter 3, elites place only 1 percent of their party labels in the "future." While this is not unheard of—indeed, politics is normally presentistic to the core—it is certainly noteworthy as the United States heads into a "new, information economy," characterized by a conversion of professions, lifestyles, and behavioral patterns. At the time this book was written, virtual space, virtual products, and virtual politics command resources, attention, and fascination. How will party labels fare as this new, timeless environment continues? In such a world, how will presentistic institutions— such as political parties—interact with a society fascinated by tomorrow? It will be interesting to see what types of discourse the burgeoning economy stimulates. It is entirely possible that technology elites and the culture they create for users who enjoy their projects may treat government as being irrelevant, leaving it to the patriotic few who are willing to run for public office and embrace party traditions. Or, of course, there could be few changes inspired by a forward-looking culture; from this perspective, the patterns of passivity discussed by Samuel Huntington and Daniel Boorstin may be so strong that even economic and futuristic cultural shifts cannot challenge them. Again, in forecasting what parties will come to mean, the safest bet is to watch the political and economic interests of elites. For, as Burnham has written, changes to the system are likely to be overwhelmed in their early stages by a "counterrevolution" among those "whose values and perceived material interests would be placed in the gravest jeopardy."[9]

A third entity that is conspicuous by its absence is the *conservative* label—largely because it appears so infrequently in the discourse, constituting just 8.5 percent of all labels in the samples drawn.[10] Although its rare use in this study might suggest that we ignore it, George W. Bush's treatment of the *conservative* label in the late 1990s merits mention. Journalist Thomas Bray has noted that W. Bush crafted a 1990s version of his father's "kinder gentler" politics in order to attract female voters and distance himself from the stereotype of a conservative as a "mean-spirited hardhead." Bray is sympathetic to this approach, probably because he, too, has felt the charge that conservatives are not empathic:

> I can sympathize with Bush's desire to hang a politically correct modifier on his conservatism. The media, through which he and other candidates must try to reach the American people, resist the notion that conservatism is a legitimate thought pattern. A few years ago, I received a minor award for editorial writing in which the judges averred that "Though conservative, he shows sensitivity to the concerns of others." I

was tempted to send back a thank you letter noting that "Though liberal, you showed wisdom in making your award."[11]

Bray's article suggests that there is "some action" surrounding the *conservative* label, as it has been slightly questioned by the media and recently adorned with a "politically correct" modifier by the Bush campaign. But Bray's article also reminds us that, because this label is not richly charged, *conservative* has not been challenged as *liberal* has, which could mean that (1) Democrats are loathe to critique their more conservative peers in a conservative era, (2) Democrats have simply employed different labels (i.e., "right wing") to critique Republicans, or (3) some of both. Consequently, a series of issues that could be employed to add political baggage to the *conservative* label (i.e., the prison-building boom as a conservative plot to imprison black men, market-based health reforms as being cruel to the poor and elderly, public assistance reforms as being genocide to this same demographic) have not been affixed to the term in any systematic or public way. In the absence of such efforts, W. Bush's work to "revitalize" this word may be making it even more palatable and powerful in the future.

Another pattern found in the data is the relative reluctance of candidates to employ party labels over the years. As chapter 5 discusses, journalists are more likely than candidates to traffic in partisan language, a finding that could reveal information about the constraints or demands of the genres, the styles of the genres, or a strain of paranoia on the parts of candidates. That is, politicians may have an intuitive hunch that there is a high correlation between "partisanizers" (candidates who employ an unusually high number of party labels) and electoral defeat, and this datum may lead them to limit their use of partisan language. But is this really a wise option for candidates? Is there still a place for party cues in presidential campaigns?

From a scholarly perspective, the answer is yes. Research from theoretical and empirical scholars suggests that party cues serve as an efficient way for citizens to understand, discuss, and navigate a highly complex political system. In his work on political language, for example, Murray Edelman writes, "It is characteristic of large numbers of people in our society that they see and think in terms of stereotypes, personalization, and oversimplifications, that they cannot recognize or tolerate ambiguous and complex situations, and that they accordingly respond chiefly to symbols that oversimplify and distort."[12] And as discussed in chapter 2, studies show that party identifiers recall information framed in partisan terms better than they do with the same information framed alternatively and that biases in the accuracy of their perceptions and the extent of their recall systematically favor the party with which they identify.[13] In other words, both theory and data show that partisan cues have utility in the system.

So does the language of voters. In reading a large number of interactive transcripts posted to the online version of the *Washington Post* regarding the 2000 presidential campaign, it appears that many citizens crave order in their political lives. In late 1999, at least, many citizens wanted Republicans to act like Republicans, Democrats to act like Democrats, and the media to help simplify the political duties of citizenship, not complicate it. Consider, for example, the following question submitted to Ken Rodin (of the *Washington Post*) regarding the Republican presidential campaign debates in the fall of 1999:

> *Question:* Why do the TV networks insist on including in the debates candidates who have absolutely no chance of winning the Republican nomination? Do all the networks have any discretion at all, or must they give time to any publicity-seeking buffoon who announces his candidacy? Wouldn't it be much more meaningful if George W. Bush could debate John McCain one-on-one? I suppose Steve Forbes would have to be included if only because of his seemingly unlimited resources, but the others are simply wasting everybody's time, including theirs.[14]

While this is just one citizen's voice, it seems logical that many others in the information-rich environment of the new millennium would view party cues as being efficient. The interesting paradox, of course, is that citizens do not like the behavior of parties (i.e., their bargaining, politicking), but they seem to appreciate the order they bring to the political process.

The concept of "order" raises a final point that I did not directly measure but that might be stressed in future studies of political parties. Researchers have long praised parties for their ability to lend stability to the United States, to nurture compromise, and to help democracy work. Consider the following statements advanced by political scholars Herbert Agar (1950) and Willmore Kendall and Austin Ranney (1956), respectively:

- "These [American] parties are unique. They cannot be compared to parties of other nations. They serve a new purpose in a new way. Unforeseen and unwanted, they form the heart of the unwritten constitution and help the written one to work. It is through the parties that the clashing interesting of a continent find grounds for compromise . . . over such an area [the United States], where there is no unity of race, no immemorial tradition, no throne to revere, no ancient roots in the land, no single religion to color all minds—

where there is only language in common, and faith, and pride of the rights of man—The American party system helps build freedom and union."[15]

- "It is the party system, more than any other American institution, that consciously, actively, and directly nurtures consensus by drawing its leaders, workers, and candidates from all strata of society, appealing to voters broadly rather than to narrow interests, and promising most groups some but not all of what they seek."[16]

In theory, political parties have the capacity to build such unions, something that, according to the data, was sorely needed in the frenetic third era of partisanship and in the polarization to follow campaign 2000, years when the country may be far more familiar with political differences than with commonalities. This disparateness is witnessed in politics—that is, "today's highly charged atmosphere of talk radio, single issue groups, heightened ideological awareness, political action committees, and attack ads"[17]— as well as in the changing demographic makeup of the nation. Immigration statistics, for example, show that the United States is rapidly becoming a more ethnically diverse place.[18] Specifically,

- Every hour, about 125 new immigrants arrive in the United States— three thousand a day, nearly 1.1 million a year, more than ever in the nation's 223-year history. Most—about 70 percent—will stay in the country and become Americans.
- Communities do not look the way they did twenty-five years ago. Hmong Laotians are in the Midwest; Brazilians work in the summer resort community of Martha's Vineyard; Hondurans are building stone walls for suburban houses and horse farms in southeastern New York state.
- People of Hispanic origin have or soon will overtake African Americans as the nation's largest minority. The percentage of the population that is African American is projected to increase from 12 percent in the year 2000 to 15 percent in the year 2050, while Hispanic Americans will make up 24 percent of the U.S. population in fifty years, up from an estimated 11 percent in 2000.
- Many minorities are clustered in key swing states for the electoral college; in campaign 2000, for instance, most Cuban immigrants in the key swing state of Florida supported Bush; by campaign 2004 that state saw "a huge influx of Puerto Ricans, Mexicans and people from Central and South America" that "diluted the political clout of

Cubans, loosening the Republican lock on the Hispanic vote" and put over 169,000 potential Democratic votes in a state that W. Bush carried by just over five hundred in 2000.[19]

As these new groups arrive in the United States, they inevitably will vie for their civil liberties, their rightful places in society. Indeed, researchers claim that the newly arrived are doing so differently in the 1990s and twenty-first century than in earlier eras. As environmental planner Daphne Spain states, "a century ago, immigrants were expected to assimilate, to disappear into the U.S. culture. We didn't have the words 'multiculturalism' and 'pluralism' then. The assumption was that the ideal part of the American dream was to speak English, own a home, work and send your kids to an American school. Now, assimilation is not being taken for granted as the automatic goal of immigrants."[20]

The face of the nation is therefore changing, lending some evidence to Michael Schudson's notion that politics is now everywhere.[21] In his historical analysis of citizenship, Schudson contends that the civil rights movement created an era of "rights-bearing" citizenship that has resulted in a highly individualized, highly politicized state; furthermore, the movement was accompanied by a "Silent New Deal," in which "between the years of 1964–1975 the federal government put more regulatory laws on the books (many of which to protects individuals' rights) than it had in the country's entire prior history."[22] The rights revolution, in Schudson's mind, has affected citizenship so much that women and minorities practice politics whenever they walk into a room and expect equal treatment, that gays and lesbians practice politics when they expect be legally married, and that children practice politics when they read food labels at the supermarket.[23] Schudson's observations remind us how politically charged life in the United States has become since the 1960s, as well as how the rights revolution has challenged the delicate harmony of the 1950s. In today's particularized and charged environment, it is difficult for Americans to imagine a national collective or to spring forth with a desire to cooperate with one another. Such realities highlight the need for a force that can draw diverse citizens and interests together, one that can nurture consensus and facilitate democratic decision making. Such realities, that is, underscore the need for groups such as political parties.

Having described the attributes of the party labels over time, how can these patterns be condensed and described in the language of branding? What has been learned about label use that can be exported to other projects? To return to the discussion of naming and branding in chapter 1 and the shortcuts and assumptions listed in chapter 2, three concepts help to distill the patterns exposed here to make sense of the symbolic capital of these labels: *visibility* (conceived of as the number of times a label is used), *potency* (understood as the power and position of a label), and *likeability* (regarded as the evaluative and emotive attributions attached to a label). In reviewing the five labels discussed here, the following trends emerge.

Visibility. As displayed in chapter 3, there has been a curvilinear trend in the use of the five party labels such that these terms were most common in the 1950s, were gradually used less often during the 1970s and 1980s, and reappeared in the 1990s and in 2000. Concerning the specific labels, *party* has been used less often over time and is regularly supplanted by the constructions of *Democrats* or *Republicans; independent* has been used in patterns that oppose the general trends—that is, gradually coming into use, peaking in 1980, and steadily being used less often than it had been in Era II; *liberal* has increased over time, and *conservative* has stayed somewhat steady with an increase in campaign 2000. When compared to earlier studies on the use of party labels, then, this study shows that these terms are more prominent than previously understood (especially given the resurgence in label use in 1996 and 2000), contributing to a type of symbolic capital that has been previously unstated. Visibility, however, is just one component of understanding symbolic capital, and the mere appearance of these terms becomes more compelling when mixed with the patterns detailed in the following sections.

Potency. As detailed in chapter 3, when all labels are examined together, they are largely portrayed as being at the elite level (variable: *position*), as being actors (variables: *potency, behavior*), and as being part of the solution (variable: *role*) in the contemporary American body politic (variable: *time*). In turning to the individual words, there are more overall similarities than differences in the ways in which *party, Democrat,* and *Republican* are constructed. The *independent, liberal,* and *conservative* labels are less likely to be actors and are split on whether they are part of the solution (*independent*), part of the problem (*liberal*), or uncertain (*conservative*). As detailed here, when party labels are used, particularly the bedrock terms (*party, Democrat, Republican*), they connote a definite sense of power.

Likeability. There are more interesting patterns deriving from this concept than from the others. Overall, the party labels are depicted as being generally positive actors on the scene (variables: *role, context, quality,* and *behavior*), and yet there are intriguing patterns across them. For instance, the *Democratic* label garners more overall positive assessments, partially because Democratic voices are more likely to talk about this term than are Republican voices and perhaps because the Democratic Party, as the "natural governing party," has garnered positive media attention for its view that government is something that should be constructed to help citizens. But since the 1980s, the Republican candidates in this sample (especially Ronald Reagan and George W. Bush) have delivered more optimistic constructions of citizens and its party labels and has been more likely to couple labels with positive attributes (attracting more upbeat news coverage as well). The *independent* label has similarly shifted over time: once depicted as a frustration to the major parties, independent voters had come into their own in news frames by the 1984 campaign, being increasingly associated with personal autonomy and important votes for presidential candidates. The *conservative* label has been fairly steady over the years, with positive depictions in 2000 thanks to George W. Bush's "compassionate conservative" brand, while the *liberal* label has picked up a set of complicating attributes over time.

So, when the message properties of visibility, potency, and likeability intersect, a set of symbolic patterns from the content analysis becomes more evident. It is often tempting in political conversations for candidates to believe that "all news is good news" or that "there is no such thing as bad publicity." In this project, it is helpful to look inside this colloquialism to get a sense of if this is true for party labels as brands. The answer, not surprisingly, appears to be "it depends." Consider these conclusions when the concepts are paired together.

Visibility and potency can contribute to brand strength. This is a conclusion that can be drawn when the symbolic capital for a label is visible and potent (as in the cases of *Democrat* and *Republican* and that for the *party* in the early years of the project). These terms are observable and are depicted as being strong and, in these ways, can weather some occasionally disagreeable commentary. It is important to note, though, that marketing theorists would be troubled by the lack of relational and emotive cues in constructions that are simply visible and powerful. Returning to Jack Trout's advice for brand managers, most strategic mistakes are made not in describing the brand but in ignoring the competition. Should a likeable outsider force begin to be discussed in visible and potent ways—say, as bodybuilder, then movie star, then recall candidate, then, ultimately, as Governor Arnold Schwarzenegger—the strength enjoyed by the party labels may pale in comparison (particularly in the candidate-selection process). Now, candidacies like Schwarzenegger's are rare, and most discussions of party labels are governed by individuals whose careers depend on them (and so challenges to party labels are unlikely to emerge from the mouths of these elites). Nevertheless, the vulnerability of the labels to the occasional visible, potent, and likeable challenger merits mention, particularly because the visible and potent major party labels do not score high on measures emphasizing relational or emotional connections with the electorate (as outsider and celebrity candidates do).

High visibility and low levels of likeability and potency can deplete a brand name. This is a conclusion that can be drawn when the symbolic capital for a label is visible, unlikeable, and politically ineffectual (as in the case of the term *liberal*). Republican voices, in their insistent use of the term and in their consistent constructions of it as a morally compromised and excessive force, successfully repositioned the label in party politics. The press seemed to follow, and the Democratic Party did not. As a consequence, the visibility and negativity surrounding the term caused it to atrophy. In a sense, this pattern contradicts the notion that "there is no such thing as bad publicity" for one key message property: when a label's likeability and potency are continually questioned, the label sheds prior associations and accumulates more complicated ones. Future work could assess how unlikeable or powerful a force can be before it begins to lose power. At present, though, the mixture of low likeability and few attributions of potency are the most troubling adornments for the *liberal* label.

Visibility and low levels of potency may lead to likeable publicity but may not empower a brand name. This is a conclusion that can be drawn when the symbolic capital for a term is visible, low on potency, and potentially likeable (as in the *independent* label). The *independent* label garners more positive associations than any other in the study. Intriguingly, though, these attributions are not linked to formal decision-making power, political accomplishments, or elite status. In these ways, the label is treated gingerly yet is sidelined, temporarily, from the trough of decision making. Here, the buzz has been largely positive for this label, but in the language of marketing experts, this likeable brand has not cut into the share of the market leaders— at least not yet.

The symbolic concepts of visibility, potency, and likeability are but a distillation of the many patterns reported here, and future work on party labels can examine how these factors continue to interact and what such interactions mean for the political capital of parties into the twenty-first century. Additionally, projects examining other labels can combine the codings here into assessments of those labels as brand names. In future projects, descriptive research can continue to unpack these trends, to see how various elites use these labels, and the meanings of partisanship that result from such efforts. Additionally, quantitative researchers can model these trends, looking for optimal levels of interactions between visibility, potency, and likeability, as well as test how certain pairings affect citizen understandings of labels. For the present purposes, it is important to recall that visibility is empowering when paired with potency but that its force is less certain without potent descriptors; that likeability is desirable but that likeability without potency lacks the wallop of the other pairings; and that low levels of likeability and low levels of potency are problematic. Perhaps one of the most surprising nonfindings of this project is that, outside of (1) congressional debates and (2) uses of the word *liberal*, the party labels examined here are rarely depicted as being both impotent and unlikeable with any regularity or force. Such a pairing would have been a toxic finding for party labels, particularly over time, and yet it never emerges—even given American's ambivalence about these institutions. In other words, the discourse examined here has largely avoided harmful pairings for all labels but the *L* word. That the rhetoric has not done so is one of the most subtle and consequential findings of this project.

THE PARTY IN 2004 AND BEYOND

The discussion here has largely focused on how labels have been used in the past. The next step, naturally, is to contemplate how and where the labels may move in the future, and perhaps the most obvious place to start is with the *liberal* label—the term in this project that has been repositioned the most and has attracted considerable media attention for its movement. As discussed throughout this text, American citizens are still open to many liberal policies, except when they have been coupled with the *liberal* label. In his analysis, Geoff Nunberg has observed that the democratic Left has long been vulnerable to adornment, as detractors have (1) critiqued its motive as being driven by "social pretension, condescension, or effete sentimentality"; (2) alleged that candidates have been influenced by "bourgeois affectation, ideological timidity and effeminacy"; and (3) suggested that its candidates are "eggheads" or "hostile to traditional conceptions of patriotism, personal morality and the family."[24]

Because the term *liberal* has been saddled with such affectations, Nunberg has argued that this word has become a referent for lifestyle choices and consumer preferences rather than for notions of class and ideology. This move, in his mind, means that once the term became a "preference" rather than a "class-based judgment," it became a word that was easy to deem culturally undesirable by those who would benefit, politically, by liberal policies. While the current book has largely focused on the meanings that *liberal* has acquired in four sets of discourse, Nunberg's broader, cultural attributions are important as well. Both the cultural and political meanings that have been heaped on this term have harmed it, particularly those from the 1980s to the present in the United States. As detailed in chapter 1, it is interesting that Republican strategists (such as Frank Luntz) encouraged Republicans to lay off the *L* word in 2000 to run more positive campaigns. By 2004, this "most lethal spear" in the "Republican arsenal" reappeared, especially in the close, final days of the campaign. As described in one *Washington Post* article, "President Bush's campaign spokesmen have called the Democratic ticket of Sen. John F. Kerry (Mass.) and Sen. John Edwards (N.C.) the most *liberal* ticket in U.S. history;" these spokesmen also are quoted as suggesting that "a *liberal* advocacy group" had produced analyses that "placed Kerry and Edwards at the *liberal* end of the Democratic spectrum in the Senate."[25]

Interestingly, though, print coverage addressing the *liberal* label featured some novel nuances by 2004. As previewed by the Anna Quindlen column in chapter 1, journalists looking for new ways to unveil the "strategy" of the candidates entered into a type of critique regarding Republican uses of the term in 2004 (one that was less common in years prior to those in this data set). Some moves included interviewing Democratic strategists to see how they would respond to Republican uses of the word and questioning if the public had been so oversaturated with the label that it no longer meant anything to them. It is entirely possible that these types of columns, which unmasked the efforts of the Right, may have encouraged some citizens (at least) to regard the use of the label as a piece of "mere strategy" rather than an authentic discussion of differences on issues. Consider the following types of statements, which began to uncover the term's use in 2004: "several Democratic strategists say Kerry is wise to resist being tattooed as *liberal*"; "Democratic strategists say the word [*liberal*] by itself lacks the potency it had"; "in general the label just doesn't have the same explosive power"; and "the *liberal* label is dynamite . . . but the dynamite cannot explode if most voters do not believe it is real."[26] At times, left-leaning strategists receive even longer quotations, including the one in the following passage, from Americans for Democratic Action communications director Don Kusler:

> For his part, Kusler wishes that a word that he regards as having an honorable heritage—backing civil rights at home and robust human rights policies abroad—will be one Democratic presidential nominees will again embrace. Conservatives have "been working on redefining the word 'liberal' for decades, and turning it into a four-letter word," Kusler said. "We don't want to give up the word. We've been losing the fight for the definition."[27]

Chapter 6 discusses how strategic news coverage has been helpful for the *independent* label, as it has helped to cast its voters as autonomous, central to campaigns, and as offering valuable votes to the presidential candidates. Interestingly, in 2004 at least, this strategic frame appears to usher in new voices and perspectives to the use of the *L* word (which, to date, has been largely managed by voices from the Right and the GOP). Time will tell if such news practices influence the meanings of this label.

In the meantime, forces on the Left are engaged in at least three other types of activities to take back their language and reposition *liberal* in order to give it more positive connotations. First, as discussed in chapter 1, some academics and public intellectuals are getting in on the act. Again, we turn to linguist George Lakoff's work, specifically his efforts at the Rockridge Institute in Northern California, which build from his book *Moral Politics*.[28] There, Lakoff argues that adherents to the major parties are guided by different worldviews, with Democrats embracing the notion of a "nurturant parent" (driven by an understanding that the world can be a better place, that children are born good and need to be made better, and that the job of a parent is to nurture his or her children and to raise them to be nurturers of themselves and others) and with Republicans accepting the concept of a "strict parent" (driven by an assumption that the world is a dangerous place, that there is competition, that there will always be winners and losers, and that children are born bad and have to be made good). These worldviews, contends Lakoff, contribute to how the parties think problems should be solved and situations negotiated. Democrats, working from the starting place that "people are good and can be made better," believe strongly in notions of empathy, responsibility, and community. Republicans, moving ahead from a belief that the world is dangerous, welcome notions of strength, discipline, competition, and punishment. These worldviews and understandings of how problems are best solved have appeared explicitly and implicitly in party communications, and in many instances Lakoff suggests that the Republican Party has been more successful in making a case for its views. Most relevant to the current purposes is how it has distilled its perspective (one that cherishes strength, discipline, and punishment) into a coherent brand with a central vision that is easily communicated and consistently referenced. These steps described by Lakoff are reminiscent of the marketing advice of Scott Davis, detailed in chapter 1; in engaging in said practices, Republicans stress the "value" of their brand over its "benefits" and "attributes."

In contrast, the Democratic Party has displayed a penchant for emphasizing the "attributes" of its brand by calling attention to a bevy of issues (e.g., prescription drugs, Social Security, education, the environment) and by running on independent issues like these, which can change from election to election.[29] In making this choice, the Democrats have tried to get voters to identify with the bottom layer of the brand-identity pyramid—an approach that Davis and other marketing theorists view as being more complicated than asking citizens to identify with the pyramid's apex (values). For Davis and others, promoting attributes is a tougher sell than peddling values for at least three reasons: individuals may not be inspired by any given set of attributes; opponents can encroach on these attributes and offer carbon copies of them; and, over time, such attributes may simply become less relevant (decreasing both the relationship between the public and the brand as well as the perceived value of the brand).

What can the Left do, then, to begin to advance a more competitive brand name for itself? Lakoff and the other scholars at the Rockridge Institute encourage a set of ideas. A first is for the Left to be proactive with language use and to think carefully about how to use research to become better at thinking, reasoning, and talking about issues. His advice here is for members of the Left to start discussing labels in ways that prime the "nurturant parent's values" and "worldview" so that the Democrats will, too, have a succinct brand, one that will inspire Democratic voters to vote on their collective "morality" and "identity" rather than on a laundry list of issues.[30] In branding terminology, then, he encourages Democrats to start talking about the "nurturant parent's" value system so that citizens can begin to identify with that level of the brand.

A second piece of advice is for the Left to develop a plan of response for instances in which the Republican "strict parent" theme has already been primed. Here, Lakoff advises two steps: first, approach that frame by calling attention to the "values" of the Left's worldview (including promise and hope); and, second, break through the Republican frame by emphasizing images of empathy, responsibility, and community. Lakoff encourages voices on the Left to sum such discussions by invoking the "notion of protection." In his mind, "you have to be a strong, protective parent if you're a nurturer," and the Left has to come across "as a strong protector."[31] Thus, Lakoff believes that by approaching the Republican frame with hope, by working though it with the prized images of the "nurturant parent," and by emphasizing the value of "protection," voices in the Democratic Party can work to strengthen their labels. In his mind, this higher-level approach, as well as the best practices of branding, is superior to trying to beat the GOP frame with the intricacies of a Democrat's prized policy position—a habit, often a losing one, for the "natural governing" party (already vulnerable by

Republican charges that Democrats love government and the idea of government more than they love their constituents).

A third suggestion that he has proposed resides outside of language. It consists of encouraging progressives to depart from the "nurturant philosophy" long enough to reinvest in themselves through the form of building think tanks and a message infrastructure to support the dissemination of their message.[32] As he puts it, over the last thirty-five years, "the right has put together over 43 think tanks. They've spent two to three billion dollars doing it. We're nowhere near that. They have this enormous apparatus and they've spent 35 years figuring out all these frames and figuring out the language. . . . One of the great mistakes of the Democratic party has been to try to describe what it means to be a Democrat in terms of programs, instead of in terms of values, principles and directions."[33] He sums that although his organization is trying to fill in such frames, much more can be done on this scene.

Still another approach advocated by some on the Left is the introduction of a new term: *progressive.* As linguist Nunberg has advised, "there's a lot to be said for progressive: it conveys the right message to sophisticated left-of-center voters without connoting anything negative to the majority of the electorate. (To most, it still doesn't connote much of anything at all.)" Nunberg elaborates that it has been appearing in "the pages of conservative publications such as the *National Review,* very often set in quotation marks, the refuge of those who have allowed the other side to stake out the linguistic territory."[34] Simply introducing the word, however, will not be enough, in Nunberg's mind. This new term would have to be invented to "convey a sense of fairness, strength, pride and common purpose, and to reconnect with people who no longer feel it has any relevance to their lives."[35] E. J. Dionne, too, has discussed the merits of adding *progressive* to public communications. His advice is as pragmatic as it is symbolic, though: as he has observed, this word polls better than *liberal* does.[36]

Yet another activity taken up on the Left has been locating new strategies for the dissemination of its language. A first strategy has been to use technology, an instinct that has emerged with new force in light of the successes of former governor Howard Dean in the surfacing stage leading to the 2004 presidential election. At that time, "Dean meet-ups" (face-to-face meetings that are initially organized and advertised online) became a campaign phenomenon. As one column reported, "on the first Wednesday in August, 2003, for instance, over 480 events took place on the same day in every U.S. state, with nearly 80,000 people attending to support the Dean campaign (the next most popular meet-up Democrat, John Kerry, has 8,000 members)." The network that this organization was able to assemble was unprecedented for a preprimary context. It generated buzz and excitement with Democratic voters as well as considerable media attention that began to anoint Dean, months ahead of the primary contests, as being the viable Democratic challenger.[37] So remarkable were these efforts that Phil Noble, founder of Politics Online, commented, "Howard Dean, a nobody from nowhere with no chance, used the Internet basically in the course of seven months to become the leading candidate of the Democratic party for president."[38]

A second instinct was to blend technology with face-to-face and traditional group mobilization efforts. Consider the following groups, who organized to spread the Democratic message in 2004:

- MoveOn.org, an activist website and e-mail list of an estimated 1.8 million members, worked to mobilize left-leaning voters, efforts that led Internet researcher Michael Cornfield to coin them as being "easily the largest political-action committee in the country. . . . It's the Christian Coalition of the left."[39]
- America Coming Together, a voter-mobilization outfit started by a group of veteran progressive activists, deployed an army of more than fourteen hundred door-to-door canvassers in seventeen battleground states to register and educate voters.[40]
- A coalition of Left groups, ranging from National Abortion and Reproductive Rights Action League to the Teamsters, organized to knock on doors and personally invite individuals to turn out.[41]
- An organization such as the National Education Association asked its 2.7 million members to "host 'house parties' before November to build opposition to President Bush's No Child Left Behind education law."[42]

All of these more immediate venues provided promising opportunities, particularly because recent research from the field of political science contends that face-to-face mobilization efforts can increase turnout in local elections[43] and that personal contacts are very important for voters who feel that they are "in the minority" in a given district (where the social pressure of feeling outside of the majority may suppress turnout).[44] While most of these efforts have been directly connected to campaign 2004, and while the lasting effects of organizations such as MoveOn.org are uncertain, the energy and commitment to organizing and finding means of disseminating the message of the Left has been considerable and represents steps to curb the reified lead of the Republican campaign and communications machine (detailed in chapter 1). These groups were not successful in tipping the 2004 presidential contest for their candidate, but if they continue to organize, they may spell success for the Democrats in the future and may contribute to enriched meanings of their party's labels.

Such efforts will take place, however, alongside an active and organized Republican Party that has benefited by its long-term game plan; by a worldview that it has distilled into a brand; by a set of wordsmiths who have helped its communications stay optimistic, proactive, consistent, and easy to follow; and by an information infrastructure that "echoes" the party's carefully chosen words.[45] In the aftermath of campaign 2000, in which the Republican Party's candidate won the presidency without winning the popular vote, the party had a politically charged moment. To protect its president from a 2004 election that would be as close as the 2000 contest, the Republican Party worked to organize a well-funded grassroots infrastructure to get its message out. There were at least two priorities here: one, working to motivate a base vote in churches across the country (Karl Rove has stated that "W. Bush lost the popular vote in 2000 in part because four million evangelicals stayed home") and, two, recruiting an army of grassroots volunteers who could go forth and proselytize the unredeemed.[46] According to the *Washington Post*, the Bush campaign had as its goal registering and turning out three million new Republican voters in a "massive ground war" that would require the partnership of the Republican National Committee and the state Republican Parties.[47] As the Republicans' victory in the 2004 election attests, by November 2, 2004, they were successful in getting 1.2 million volunteers to contact eighteen million voters and in getting their candidate elected with a nearly 3.6 million majority of the popular vote.[48] What does all of this mean for the future of the terms *Republican* and *conservative*? Given the Right's track record, its political resources, and its opposition's reluctance (so far at least) to adorn its labels, the future of these terms appear to be the GOP's to manage.

While the close campaigns in 2000 and 2004 have brought energy to the Democratic and Republican parties, the campaigns have also presented some complications for political independents. Overall interest in third-party candidates was estimated to be at an all-time low in 2004, perhaps because many traditional independent voters saw a real difference between the candidates in this contest. While independents were certainly constructed as being important in campaign 2004, another theme surrounded them: their desire to have their vote "count," especially after votes for third-party candidate Ralph Nader, which may have been cast as a symbolic protest, had real political effects in helping George W. Bush win in 2000. Notice the urgency in these former third-party voters quoted in news coverage in 2004. First, a woman who voted for a Ralph Nader in 2000 explains her situation to a reporter this way:

> "I assumed wrongly that it was going to be business as usual, gridlock as usual and money games in Washington (in 2000)," said (Denise) Van-Sickle, a 44-year-old resident of Blue Springs, Mo. Instead, she said, President Bush has taken the country into a war she doesn't support and made other bad decisions. "We are standing at a very important critical moment in history," said VanSickle, who is now volunteering for the Kerry campaign. "This is much bigger than the 2000 election."[49]

Another Nader voter from 2000 was quoted in 2004 as saying,

> "Last time I kind of admired what he was doing," said Elizabeth Allen, a 51-year-old from Austin who voted for Nader in 2000 but is now volunteering for Kerry in Missouri. "This time I think he's acting like a spoiled brat."[50]

Should America continue to witness close elections and should such types of news frames continue, these discussions could chip away at the prized autonomy and nonalignment of the *independent* label, for as the horse race between the two major party candidates becomes serious, these independent voters appear to return to the construction that depicts their Era I role: that of unruly political siphons and spoilers.

This type of pattern would not surprise scholars Walter Stone and Ronald Rapoport. Indeed, commenting on a political irony of the *independent* label, they observe,

> It is surprising that the influence of the [H. Ross] Perot movement on the major parties in the U.S. has been largely ignored. Perot's was the most successful independent candidacy in 80 years, and many scholars have speculated on the effects of third parties on major-party change. By increasing the Republican vote in presidential and congressional elections since 1992, the Perot movement has worked at the margins of American politics to produce a closely balanced party system in the years following 1992. That balance is reflected in the first partisan tie in the U.S. Senate since 1880, the razor-thin margin the Republicans have in the House, and the excruciatingly close outcome of the presidential election. Ironically, a candidate who first ran as an independent, who attacked both parties for their failures to address crucial policy questions

and to get beyond their own partisan interests, *has helped create a new era in American politics in which partisanship is likely to be heightened and political conflict is more likely to turn on a partisan axis than at any time in the last century.*[51]

The future of the *independent* label, then, may depend on the symbolic and political capital of the two major parties. In attending to the coverage of the 2004 campaign, reporters appear to be careful in making distinctions between *independent* and *third party* voters (who may or may not vote for Ralph Nader) and *swing* voters (who would be expected to contribute their vote to one of the major party candidates after coming to a decision on the key concerns of 2004—the economy, the war in Iraq, and the question of values). In many instances, the former voters are treated with suspicion or are covered in articles apart from the mainstream of the campaign; the latter voters, in contrast, are central to telling the story of which candidate might ultimately win. These types of news frames may be more influential for the meanings of the *independent* label than for the other terms in this analysis. Because the term *independent* does not have a regularly elected team of elites who have a vested interest in protecting its usage, this label may be more prone to be influenced by political events and news frames than any of the other words in this study.

Additional means of understanding the future role of party labels include looking to other data sets not examined here. Given that citizens approve of democracy but prefer not to examine it in detail, it would also be interesting to track the meanings of party that slip into "popular" media, such as television entertainment programming and television advertisements— that is, the types of messages individuals encounter when they are relaxing. Take the partisan meanings found in the political advertisements that interrupt prime-time television programming. Research on campaign spots—one of the most condensed and most viewed forms of campaign discourse— predicts that citizens would experience one of two types of party meanings in such circumstances. On one hand, personal ads (or segments focusing on the candidate) might dull the meanings of partisanship for citizens since most candidates are reluctant to employ party labels or ideological language in their promotional spots. Attack ads, in contrast, could sharpen partisanship because candidates often use such ads to portray their opponents as being "unyielding ideologues." Research on party meanings in advertisements could test these expectations and provide a deeper understanding of the types of partisanship citizens encounter when watching television.

Additionally, knowing more about the meanings of parties as constituted in other popular venues (i.e., popular films, political cartoons, political jokes, and satire) would be helpful. Preliminary research on films and cartoons suggests that such genres offer exaggerated portrayals of partisan personalities and conflict. In this way, these media are not likely to be a salvation for the parties, although these genres do deserve a closer look. Certainly, the popularity of politics in film and in prime-time television programming suggests that there is something about politics that viewers find compelling. Because political themes appear in so many popularized outlets, understanding the range of meanings presented there, as well as how citizens receive such messages, can only enrich the current analysis.

Comparative research, too, might offer insight into the feelings that Americans have about parties. That is, do other democratic nations display a similar ambivalence about parties? Do they employ labels in similar or different ways? Since the creation of parties is generally agreed to be a minimal condition for democracy, it would be interesting to study how other democratic systems view them. One intriguing line of research on how parties are emerging in the newly competitive Russian system, for example, shows that parties are developing in Russia and that Russians—like Americans—display a reluctance to warmly embrace them.[52] Moreover, comparative researchers Joshua Tucker and Ted Brader remind us that "political parties may lend stability at a cost to democracy (e.g., Mexico or Japan), or promote democracy while undermining it (e.g., Weimar Germany)."[53] Understanding the meanings of party in a variety of regimes would surely improve the depth of the current analysis.

CONCLUSION

Political parties may never be loved in the United States, largely because they stand for things that Americans do not like, things such as conflict, politics, and bargaining. Yet even though parties may never be treasured, this project shows that they have been hard to resist. American elites have a strong tradition of talking about parties and have generally used party terms in ways that contribute to parties' political potency in the United States, patterns that spell good news for the party system and the two major parties, even when the conversation has sometimes turned sour.

In attending to the symbolic capital of the individual labels studied here, I have found key findings that detail impressive levels of stability for the terms *party*, *Democrat*, and *Republican* (words that are largely protected by government elites); symbolic gains of the term *independent* (despite uncertain levels of political capital); the demise of the term *liberal* (despite public support for traditionally liberal policies); and a relative steadiness of the term *conservative* (a word that has not been attacked by the Left as *liberal* has been by the Right). In the main, these terms have also generally been constituted as being those of elites, a construction that revives the terms' political capital but, save the *independent* label, puts them "out of touch" with the information-age voter.

In examining these terms over time, a key conclusion is that Republican candidates and legislators have exercised considerable discipline in demoting the term *liberal*, in placing the *Republican* brand name closer to citizens, and in forestalling critique of the term *conservative* over the past thirty years. While a central tenet of this analysis is that neither party can dictate the uses of its words—indeed, cultural and political forces are operating on all of these words at any given time—this project shows that brand consistency yielded a net symbolic gain for the Republican Party in 2004. Because Americans are more likely to come to know parties through language than through partisan activities, and because one party has been more organized in its label use than the opposition has, listening to the talk of the party has uncovered lessons about public understandings of these organizations in the current moment and, perhaps, the future.

A broader conclusion is that the discussion of the two major parties (terms *party*, *Democrat*, and *Republican*) contributes to the political stability of the American system. On this point, it is notable that members of the organized Republican message team have not attacked the terms *party* or *Democrat* as they have the ancillary term *liberal*. Perhaps there is something in their minds about their opponent's primary label that commands respect or at least pause. Such pause is similarly noted in studying how elites have discussed the bedrock party terms when the major parties have been politically compromised in the United States, especially during Era II, 1960–1979. At that time, these elite voices were incredibly careful in using these labels, regularly returning to their potential even in a complicated moment. An example of this trend appears in the following statement from David Broder's widely read and curiously entitled book *The Party's Over*. When discussing the plight of the party system in the late 1960s and early 1970s, Broder included this optimistic scenario among his musings:

It is my conviction—and the central argument of this book—that if we engage ourselves in politics, and particularly concern ourselves with the working of those strangely neglected institutions, the *political parties*, that we may find the instrument of national self-renewal is in our own hands.[54]

Chapter 3 addresses how scholars have inadvertently praised parties while critiquing them, one of the more subtle and yet consequential patterns unearthed here. Another example of such potentially inadvertent praise appears in the "resilience" of parties emphasized in Frank Sorauf's textbooks:

> Nevertheless, the reign of the existing *parties*, and more generally, of the American *two-party system* seems secure. The *parties'* support may not be what it was, but their resilience is still remarkable. Talk of the imminent decline of the *Republicans* after Watergate and the losses of 1974 and 1976 was silenced by the *party's* resurgence in the 1978 and 1980 elections. Similar talk of *Democratic* decline in the 1980s must be tempered by recognition of the *party's* continuing strength in Congress and the state houses, not to mention a *Republican party* without Ronald Reagan at the top of the ticket after 1984. Changes in the parties and in their appeals, it appears, will have to take place within the *party* system we have known for more than a century.[55]

This broader argument advances what may seem to be an obvious point: the major parties enjoy political capital because voices in the United States continue to discuss parties in light of their potency in the system. As long as elites continue to bow symbolically to political parties—thereby giving them the limelight time and time again—it stands to reason that they will not be far from power in the polity. Americans favor order, and so the death-watch of parties can be looked at as being just another way that elites construct order in their lives. No doubt, this project, too, perpetuates the symbolic purchase of party labels when it reveals how they play a much more powerful role in American politics than had as yet been acknowledged. Thus, as long as political elites—or citizens, for that matter—discuss the potency of the party system (for good or ill), the parties will never be far from governing the political imaginary. Indeed, the talk of the party will prevent it.

NOTES

1. E. E. Schattschneider, *Party Government* (New York: Holt, Rinehart and Winston, 1942), 1.

2. See John R. Hibbing and Elizabeth Theiss-Morse, *Congress as Public Enemy: Public Attitudes toward American Political Institutions* (Cambridge: Cambridge University Press, 1995), 9.

3. Roderick P. Hart, *Campaign Talk: Why Campaigns Are Good for Us* (Princeton, N.J.: Princeton University Press, 2000); Samuel Popkin, *The Reasoning Voter* (Chicago: University of Chicago Press, 1991).

4. Gerald Pomper, *Passions and Interests: Political Party Concepts of American Democracy* (Lawrence: University of Kansas Press, 1992), 82, 84.

5. L. Sandy Maisel and Kara Z. Buckley, *Parties and Elections in America: The Electoral Process* (Lanham, Md.: Rowman & Littlefield, 2004); Anthony Corrado, "Financing the 2000 Presidential General Election," in *Financing the 2000 Election*, ed. David B. Magleby (Washington, D.C.: Brookings, 2002).

6. "$600 Million Tab for Decision 2004 Ads," www.msnbc. msn.com/id/ 6376861 (31 October 2004).

7. Glen Justice, "Despite New Financing Rules, Parties Collect Record $1 Billion," *New York Times*, www.nytimes.com/2004/10/26/politics/campaign/26money .html (25 October 2004).

8. Walter Dean Burnham, *Critical Elections and the Mainsprings of Politics* (New York: Harper, 1970), 133.

9. Burnham, *Critical Elections*, 189.

10. More specifically, *conservative* represented 7 percent of labels in textbooks; 9.2 percent in speeches; and 1.2 percent in congressional debates. Because there were so many news articles housed in the Campaign Mapping Project, I was able to collect the desired number of *conservative* labels for that genre (16.7 percent).

11. Thomas J. Bray, "Is Conservatism a Four-Letter Word?" *Detroit News*, 14 March 1999, 6B.

12. Murray Edelman, *The Symbolic Uses of Politics* (Urbana: University of Illinois Press, 1964), 31.

13. Milton Lodge and Ruth Hamil, "A Partisan Schema for Information Processing," *American Political Science Review* 83, no. 2 (1986): 399–419.

14. See question submitted by A. S. Jacobs, Overland Park, Kans., in Ken Rudin, "Are the Media Biased?" *Washington Post,* http://washingtonpost.com/wp-srv/ politics/campaigns/junkie/junkie.htm? (17 December 1999).

15. Herbert Agar, *The Price of Union* (Boston: Houghton Mifflin, 1950), quoted in David Broder, *The Party's Over: The Failure of Politics in America* (New York: Harper and Row, 1972), 181–82.

16. Willmore Kendall and Austin Ranney, *Democracy and the American Party System* (New York: Harcourt Brace, 1956), 509.

17. John F. Bibby, "In Defense of the Two-Party System," in *Multiparty Politics in America*, ed. Paul S. Herrnson and John C. Green (Lanham, Md.: Rowman & Littlefield, 1997), 73–84, 76–77.

18. According to the U. S. Department of the Interior, the term *diversity* is used "broadly to refer to many demographic variables, including, but not limited to, race,

religion, color, gender, national origin, disability, sexual orientation, age, education, geographic origin, and skill characteristics. America's diversity has given this country its unique strength, resilience, and richness"; see www.doi.gov/diversity/ 9definitions.htm (15 December 1999).

19. Hollis Engley, "Immigration Changes the Face of America," *USA Today*, www .usatoday.com/2000/diverse/divrs01.htm (21 October 1999); Abby Goodnough, "Hispanic Vote in Florida; Neither a Bloc nor a Lock," *New York Times*, www.nytimes .com/2004/10/17/politics/campaign/17florida.html?fta=y (17 October 2004).

20. Quoted in Engley, "Immigration Changes."

21. Michael Schudson, *The Good Citizen: A History of American Civic Life* (New York: Free Press, 1998), 280–81.

22. Schudson, *Good Citizen*, 265.

23. Schudson, *Good Citizen*, 299.

24. Geoffrey Nunberg, "The Liberal Label: The Substance Is Alive and Well, but the Brand Is in Trouble," *American Prospect* 14, no. 8 (2003): 36.

25. John F. Harris, "Truth, Consequences of Kerry's 'Liberal' Label," *Washington Post*, 19 July 2004, 1A.

26. Harris, "Truth Consequences."

27. Harris, "Truth Consequences."

28. George Lakoff, *Moral Politics: How Liberals and Conservatives Think* (Chicago: University of Chicago Press, 2002).

29. "Interview with George Lakoff," *Alternet.org*, www.alternet.org/story/17574 (15 January 2004).

30. "Interview with George Lakoff."

31. "Interview with George Lakoff."

32. Bonnie Azab Powell, "Framing the Issues: UC Berkeley Professor George Lakoff Tells How Conservatives Use Language to Dominate Politics," *UC Berkeley News*, www.berkeley.edu/news/media/releases/2003/10/27_lakoff.shtml (27 October 2003).

33. George Lakoff, "How to Talk Like a Conservative If You Must," interview with Dave Gilson, www.motherjones.com/news/qa/2004/10/10_401.html (18 October 2004).

34. Nunberg, "Liberal Label."

35. Nunberg, "Liberal Label."

36. E. J. Dionne, *Stand Up, Fight Back: Republican Toughs, Democratic Wimps, and the Politics of Revenge* (New York: Simon and Schuster, 2004).

37. Ann Mack, "Politicians Log On," *Media Week* 26 (2004): 24–28.

38. Edward Miliband, "Meet-Up at the White House?" *New Statesman*, 25 August 2003, 19.

39. Chris Taylor and Karen Tumulty, "MoveOn's Big Moment," *Time*, 24 November 2003, 32.

40. Vince Beiser, "Big Money for Grass-Roots Campaign," *Rolling Stone*, 2 September 2004, 44.

41. Mark David, "Winning Votes from the Ground Up," *Campaigns and Elections* 24, no. 7 (2003): 10.

42. "Pro-Kerry NEA Plans 'House Parties' vs. Bush," *USA Today*, 6 July 2004, 9D.

43. Donald P. Green, Alan S. Gerber, and David W. Nickerson, "Getting Out the Vote in Local Elections: Results from Six Door-to-Door Canvassing Experiments," *Journal of Politics* 65, no. 4 (2003): 1083–107.

44. Jim Gimpel, "Computer Techology and Getting Out the Vote," *Campaigns and Elections* 24, no. 8 (2003): 39–41.

45. Jeff Faux, *The Party's Not Over: A New Vision for the Democrats* (New York: Basic Books, 1996), 208.

46. Elisabeth Bumiller, David M. Halbfinger, and David E. Rosembaum, "Turnout Effort and Kerry, Too, Were GOP's Keys to Victory," *New York Times*, www.nytimes.com/2004/11/04/politics/campaign/04reconstruct.html (4 November 2004); Ken Herman, "Bush Campaign Effort Aimed at Churches Is Criticized," *Austin American Statesman*, 2 July 2004, A11.

47. Dan Balz and Mike Allen, "2004 Is Now for Bush's Campaign," *Washington Post*, 30 November 2003, A1.

48. Julia Malone, "In Campaign Waged One Voter at a Time, GOP Gave Bush Not Only Electoral Vote but 3.5 Million Majority of Popular Vote," *Austin American Statesman*, http://www.statesman.com/news/content/auto/epaper/editions/thursday/news_14982e64728e21f2001a.html (4 November 2004).

49. Deidre Shesgreen, "Little Attraction to Third Parties in Polarized Country," *Austin American Statesman*, 31 October 2004, 7A.

50. Shesgreen, "Little Attraction," 7A.

51. Walter Stone and Ronald Rapoport, "It's Perot Stupid! The Legacy of the 1992 Perot Movement in the Major-Party System, 1994–2000," www.apsanet.org/PS/march01/stone.cfm (March 2001).

52. Robert Dahl, *Dilemmas of Pluralist Democracy* (New Haven, Conn.: Yale University Press, 1982), 11.

53. See Joshua Tucker and Ted Brader, "Congratulations, It's a Party! The Birth of Mass Political Parties in Russia, 1993–1996," paper presented at the annual meeting of the American Political Science Association, Boston, Mass., 3–6 September 1998, 3.

54. David Broder, *The Party's Over: The Failure of Politics in America* (New York: Harper and Row, 1972), xi.

55. Frank Sorauf and Paul Allen Beck, *Party Politics in America*, 6th ed. (Glenview, Ill.: Scott Foresman, 1988), 65.

METHODOLOGICAL APPENDIX

The book presents findings from an extensive content analysis that keys on six pivotal terms (*Democrat, Republican, independent, party, liberal,* and *conservative*—and their derivatives) found in four genres of political discourse (presidential campaign speeches, newspaper coverage, congressional debates, and civics textbooks), 1948–2000.[1] These party labels were selected because they serve as the obvious (*Democrat, Republican, party*) and nonobvious (*independent, liberal,* and *conservative*) markers of partisanship in the United States. Admittedly, there are important denotative and connotative distinctions between the terms *liberal* and *Democrat* and *conservative* and *Republican,* not the least of which is that the former word in each pairing refers to an ideological position, whereas the latter references a formal, organized political group. Nevertheless, because the terms *liberal* and *conservative* have come to be used as proxies for the parties, they have been included here to enrich the project. These genres of discourse were selected because they represent the remarks of four elites who collectively manage the meanings of party in the American polity. Furthermore, this period was selected to offer a longitudinal understanding of the concept, to provide an understanding of party meanings before the widespread use of television and before the party reforms of the late 1960s and early 1970s, and to give a nuanced insight into these labels heading into the 2004 presidential campaign.

TEXTS

This project has analyzed party labels in two moments: in a *campaigning condition* and in a *governing condition.*[2] To study party labels during high-profile campaigns, speeches from twenty-eight Democratic and Republican presidential candidates, as well as articles from seven news outlets (the *New York Times, Washington Post, Chicago Tribune, Los Angeles Times, Christian Science Monitor, Atlanta Journal-Constitution,* and Associated Press wire stories), were drawn from the database of the Campaign Mapping Project—directed by Roderick Hart and Kathleen Hall Jamieson.[3] To study party labels during noncampaign periods, congressional debates were photocopied from the *Congressional Record,*[4] and high school and college civics textbooks were randomly collected from (1) a list provided by the Texas Education Agency's *Current Adoption Textbooks* (an annual publication that lists the textbooks approved for use in Texas classrooms) and (2) the lists provided by political scholar J. M. Sanchez in studies of the portrayal of the presidency in college textbooks.[5]

Two sets of analyses were conducted on the labels during these moments. For the campaign condition (where I had access to the corpus Campaign Mapping Project, a textbase of 624 presidential speeches and 7,309 news articles covering these speeches), quantitative tests were run on all appearances of the labels in the textbase. Such analyses map trends in word usage. Then, for both the campaign and the governing conditions, a stratified random sample of all labels was drawn and subjected to human coding techniques.[6] While it was my goal to gather an even number of labels per voice, genre, and year in this study, three of the labels (*independent, liberal,* and *conservative*) simply did not appear often enough in three of the genres (speeches, textbooks, and debates) to gather the stratified random sample described here. Accordingly, this study subjected an imperfect sample to qualitative and quantitative analysis (see table A.1).

Because of these imperfections in the stratified sample, statistical analyses were conducted and interpreted with caution, and in many places simple percentages of the labels are presented. At other times, however, I was interested in making statements about the proportions of party labels in the

Table A.1.   Party Labels in Content Analysis

	Speeches	News	Debates	Books	Total
Democrat	140	140	228	160	668
Republican	140	140	357	155	792
Independent	113	140	5	54	312
Liberal	124	140	44	52	360
Conservative	68	140	10	44	262
Party	138	140	204	167	649
Total	723	840	848	632	3,043

Campaign Mapping Project data. In those instances, *density ratios* were reported, and such ratios were calculated by dividing the number of appearances of a particular label by the total number of words in a sample of interest and multiplying this figure by one hundred. (For example, the density ratio for the number of Democratic labels in news coverage would be calculated as follows: total number of Democratic labels in news coverage/ total number of words in news coverage × 100.) These density ratios present larger patterns than can be witnessed in the coded stratified sample.

CODING UNIT AND SCHEME

The unit of analysis for the content analysis is the party label as located in a forty-one-word cluster (with twenty words of verbal content preceding and following the label). All of the texts for the campaign condition were scanned and introduced to a Keyword-in-Context program. The keywords program located the six terms of the study and reproduced them with the twenty words preceding and following the party label; a research team did the same manually for the governing condition. All coding decisions were mutually exclusive for each variable. Yet potential redundancy was intentionally introduced to this research design. These redundancies were tolerated to capture the complexity of statements on partisanship and are not statistically problematic, as I did not advance directional hypotheses and am not concerned with potential covariation polluting my findings.

There are two parts to the following coding scheme. First, it features a series of simple descriptive measures. These include the following: label (*Democrat, Republican, independent, liberal, conservative, party*); genre (presidential speech, newspaper article, congressional debate, civics textbook); year (recorded); and party task (primary task of party in statement—not applicable, mobilization, campaign, governing, mixed; see table A.2).

Also examined was a series of variables derived from many of the insightful observations of party in the political science literature. Several of these variables come from debates in the literature on parties and were created to test the extent to which the discussion of party labels supports the theories of party advanced by political scholars (described in chapter 2).

An obvious initial concern for this study is the social or political job being performed by parties. Otherwise stated, are parties potent, as Joseph Schlesinger might suggest, or are they powerless, as David Broder and others hypothesize?[7] To measure the tension between these positions, both *role* (the job performed by the party; see table A.3) and *potency* (the extent to

Table A.2. Party Labels by Genre by *Task* Variable (in percentages)

	Democrat	Republican	Independent	Liberal	Conservative	Party
Presidential speech						
Mobilization	5.0	2.1	1.8	3.2	0.0	11.6
Campaign	62.1	62.1	53.1	21.8	50.0	52.2
Governing	22.1	27.9	31.0	44.4	33.8	22.5
Mixed	1.4	1.4	0.9	1.6	5.9	1.4
Not applicable	9.3	6.4	13.3	29.0	10.3	12.3
Newspaper article						
Mobilization	7.1	2.9	7.1	10.0	15.7	16.4
Campaign	76.4	82.9	82.9	62.1	58.6	69.3
Governing	8.6	7.9	3.6	13.6	13.6	7.1
Mixed	5.0	2.1	4.3	3.6	4.3	3.6
Not applicable	2.9	4.3	2.1	10.7	7.9	3.6
Congressional debate						
Mobilization	3.1	3.1	0.0	18.2	0.0	8.3
Campaign	8.8	4.8	0.0	6.8	30.0	10.3
Governing	74.6	80.4	80.0	52.3	40.0	53.9
Mixed	6.1	4.8	0.0	9.1	0.0	9.3
Not applicable	7.5	7.0	20.0	13.6	30.0	18.1
Civics textbook						
Mobilization	20.0	18.1	7.4	28.8	36.4	12.0
Campaign	50.6	47.1	74.1	23.1	29.5	37.1
Governing	16.9	16.8	1.9	11.5	20.5	27.5
Mixed	4.4	6.5	5.6	13.5	6.8	11.4
Not applicable	8.1	11.6	11.1	23.1	6.8	12.0

which the party acts or is acted upon in our democratic state; see table A.4) were measured via the following coding categories.

Role: social or political job being performed by the party.

0. unclear ("Rep. John Anderson is the Republican nominee from Illinois")
1. part of the solution ("Our aims have been drawn from the finest of Republican traditions")
2. part of the problem ("The Whip complained, again, about the Democratic leadership")
3. as conflicted ("Third parties have nurtured ideas that sometimes seem far-fetched but nevertheless sometimes took hold")

Potency: the speaker's calculation of the force exerted by, or upon, the party.

0. unclear ("What are the goals of our party?")
1. as actor ("As Republican leader, I've always wanted to do that")
2. as recipient ("I am not too concerned with partisan denunciation")
3. balanced ("The party will never be indolent as long as it looks forward and not back")

A related concern regards where these parties reside in time. Are parties remembered as relics of the past? Are they fixtures of today? Or are they seen as important players in the future? As various scholars note, research on parties should be sensitive to history, which thereby prompts the following *time* variable (see table A.5).

Time: the party's moment in history as implied by the speaker (not a simple measure of a predicate's "tense").

0. in present ("Bush is in-line with his party")
1. in past ("The Republicans wanted to do that")
2. as potential ("Our party shall always remain committed to a secure future")

The valence of partisanship is also an important element to consider. As linguists might argue, unless parties are talked about in a positive way, it is unlikely that they will be conceived of in a positive manner—hence, the creation of the variable *context* (see table A.6).

Table A.3. Party Labels by Genre by _Role_ Variable (in percentages)

	Democrat	Republican	Independent	Liberal	Conservative	Party
Presidential speech						
Unclear	37.9	36.4	25.7	43.5	32.4	39.9
Part of solution	45.0	33.6	70.8	7.3	36.8	39.1
Part of problem	13.6	29.3	1.8	47.6	29.4	20.3
As conflicted	3.6	0.7	1.8	1.6	1.5	0.7
Newspaper article						
Unclear	77.1	57.1	73.6	54.3	64.3	50.0
Part of solution	15.0	23.6	23.6	17.9	27.1	26.4
Part of problem	6.4	17.1	2.1	27.1	7.1	22.9
As conflicted	1.4	2.1	0.7	0.7	1.4	0.7
Congressional debate						
Unclear	37.3	28.3	80.0	25.0	50.0	33.3
Part of solution	32.9	28.6	20.0	20.5	30.0	36.3
Part of problem	19.7	34.7	0.0	45.5	20.0	25.5
As conflicted	10.1	8.4	0.0	9.1	0.0	4.9
Civics textbook						
Unclear	38.1	34.2	35.2	42.3	31.8	26.3
Part of solution	33.1	38.1	31.5	34.6	31.8	46.7
Part of problem	11.3	10.3	9.3	7.7	11.4	12.0
As conflicted	17.5	17.4	24.1	15.4	25.0	15.0

Table A.4. Party Labels by Genre by *Potency* Variable (in percentages)

	Democrat	Republican	Independent	Liberal	Conservative	Party
Presidential speech						
Unclear	29.3	27.9	24.8	35.5	33.8	34.8
As actor	55.7	53.6	48.7	52.4	35.3	46.4
As recipient	15.0	17.9	26.5	12.1	30.9	18.8
Balanced	0.0	0.7	0.0	0.0	0.0	0.0
Newspaper article						
Unclear	7.9	22.1	10.0	32.1	27.1	9.3
As actor	56.4	51.4	54.3	34.3	49.3	47.1
As recipient	35.7	25.7	35.7	33.6	23.6	43.6
Balanced	0.0	0.7	0.0	0.0	0.0	0.0
Congressional debate						
Unclear	11.0	10.4	20.0	2.3	10.0	15.2
As actor	56.1	58.0	0.0	47.7	50.0	45.6
As recipient	32.5	31.4	80.0	50.0	40.0	32.8
Balanced	0.4	0.3	0.0	0.0	0.0	6.4
Civics textbook						
Unclear	26.9	16.8	31.5	40.4	34.1	28.7
As actor	23.1	42.6	33.3	21.2	20.5	34.7
As recipient	45.0	32.9	33.3	38.5	40.9	30.5
Balanced	5.0	7.7	1.9	0.0	4.5	6.0

Table A.5. Party Labels by Genre by *Time* Variable (in percentages)

	Democrat	Republican	Independent	Liberal	Conservative	Party
Presidential speech						
In present	69.3	68.6	93.8	87.1	86.8	78.3
In past	25.7	24.3	3.5	10.5	5.9	19.6
As potential	5.0	7.1	2.7	2.4	7.4	2.2
Newspaper article						
In present	92.9	95.7	93.6	93.6	89.3	96.4
In past	7.1	4.3	6.4	6.4	10.0	3.6
As potential	0.0	0.0	0.0	0.0	0.7	0.0
Congressional debate						
In present	85.5	91.6	80.0	86.4	80.0	80.9
In past	14.5	8.1	20.0	13.6	20.0	18.1
As potential	0.0	0.3	0.0	0.0	0.0	1.0
Civics textbook						
In present	42.5	38.1	63.0	50.0	54.5	79.6
In past	56.9	61.9	37.0	48.1	45.5	20.4
As potential	0.6	0.0	0.0	1.9	0.0	0.0

Table A.6. Party Labels by Genre by *Context* Variable (in percentages)

	Democrat	Republican	Independent	Liberal	Conservative	Party
Presidential speech						
Unclear	6.4	10.0	8.0	8.9	1.5	15.2
Identity condition	9.3	13.6	13.3	23.4	13.2	18.8
Positive	35.7	25.7	53.1	8.1	23.5	31.9
Negative	14.3	23.6	3.5	36.3	23.5	27.1
Balanced	34.3	27.1	22.1	23.4	38.2	12.3
Newspaper article						
Unclear	2.1	3.6	2.9	4.3	2.1	2.9
Identity condition	30.7	36.4	60.7	37.1	52.9	39.3
Positive	23.6	18.6	18.6	11.4	15.7	16.4
Negative	26.4	30.0	9.3	40.0	20.0	27.1
Balanced	17.1	11.4	8.6	7.1	9.3	14.3
Congressional debate						
Unclear	6.6	7.8	0.0	9.1	10.0	8.8
Identity condition	28.9	24.6	0.0	18.2	30.0	31.9
Positive	25.9	20.7	0.0	13.6	30.0	24.0
Negative	27.6	34.7	60.0	38.6	30.0	24.5
Balanced	11.0	12.0	40.0	20.5	0.0	10.8
Civics textbook						
Unclear	38.1	38.1	44.4	42.3	61.4	55.1
Identity condition	11.9	11.0	16.7	5.8	4.5	4.2
Positive	26.3	26.5	20.4	26.9	11.4	21.0
Negative	18.8	17.4	16.7	19.2	18.2	15.6
Balanced	5.0	7.1	1.9	5.8	4.5	4.2

Context: the speaker's attribution of the social scene affecting the collective.

    0. unclear ("The GOP wants to put that bill on the president's desk")
    1. identity condition ("Anderson, a GOP from IL, expressed that sentiment")
    2. positive ("A party that can unite itself will unite America")
    3. negative ("Humphrey rejected the advice of his own party")
    4. balanced ("The democratic party, in good times and bad")

Parties are not isolated in the American political climate, and they must work with a variety of political entities. These include the parties themselves, individual candidates, interest groups, and voters.[8] The variable *association*, therefore, tracks those persons with whom American political parties share space (see table A.7).

Associations: a reference to some social entity with which the party interacts (for good or ill).

    0. no other entity mentioned ("The party's platform calls for balancing the budget")
    1. same party ("as well as some in his own party")
    2. different party ("The Taxpayer Party threw its support to the Republican Party")
    3. politician of same party ("fellow Democrats—Gene McCarthy and George McGovern")
    4. politician of other party ("Texas Democrats disagreed with Nixon")
    5. voters/citizens ("Suburban voters will offer the Republican Party")
    6. political interest group ("'Project 500' attacked the party")
    7. party undifferentiated ("Parties mobilize voters")
    8. world ("The Democrat spoke with the Canadian Ambassador")
    9. media ("The Republican was swamped by journalists")
   10. other

For a period of years, party was thought to exist in three places: in government, as an organization, and in the electorate.[9] Recently, there has been a movement away from this trilogy to define *party* as a group of office seekers.[10] Gerald Pomper regards this shift in thinking as being important, and he writes, "Useful concepts of political parties must emphasize, not neglect, how parties connect mass electorates with elite officials."[11] The variable *position*, then, observes whether partisan labels link voters to the party[12] or

Table A.7. Party Labels by Genre by Association Variable (in percentages)

	Democrat	Republican	Independent	Liberal	Conservative	Party
Presidential speech						
None	5.0	4.3	4.4	15.3	10.3	6.5
Same party	13.6	19.3	0.9	4.0	8.8	13.8
Different party	41.4	30.0	52.2	12.1	27.9	28.3
Politician of same party	15.7	12.1	1.8	6.5	8.8	15.2
Politician of different party	5.7	8.6	2.7	16.9	20.6	4.3
Voters	15.7	21.4	29.2	44.4	20.6	22.5
Interest group	0.0	0.0	0.9	0.0	0.0	0.7
Other	2.9	4.2	8.0	0.8	2.9	8.6
Newspaper article						
None	6.4	2.1	3.6	7.9	5.0	4.3
Same party	6.4	5.0	2.1	8.6	10.7	10.7
Different party	12.9	17.1	27.1	10.7	13.6	10.0
Politician of same party	16.4	30.0	5.0	27.9	26.4	32.9
Politician of different party	29.3	18.6	24.3	10.7	11.4	1.4
Voters	25.0	24.3	28.6	27.9	25.0	21.4
Interest group	0.0	0.0	4.3	3.6	4.3	0.7
Other	2.1	2.8	5.4	2.8	3.6	2.8

(continued)

Table A.7. (*continued*)

	Democrat	Republican	Independent	Liberal	Conservative	Party
Congressional debate						
None	16.7	23.5	40.0	29.5	30.0	17.2
Same party	13.2	13.2	0.0	29.5	10.0	15.7
Different party	46.1	33.6	0.0	18.2	30.0	23.0
Politician of same party	5.7	4.2	0.0	0.0	0.0	4.4
Politician of different party	1.8	4.8	0.0	0.0	0.0	1.5
Voters	11.4	17.9	20.0	18.2	10.0	6.9
Interest group	0.0	0.3	0.0	0.0	0.0	0.0
Other	3.5	2.8	5.0	2.8	3.6	2.8
Civics textbook						
None	19.4	9.7	18.5	23.1	11.4	31.7
Same party	13.1	16.1	5.6	3.8	4.5	9.0
Different party	34.4	46.5	27.8	30.8	45.5	7.8
Politician of same party	14.4	11.6	13.0	7.7	11.4	2.4
Politician of different party	8.1	7.1	9.3	9.6	9.1	1.2
Voters	2.5	3.2	14.8	15.4	11.4	10.8
Interest group	3.1	0.6	0.0	3.8	0.0	3.0
Other	5.1	5.2	11.2	5.7	6.8	34.1

whether party is viewed as an instrument of elites (see table A.8).[13] If the latter is the case, it is not surprising that Americans would often feel separated from their political parties.

Position: the party's position in the governmental process as implied by the speaker.

> 0. elite—organization, bureaucracy, candidates ("Democrats will vote to override the President's veto")
> 1. mass—voters, media ("Reform Party supporters")
> 2. global/undifferentiated ("I accept the nomination of our party")

Many scholars note that a key role of the party is to process interest group demands or social interests.[14] Over the years, however, "social interests" has become almost a pejorative phrase, as many politicians like to claim that they are above such "special interests" (a vernacular term for many social concerns). Pomper raises an interesting point regarding interests, asserting that partisans can possess collective goals (ones that provide benefits for an entire group—e.g., broad programs, ideologies, and public goods) or coalitional goals (modest goals that reward members of a coalition—e.g., patronage, party platforms featuring tax cuts, stances on abortion).[15] These thoughts raise several questions, including the following: Do parties look out for the greater, common good? Or are they more interested in coalitional goals? The variable *goals* was created to search for statements emphasizing these broader (as opposed to narrower) goals.

Goals: the party's goals for the American body politic as implied by the speaker.

> 0. no goal mentioned ("the Democratic candidate from New York")
> 1. a broad (collective) goal—ideological, theoretical, or community focus; lofty promises for the public good ("Democrats stand for liberty, the protection of all")
> 2. a narrow (coalitional) goal—utility maximizers, narrow interests, specific platforms ("Conservatives demand Capital Gains Tax cuts today")

The literature on political parties is mixed as to what, exactly, parties do. Many claim that parties play instrumental roles in the polity; some posit that they are largely psychological cues; and others contend that they serve primarily as cognitive cues. While these authors rarely pit these explanations against one another, I was curious to discover how parties are discussed in

Table A.8. Party Labels by Genre by *Position* Variable (in percentages)

	Democrat	Republican	Independent	Liberal	Conservative	Party
Presidential speech						
Elite	62.1	84.3	19.5	79.8	75.0	86.2
Mass	26.4	8.6	59.3	12.1	8.8	2.9
Global/undifferentiated	11.4	7.1	21.2	8.1	16.2	10.9
Newspaper article						
Elite	61.4	70.7	29.3	55.7	60.7	65.0
Mass	27.1	19.3	65.7	32.1	30.0	17.1
Global/undifferentiated	11.4	10.0	5.0	12.1	9.3	17.9
Congressional debate						
Elite	93.4	95.8	60.0	75.0	50.0	78.4
Mass	3.5	2.0	0.0	13.6	10.0	5.4
Global/undifferentiated	3.1	2.2	40.0	11.4	40.0	16.2
Civics textbook						
Elite	81.9	84.5	44.4	51.9	43.2	61.7
Mass	13.8	12.9	51.9	25.0	36.4	5.4
Global/undifferentiated	4.4	2.6	3.7	23.1	20.5	32.9

political discourse. The variable *behavior* (see table A.9) was created to trace whether Americans talk about parties as institutions that think, feel, or act.

Behavior. How does the speaker conceptualize the party as that measured by party-linked verbs?[16]

0. unclear ("Third-party appeal is growing")
1. party as intellectual body (rational choice theorists—opine, think) ("Republicans questioned")
2. party as acting body (policymaking construct—funded, voted) ("The party would restore"; "The party has labored")
3. party as feeling body (psychological/affective construct—believed, felt) ("Democrats care deeply")

Finally, the qualities and liabilities of party were also measured. During the fifty-year span that this project covers, the American electorate has witnessed an increase in television viewing and a decrease in partisan attachments. How has this trade-off influenced the ways in which Americans refer to parties? What types of adjectives have speakers associated with *party* over time? The variable *quality* was designed to answer these questions by recording the adjectives and adjective-derived adverbs used to modify *party* in political discourse (see table A.10).

Quality: What qualities of the party are stressed by the speaker?[17]

0. none ("The Democrats voted")
1. action—excited or placid ("The Republicans hurriedly called for a vote")
2. emotion—positive or negative ("Upbeat liberals will return to fight another day")
3. unity—diverse or congealed ("The United Party appears strong")
4. clarity—clear or confused ("Once again, the president's success left the Republicans baffled")

After analyzing my texts with this coding system, I ran a series of descriptive and nonparametric statistics on these data to answer the study's research questions. I also clustered these variables into three concepts, discussed in chapter 7.[18] Six coders aided in the data analysis; the reliability statistics for this group were all over .87 for all variables.

While this content analysis has covered much territory, it is but one approach to studying party labels. Other researchers interested in this topic might have selected different data sets (popular, as opposed to elite, voices;

Table A.9. Party Labels by Genre by *Behavior* Variable (in percentages)

	Democrat	Republican	Independent	Liberal	Conservative	Party
Presidential speech						
Unclear	60.7	59.3	44.2	59.7	67.6	62.3
Intellectual body	11.4	16.4	26.5	16.9	20.6	12.3
Acting body	22.9	17.9	22.1	19.4	7.4	16.7
Feeling body	5.0	6.4	7.1	4.0	4.4	8.7
Newspaper article						
Unclear	39.3	52.1	36.4	35.0	35.0	45.0
Intellectual body	13.6	22.9	25.7	33.6	28.6	12.9
Acting body	41.1	25.0	31.4	26.4	30.0	33.6
Feeling body	5.7	0.0	6.4	5.0	6.4	8.6
Congressional debate						
Unclear	34.6	36.1	80.0	27.3	0.0	37.3
Intellectual body	18.4	19.3	0.0	43.2	80.0	14.7
Acting body	45.2	42.3	20.0	25.0	20.0	45.6
Feeling body	1.8	2.2	0.0	4.5	0.0	2.5
Civics textbook						
Unclear	59.4	45.8	51.9	51.9	54.5	52.1
Intellectual body	3.8	7.7	11.1	17.3	25.0	5.4
Acting body	35.0	43.9	35.2	25.0	18.2	41.9
Feeling body	1.9	2.6	1.9	5.8	2.3	0.6

Table A.10. Party Labels by Genre by *Quality* Variable (in percentages)

	Democrat	Republican	Independent	Liberal	Conservative	Party
Presidential speech						
None	67.1	60.0	56.6	71.8	75.0	62.3
Action	1.4	2.1	1.8	4.8	0.0	0.7
Emotion	3.6	8.6	5.3	4.0	7.4	11.6
Unity	25.7	24.3	29.2	2.4	7.4	21.7
Clarity	2.1	5.0	7.1	16.9	10.3	3.6
Newspaper article						
None	39.3	49.3	37.1	25.0	39.3	42.1
Action	5.7	0.7	1.4	6.4	4.3	0.7
Emotion	32.1	7.9	32.1	29.3	22.1	22.9
Unity	20.7	40.7	26.4	32.9	30.7	32.9
Clarity	2.1	1.4	2.9	6.4	3.6	1.4
Congressional debate						
None	46.5	42.9	80.0	61.4	60.0	51.5
Action	13.2	18.5	0.0	4.5	0.0	8.3
Emotion	13.6	17.6	20.0	13.6	10.0	8.8
Unity	24.6	19.3	0.0	15.9	10.0	30.9
Clarity	2.2	1.7	0.0	4.5	20.0	0.5
Civics textbook						
None	56.3	46.5	51.9	59.6	45.5	53.3
Action	18.1	21.3	18.5	11.5	11.4	24.0
Emotion	6.3	11.6	3.7	9.6	11.4	3.6
Unity	16.3	14.2	18.5	11.5	13.6	14.4
Clarity	3.1	6.5	7.4	7.7	18.2	4.8

or portrayals in other media, such as film, advertising, and literature), different eras (party meanings before 1948), larger data sets (to have greater statistical power and to increase the generalizability of the study), or smaller
data sets (to study individual texts in greater depth). This approach allowed
me to examine and describe a considerable number of texts, but it did not
allow these texts to be submitted to empirical verification or intense rhetorical scrutiny. Although this is a trade-off, to be sure, I believe that because
scholars have yet to study patterns in label use, a message-based approach is
a good fit for this study, trading the effects favored by behavioralists for a
richer description of these texts. Even though many of the patterns in language use may be resisted or subverted by citizens, the patterns described
here do represent a mapping of how such terms have been used over time—
a first step toward unpacking how they have been used and what they may
have meant to American citizens in the 2004 presidential contest.

NOTES

1. This project employs a content analytic approach, a technique that lets researchers classify items objectively and systematically according to explicit rules and
criteria. Key benefits of this approach include the following: the application of a
consistent coding scheme to a large number of representative texts; the creation of
content categories to answer theoretical puzzles in the extant literature on parties;
and the calculation of reliability measures to ensure consistency of coding over time
and between coders. See Klaus Krippendorff, *Content Analysis: An Introduction to Its
Methodology* (Newbury Park, Calif.: Sage, 1980).

2. Frank Sorauf and Paul Allen Beck, *Party Politics in America*, 6th ed. (Glenview,
Ill.: Scott Foresman, 1988).

3. The Campaign Mapping Project was a multiyear research project directed by
Roderick Hart (University of Texas) and Kathleen Hall Jamieson (University of
Pennsylvania) and funded by the Ford and Carnegie foundations. The purpose of
the project was to (1) assemble the campaign material produced during presidential
election campaigns in the United States between 1948 and 2000, (2) create a measuring instrument (the campaign quality index) capable of assessing how well modern campaigns are carrying out the democratic mandate, and (3) monitor ongoing
presidential campaigns and issue warnings about debilitating election practices. To
meet these goals, the Hart- and Jamieson-led research teams gathered seven sets of
discourse found between September 1 and election day for each of the campaigns:
speeches, television advertisements, print and broadcast coverage, debates, and letters
to the editor. While the original project collected texts from 1948 to 1996, research
teams at the University of Texas, guided by Hart, have continued to collect these

texts in 2000 and 2004 to extend the scope of the textbase. The current project presents a content analysis of the data from 1948 to 2000 and considers the texts from 2004 in making sense of that presidential campaign.

4. Admittedly, the *Congressional Record* serves as an imperfect account of these debates. Because legislators may amend their remarks before they are printed, the *Congressional Record* is an imprecise—but conservative—data source. Because it is more conservative then the debates and is the closest account of such speeches available, these amendments are tolerated.

5. See Deborah Smith-Howell, "Using the Past in the Present: The Rhetorical Construction of the Presidency" (unpublished doctoral project, University of Texas at Austin, 1993), 46. Guided by Smith-Howell, this project examined the following textbooks.

High School Texbooks

Abbott, Frank. *American Government*. Boston: Allyn & Bacon, 1949.

Aker, Homer F. *You and Your Government*. San Francisco: Harr Wagner, 1948.

Gillespie, Judith A., and Stuart Lazarus. *American Government: Comparing Political Experiences*. Englewood Cliffs, N.J.: Prentice-Hall, 1979.

Gross, Richard E. *American Citizenship: The Way We Govern*, with Arnold W. Seibel. Menlo Park, Calif.: Addison Wesley, 1979.

Robert E. Keohane, Mary Pieters Keohane, and Joseph D. McGoldrick. *Government in Action*. New York: Harcourt Brace, 1953.

McClenaghan, William A. *Magruder's American Government*. Boston: Allyn & Bacon, 1993 (originally published in 1964).

Mehlinger, Howard D., and John J. Patrick. *American Political Behavior*. Lexington, Mass.: Ginn, 1980.

Posey, Rollin Bennett, and A. G. Huegli. *Government for Americans*. Evanston, Ill.: Row, Peterson, 1953.

Remy, Richard C. *United States Government: Democracy in Action*. New York: Glencoe, 1993.

College Textbooks

Bardes, Barbara A., Mack C. Shelley, and Steffen W. Schmidt. *American Government and Politics Today: The Essentials*. 4th ed. St. Paul, Minn.: West, 1994.

Burns, James MacGregor, J. W. Peltason, and Thomas E. Cronin. *Government by the People*. 2nd ed. Englewood, N.J.: Prentice Hall, 1966.

Dye, Thomas R., and L. Harmon Zeigler. *American Politics in the Media Age*. Pacific Grove, Calif.: Brooks/Cole, 1983.

Ladd, Carl Everett. *The American Polity: The People and Their Government*. 3rd ed. New York: W. W. Norton, 1985.

Lineberry, Robert L., George C. Edwards, and Martin P. Wattenberg. *Government in America: People, Politics, and Policy*. 4th ed. New York: Harper Collins, 1989.

Lowi, Theodore J., and Benjamin Ginsberg. *American Government: Freedom and Power*. New York: W. W. Norton, 1990.

Saye, Albert Berry, and John F. Allums. *Principles of American Government*. Englewood Cliffs, N.J.: Prentice Hall, 1966.

Sherrill, Robert. *Why They Call It Politics: A Guide to America's Government.* San Diego: Harcourt Brace Jovanovich, 1972.

Wasserman, Gary. *The Basics of American Politics.* New York: Harper Collins, 1979.

Woll, Peter, and Sydney Zimmerman. *American Government: The Core.* New York: Random House, 1989.

See also, J. M. Sanchez, "Mediocrity at the Helm: Evaluations of the President in Political Science Textbooks," *Social Science Journal* 33, no. 1 (1996): 97–112.

6. Specifically, I set out to code the following texts from my stratified sample. For speeches, five of each of the party labels per candidate per year, which adds to ten of each label per year, sixty labels per year, and 840 labels in this genre. Only 723 labels were collected (largely due to the lack of *independent, liberal,* and *conservative* labels in the corpus Campaign Mapping Project database). For news coverage, ten of each of the labels per year, which adds to sixty labels per year and 840 labels in this genre. All 840 labels were collected. For congressional debates, all labels in the four debates were coded (*n* = 848). For civics textbooks, seven of each of the party labels per book, which adds to forty-two per book and 632 labels total. Most books featured the *Democratic, Republican,* and *party* labels, and far fewer featured the *independent, liberal,* and *conservative* labels. In all, 3,043 labels were coded: speeches (*n* = 723), news (*n* = 840), debates (*n* = 848), and books (*n* = 632).

7. David Broder, *The Party's Over* (New York: Harper and Row, 1972); Morris P. Fiorina, *Divided Government* (New York: Macmillan, 1992); Joseph A. Schlesinger, "The New American Political Party," *American Political Science Review* 79 (1985): 1152–69, 1153.

8. V. O. Key Jr., *Politics, Parties, and Pressure Groups* (New York: Crowell, 1946); Martin P. Wattenberg, *The Decline of American Political Parties, 1952–1996* (Cambridge, Mass.: Harvard University Press, 1998).

9. Frank Sorauf and Paul Allen Beck, *Party Politics in America*, 6th ed. (Glenview, Ill.: Scott Foresman, 1988).

10. John Aldrich, *Why Parties? The Origin and Transformation of Party Politics in America* (Chicago: University of Chicago Press, 1995).

11. Gerald Pomper, *Passions and Interests: Political Party Concepts of American Democracy* (Lawrence: University of Kansas Press, 1992), 5.

12. Samuel Eldersveld, *Political Parties in American Society* (New York: Basic Books, 1982).

13. Gerald M. Pomper, "The Alleged Decline of American Parties," in *Politicians and Party Politics*, ed. John Grey Geer (Baltimore: Johns Hopkins University Press, 1998).

14. V. O. Key, *Southern Politics* (New York: Knopf, 1949).

15. Pomper, *Passions and Interests.*

16. Roderick P. Hart, Deborah Smith-Howell, and John Llewellyn, "The Mindscape of the Presidency: *Time* Magazine, 1945–1985," *Journal of Communication* 41, no. 3 (1991): 6–25.

17. Hart, Howell, and Llewellyn, "Mindscape."

18. These clusters include the concepts of visibility—the public nature of the labels (as measured through the number of times in which a term is used); potency—the perceived strength of the labels (as measured through the variables *potency, task, time, position, behavior*); likeability—the public evaluation of the labels (as measured through the variables *role, context, position,* and *quality*).

BIBLIOGRAPHY

"$600 million tab for Decision 2004 ads." *MSNBC*, 31 October 2004. At www .msnbc.msn.com/id/6376861/.

Achenbach, Joel. "The Cable-ized Cabal." *The Washington Post*, 24 September 1999. At www.washingtonpost.com/wp-srv/columnists/achenbach/achenbach.htm.

"Adlai Defends Tideland Stand in Texas Swing; Charges Carpetbaggers Misstate Position." *Chicago Tribune*, 18 October 1952, 1(A).

"Adlai Takes Ike's Challenge." *Washington Post*, 3 October 1956, 1(A).

Agar, Herbert. *The Price of Union*. Boston: Houghton Mifflin, 1950.

Aldrich, John. *Why Parties? The Origin and Transformation of Party Politics in America*. Chicago: University of Chicago Press, 1995.

Alterman, Eric. *What Liberal Media? The Truth about Bias in the News*. New York: Basic Books, 2003.

"Arkansas to Back Truman After All." *New York Times*, 8 October 1948, 3(A).

Atkin, Douglas. *The Culting of Brands: When Customers Become True Believers*. New York: Portfolio, 2004.

Bader, John B., and Charles O. Jones. "The Republican Parties in Congress: Bicameral Differences." In *Congress Reconsidered*, 5th ed., edited by Lawrence C. Dodd and Bruce I. Oppenheimer, 291–314. Washington D.C.: Congressional Quarterly Press, 1993.

Balz, Dan, and Mike Allen. "2004 Is Now for Bush's Campaign." *Washington Post*, 30 November 2003, 1(A).

Bartels, Larry M. "Partisanship and Voting Behavior, 1952–1996." *American Journal of Political Science* 44 (2000): 35–50.

———. "Beyond the Running Tally: Partisan Bias in Political Participation." *Political Behavior* 24, no. 2 (June 2002): 117–51.

Baumer, Donald C., and Howard J. Gold. "Party Images and the American Electorate." *American Politics Quarterly* 23, no. 1 (1995): 33–61.

Beatty, Sally. "Bank of America Puts Ads in ATMS." *Wall Street Journal*, 25 July 2002, 8(B).

Beiser, Vince. "Big Money for Grass-Roots Campaign." *Rolling Stone*, 2 September 2004, 44.

Belch, George E., Michael A. Belch, and Angelina Villareal. "Effects of Advertising Communications: Review of Research." *Research in Marketing* 9 (1987): 59–117.

Bennett, W. Lance. *News: The Politics of Illusion*. 2nd ed. New York: Macmillan, 1988.

Berger, Peter, and Thomas Luckman. *The Social Construction of Reality*. Garden City, N.Y.: Doubleday, 1966.

Bibby, John F. "In Defense of the Two-Party System." In *Multiparty Politics in America*, edited by Paul S. Herrnson and John C. Green, 73–84. Lanham, Md.: Rowman & Littlefield, 1997.

"Big Surprises in TV Viewing Study." *PR Newswire*, 5 May 2004. At www .prnewswire.com.

Birner, Regina, and Heidi Wittmer, "Converting Social Capital into Political Capital: How Do Local Communities Gain Political Influence? A Theoretical Approach and Empirical Evidence from Thailand and Colombia." Presented at "Constituting the Commons: Crafting Sustainable Commons in the New Millennium," the Eighth Conference of the International Association for the Study of Common Property, Bloomington, Ind. (31 May–4 June 2000). At dlc.dlib.indiana.edu/archive/00000221/ (accessed 17 July 2004).

Blackwell, Roger, and Tina Stephan. *Brands That Rock: What Business Leaders Can Learn from the World of Rock and Roll*. New York: John Wiley & Sons, 2003.

Boorstin, Daniel. "The Genius of American Politics." In *The American Polity Reader*, edited by Ann G. Serow, W. Wayne Shannon, and Everett C. Ladd, 19–23. New York: W. W. Norton, 1990.

Booth, John A., and Patricia Bayer Richard. "Civil Society, Political Capital, and Democratization in Central America." *The Journal of Politics* 60 no. 3 (1998): 780–800.

Bourdieu, Pierre. *The Logic of Practice*. Cambridge: The Polity Press, 1990.

———. *Outline of a Theory of Practice*. Cambridge: Cambridge University Press, 1977.

Bosmajian, Haij. *The Language of Oppression*. Lanham, Md.: University Press of America, 1983.

"Both Sides Woo Reagan Democrats." *Atlanta Journal-Constitution*, 19 September 1988, 1(A).

Brady, Diane. "Sleepless at Starwood." *Business Week*, 21 July 2003, 56.

Bray, Thomas J. "Is Conservatism a Four-Letter Word?" *The Detroit News*, 14 March 1999, 6(B).

Brock, David. *The Republican Noise Machine: Right Wing Media and How it Corrupts Democracy*. New York: Crown, 2004.

Broder, David. *The Party's Over*. New York: Harper and Row, 1972.

———. "Voters Of Two Minds." *Washington Post*, 26 September 1999, 7(B).

Bumiller, Elisabeth, David M. Halbfinger, and David E. Rosembaum. "Turnout Effort and Kerry, Too, Were G.O.P.'s Keys to Victory." *New York Times*, 4 November 2004. At www.nytimes.com/2004/11/04/politics/campaign/04reconstruct.html.

Burke, Edmund. *Works*. vol. 1 London: G. Bell and Sons, 1897.

Burke, Kenneth. *A Rhetoric of Motives.* Berkeley: University of California Press, 1950.

———. *Language As Symbolic Action.* Berkeley: University of California Press, 1966.

———. *On Symbols and Society.* Chicago: University of Chicago Press, 1989.

Burnham, Walter Dean. "The Changing Shape of the American Political Universe." *The American Political Science Review* 59, no. 1 (March 1965): 7–28.

———. *Critical Elections and the Mainsprings of American Politics.* New York: Norton, 1970.

———. *American Politics in the 1970s: Beyond Party?* New York: Oxford University Press, 1974.

Burns, James MacGregor, Jack W. Pelatson, and Thomas E. Cronin. *Government By the People.* 11th ed. Englewood Cliffs, N.J.: Prentice Hall, Inc., 1981.

"Bush: No Regrets on Campaign's Tone; Tactics Against Opponent Aren't Personal." *Washington Post,* 1 November 1988, 1(A).

Bush, George H. W., "Campaign Speech." Kingsburg, Calif., 14 September 1988. Annenberg/Pew Archive of Presidential Discourse. Philadelphia: Annenberg School for Communication, University of Pennsylvania, 2000. CD-ROM.

———. "Acceptance Speech at the Republican National Convention." Houston, Tex., 20 August 1992. Annenberg/Pew Archive of Presidential Discourse. Philadelphia: Annenberg School for Communication, University of Pennsylvania, 2000. CD-ROM.

———. "Remarks to the Community." Gastonia, N.C., 21 October 1992. Annenberg/Pew Archive of Presidential Discourse. Philadelphia: Annenberg School for Communication, University of Pennsylvania, 2000. CD-ROM.

Bush, George W. "Acceptance Address to the Republican Nominating Convention" Philadelphia, Pa., 3 August 2000. Campaign Mapping Project Database, University of Texas at Austin.

———. "Speech to California Republican Party Convention via Satellite" Austin, Tex., 16 September 2000. Campaign Mapping Project Database, University of Texas at Austin.

———. "Campaign Speech." 30 October 2000. Campaign Mapping Project Database, University of Texas at Austin.

Byrd, Joan. "Giving People What They Deserve: Why Cover Minor Political Parties?" *Media Studies Journal* 12, no. 2 (1998): 26–30.

"California Still Tuning Out Dole; Message Falters in Vote Rich State." *Chicago Tribune,* 29 September 1996, 3(A).

Campbell, Angus, Phillip Converse, Warren Miller, and Donald Stokes. *The American Voter.* New York: Wiley, 1960.

"Candidates Word Wrestle to a Draw." *Christian Science Monitor,* 27 September 1988, 3(A).

Cantril, Albert, and Susan D. Cantril. *Reading Mixed Signals: Ambivalence in American Public Opinion About Government.* Baltimore, Md.: Johns Hopkins Press, 1999.

Carmines, Edward G., and James A. Stimson, *Issue Evolution: Race and the Transformation of American Politics.* Princeton, N.J.: Princeton University Press, 1992.

Carney, James. "Hey—Who's That Guy Next to Karl Rove?" *Time*, 23 August 1999, 34.

"Carter Basks in Democrat Glow Here." *Chicago Tribune*, 10 September 1976, 1(A).

Carter, Jimmy. "Acceptance Speech at the Democratic National Convention." Chicago, Ill., 15 July 1976. Annenberg/Pew Archive of Presidential Discourse. Philadelphia: Annenberg School for Communication, University of Pennsylvania, 2000. CD-ROM.

———. "Acceptance Speech." Democratic National Convention, New York, N.Y., 14 August 1980. Annenberg/Pew Archive of Presidential Discourse. Philadelphia: Annenberg School for Communication, University of Pennsylvania, 2000. CD-ROM.

Chambers, William, and Walter Dean Burnham. *The American Party Systems: Stages of Political Development*. New York: Oxford University Press, 1975.

Cialdini, Robert. *Influence: The Psychology of Persuasion*. New York: Quill, 1993.

Clark, Alistair. "The Continued Relevance of Local Parties in Representative Democracies." *Politics* 24, no. 1 (February 2004): 35–46.

"Clash May Point Way for Campaign's Final Weeks; Republican Relies on Negativism, Democrat Parries and Independent Is Clearly Outsider." *Washington Post*, 14 October 1992, 1(A).

"Clinton Grabs For Prizes at Safe Pace." *Los Angeles Times*, 26 October 1996, 10(A).

"Clinton Having Success In Neutralizing 'Values' Issue." *Los Angeles Times*, 8 September 1992, 1(A).

"Clinton Regains Huge Lead, New Poll Reveals." *Chicago Tribune*, 1 September 1992, 4(A).

Clinton, Bill. "Acceptance speech." Democratic National Convention, New York City, N.Y., 16 July 1992. Annenberg/Pew Archive of Presidential Discourse. Philadelphia: Annenberg School for Communication, University of Pennsylvania, 2000. CD-ROM.

———. "Welfare Reform Speech: A Second Chance." Delivered to the Clayton County Office of Family and Children's Services, Jonesboro, Ga., 9 September 1992. Annenberg/Pew Archive of Presidential Discourse. Philadelphia: Annenberg School for Communication, University of Pennsylvania, 2000. CD-ROM.

———. "Remarks to People of Township of Union." Union, N.J., 3 November 1996. Annenberg/Pew Archive of Presidential Discourse. Philadelphia: Annenberg School for Communication, University of Pennsylvania, 2000. CD-ROM.

Cohen, Robert, and John Farmer. "Who Will Win the Independent Voters?" *Austin American Statesman*, 11 November 1999, 22(A).

Collins, Neil, and Paul Butler. "Positioning Political Parties: A Market Analysis." *Journal of Press and Politics* 1, no. 2 (1996): 63–77.

Condit, Celeste M., and John L. Lucaites. *Crafting Equality: America's Anglo-African World*. Chicago: University of Chicago Press, 1993.

Converse, Philip. "The Nature of Belief Systems in Mass Publics." In *Ideology and Discontent*, edited by David E. Apter, 206–61. New York: Free Press, 1964.

Cook, Timothy E. *Making Laws and Making News: Media Strategies in the U.S. House of Representatives.* Washington, D.C.: Brookings Institution, 1989.

Corn, David. "G.O.P.'s New Mouthwash." *Nation* 269, no. 9 (September 1996): 4–6.

Corrado, Anthony. "Financing the 2000 Presidential General Election." In *Financing the 2000 Election*, edited by David B. Magleby, 79–105. Washington, D.C.: Brookings Institution Press, 2002.

Cotter, Cornelius, et al. *Party Organizations and American Politics.* New York: Praeger, 1984.

Cronin, Thomas J. "The Textbook Presidency and Political Science." In *Perspectives on the Presidency*, edited by Stanley Bach and George T. Sulzner, 54–74. Lexington, Mass.: D.C. Heath, 1974.

Dahl, Robert. *Who Governs?* New Haven, Conn.: Yale University Press, 1961.

———. *A Preface to Democratic Theory.* Chicago: University of Chicago Press, 1963.

———. *Dilemmas of Pluralist Democracy.* New Haven, Conn.: Yale University Press, 1982.

David, Mark. "Winning Votes From the Ground Up." *Campaigns & Elections* 24, no. 7 (2003): 10.

Davidson, Roger, and Walter J. Oleszek. *Congress and Its Members.* 4th ed. Washington D.C.: Congressional Quarterly Press, 1993.

Dennis, Dion. "Inventing 'W, The Presidential Brand': The Rise of QVC Politics." *CTheory*, 11 December 2002. At www.ctheory.net/text_file.asp?pick=359.

Dennis, Jack. "Trends in Public Support for the American Party System." *British Journal of Political Science* 5 (1975): 230.

"Debate Changed 1 Mind among 12 Pittsburghers; Backers of Both Camps Voice Disappointment." *Washington Post*, 13 October 1984, 6(A).

Denzin, Norman K. *Interpretive Interactionism.* Newbury Park: Sage, 1989.

deTocqueville, Alexis. *Democracy in America.* Edited by J. P. Mayer. New York: Harper & Row, 1848/1969.

"Dewey Held to Net 14 States, Truman 6 by Western Tours." *New York Times*, 4 October 1948, 1(A).

"Dewey is Apparently Winner with Senate Result Uncertain." *Washington Post*, 31 October 1948, 1(A).

Dewey, Thomas. "Acceptance Speech." Republican National Convention, 24 June 1948.

Dionne, E. J. *Why Americans Hate Politics.* New York: Simon & Schuster, 1991.

———. "Need a Map?: The Left." *Washington Post*, 31 October 1999, 16(A).

———. "The Civics Deficit." *Washington Post*, 20 November 1999, 29(A).

———. *Stand Up, Fight Back: Republican Toughs, Democratic Wimps, and the Politics of Revenge.* New York: Simon and Schuster, 2004.

"Dole's New Battle Cry: Clinton is an Elitist 'Liberal, Liberal, Liberal.'" *Washington Post*, 9 September 1996, 12(A).

Dole, Robert. "Campaign Speech." Villanova University, 16 September 1996. Annenberg/Pew Archive of Presidential Discourse. Philadelphia: Annenberg School for Communication, University of Pennsylvania, 2000. CD-ROM.

——. "Remarks." Elizabethtown College, 2 October 1996. Annenberg/Pew Archive of Presidential Discourse. Philadelphia: Annenberg School for Communication, University of Pennsylvania, 2000. CD-ROM.

——. "Campaign Address." Macon, Ga., 23 October 1996. Annenberg/Pew Archive of Presidential Discourse. Philadelphia: Annenberg School for Communication, University of Pennsylvania, 2000. CD-ROM.

Downs, Anthony. *An Economic Theory of Democracy.* New York: Harper, 1957.

Dryzek, Jon S., and Stephen T. Leonard. "History and Discipline in Political Science." *American Political Science Review* 82, no. 4 (December 1988): 1245–60.

Dukakis, Michael. "A Strong and Secure America." Campaign Address at Georgetown University, Washington, D.C., 14 September 1988.

Edelman, Murray. *The Symbolic Uses of Politics.* Urbana: University of Illinois Press, 1964.

——. *Politics As Symbolic Action: Mass Arousal and Quiescence.* New York: Academic Press, 1971.

——. *Political Language: Words That Succeed and Policies That Fail.* New York: Academic Press, 1977.

Ehrenhalt, Alan. "In the Senate of the 1980s, Team Spirit Has Given Way to the Rule of Individuals." *Congressional Quarterly Weekly Report,* 4 September 1982, 2175–82.

——. The United States of Ambition: Politicians, Power, and the Pursuit of Office. New York: Times Books, 1992.

Ehrlich, Howard S. "Populist Rhetoric Reassessed: A Paradox." *Quarterly Journal of Speech* 63 (1977): 140–51.

Eisenberg, Eric, and Harold Lloyd Goodall Jr. *Organizational Communication: Balancing Creativity and Constraint.* New York: St. Martin's Press, 1993.

Eisenhower, Dwight. "Acceptance Address to the Republican Nominating Convention." 11 July 1952. Annenberg/Pew Archive of Presidential Discourse. Philadelphia: Annenberg School for Communication, University of Pennsylvania, 2000. CD-ROM.

——. "Remarks Made on Eisenhower Campaign Train." Flint, Mich., 1 October 1952. Annenberg/Pew Archive of Presidential Discourse. Philadelphia: Annenberg School for Communication, University of Pennsylvania, 2000. CD-ROM.

Eldersveld, Samuel. *Political Parties in American Society.* New York: Basic Books, 1982.

Emling, Shelley. "Brave New Billboards Arrive; Messages Tailored to Viewers." *Atlanta Journal-Constitution,* 16 March 2003, 1(G).

——. "Look! Up in the Sky? It's a Bird! It's a Plane! It's an Ad?" *Austin American Statesman,* 20 July 2003, 1, 6(J).

Engley, Hollis. "Immigration Changes the Face of America." *USA Today,* 21 October 1999. At www.usatoday.com/2000/diverse/divrs01.htm (accessed 21 October 1999).

Fallows, James. *Breaking the News: How the Media Undermine American Democracy.* New York: Vintage, 1997.

Faux, Jeff. *The Party's Not Over: A New Vision for the Democrats.* New York: Basic Books, 1996.

Fenno, Richard. "U. S. House Legislators in Their Constituencies: An Exploration." *American Political Science Review* 71, no. 3 (September 1977): 914.

Fineman, Howard. "Report from LA: Rebranding the Political Parties." *Newsweek*, 17 August 2000. At www.msnbc.msn.com/id/3032542/site/newsweek/ (accessed 17 August 2000).

Fiorina, Morris. "What Culture Wars?" *Wall Street Journal*, 14 July 2004, 14(A).

Fiorina, Morris P. *Divided Government.* New York: Macmillan, 1992.

Finer, S. E. *The Changing British Party System, 1945–1979.* Washington D.C.: American Enterprise Institute, 1980.

Fiske, Susan T., Donald R. Kinder, and W. Michael Larter. "The Novice and the Expert: Knowledge-based Strategies in Political Cognition." *Journal of Experimental Social Psychology* 19 (1983): 381–400.

"Ford Not Inspiring, Carter Tells Crowd." *Atlanta Journal-Constitution*, 5 November 1976, 1(A).

Francis, Diane. "Muzzling the Minority Voice in Quebec." *Macleans* 109, no. 9 (1996): 13.

Frantzich, Stephen E. *Political Parties in the Technological Age.* New York: Longman, 1989.

Fromkin, Victoria, and Robert Rodman. *An Introduction to Language.* New York: Holt, Rinehart and Winston, Inc., 1974.

Fuchs, Ester R., Lorraine C. Minnite, and Robert Y. Shapiro, "Political Capital and Political Participation." Unpublished manuscript. At www.sipa.columbia.edu /RESEARCH/Paper/99-3.pdf (accessed 17 July 2004).

Gans, Herbert. *Deciding What's News.* New York: Random House, 1979.

Geertz, Clifford. "Thick Description: Toward an Interpretive Theory of Culture." In *The Interpretation of Cultures: Selected Essays*, edited by Clifford Geertz, 3–30. New York: Basic Books, 1973.

Ghanem, Salma. "Filling in the Tapestry: The Second Level of Agenda Setting." In *Communication and Democracy: Exploring the Intellectual Frontiers in Agenda-Setting Theory*, edited by Maxwell McCombs, Donald L. Shaw, and David Weaver, 3–14. Mawhah, N.J.: Erlbaum Associates, 1997.

Gimpel, Jim. "Computer Techology and Getting out the Vote." *Campaigns & Elections* 24, no. 8 (2003): 39–41.

Gobe, Marc. *Citizen Brand: 10 Commandments for Transforming Brands in a Consumer Democracy.* New York: Alworth Press, 2002.

Gobe, Marc, and Sergio Zyman. *Emotional Branding: The New Paradigm for Connecting Brands to People.* New York: Allworth Press, 2001.

Goodnough, Abby. "Hispanic Vote in Florida; Neither a Bloc nor a Lock." *New York Times*, 17 October 2004. At www.nytimes.com/2004/10/17/politics/campaign/ 17florida.html?fta=y.

"GOP Seeks Shift in Party Loyalty in Election Today." *New York Times*, 6 November 1984, 1(A).

Gore, Al. "Acceptance Address to the Democratic National Convention." Los Angeles, Calif., 17 August 2000. Campaign Mapping Project Database, University of Texas at Austin.

"Gossip." *New York Post*, 2 August 2004. At www.nypost.com/gossip/28411.htm (accessed 2 August 2004).

"Gov. Stevenson Eases Into Role Of Aggressor; Takes Each Issue as Personal Challenge." *Chicago Tribune*, 8 September 1952, 5(A).

Green, Donald P., Alan S. Gerber, and David W. Nickerson, "Getting Out the Vote in Local Elections: Results from Six Door-to-Door Canvassing Experiments." *Journal of Politics* 65, no. 4 (2003): 1083–107.

Gross, Richard E., and Arnold W. Seibel. *American Citizenship: The Way We Govern.* Englewood Cliffs, N.J.: Prenctice-Hall, Inc., 1979.

"Group of Viewers Shifts Opinions After TV Debate." *Washington Post*, 9 October 1984, 1(A).

Harris, John F. "Truth, Consequences of Kerry's 'Liberal' Label." *Washington Post*, 19 July 2004, 1(A).

Hart, Roderick P. *Modern Rhetorical Criticism.* New York: Harper Collins, 1990.

———. *Diction 4.0: The Text Analysis Program.* Thousand Oaks, Calif.: Sage, 1997.

———. *Campaign Talk: Why Elections Are Good for Us.* Princeton, N.J.: Princeton University Press, 2000.

Hart, Roderick P., Deborah Smith-Howell, and John Llewellyn. "The Mindscape of the Presidency: *Time* Magazine, 1945–1985." *Journal of Communication* 41 no. 3 (1991): 6–25.

Hart, Roderick P., Sharon E. Jarvis, William P. Jennings, and Deborah Smith-Howell. *Political Keywords: Using Language that Uses Us.* New York: Oxford, 2005.

Herman, Ken. "Bush Campaign Effort Aimed at Churches Is Criticized." *Austin American Statesman*, 2 July 2004, 11(A).

Herrera, Richard. "Understanding the Language of Politics: A Study of Elites and Masses." *Political Science Quarterly* 111, no. 4 (winter 1996–1997): 619–37.

Hetherington, Marc. "Resurgent Mass Partisanship: The Role of Elite Polarization." *American Political Science Review* 94 (2001): 619–31.

Hibbing, John R., and Elizabeth Theiss Morse. *Congress as Public Enemy: Public Attitudes Toward American Political Institutions.* Cambridge, Mass.: Cambridge University Press, 1995.

———. "Civics is Not Enough: Teaching Barbarics in K–12." *PS: Political Science and Politics* 29, no. 1 (1996): 57–62.

Hoesktra, D. J. "The 'Textbook Presidency' Revisited." *Presidential Studies Quarterly* 12 (1982): 159–67.

Hofstadter, Richard. *The Age of Reform.* New York: Vintage Books, 1955.

———. *The Idea of a Party System: The Rise of Legitimate Opposition in the United States, 1780–1840.* Berkeley: University of California Press, 1972.

Holman, Rebecca H. "Advertising and Emotionality." In *The Role of Affect in Consumer Behavior*, edited by Robert A. Peterson, Wayne D. Hoyer, and William R. Wilson, 119–40. Lexington, Mass.: Lexington Books, 1986.

Horst, Gerald L. "Letter to the Editor; Focus: President Bush; 'W' Not Disrespectful." *San Antonio Express News*, 1 August 2004, 4(H).

Howard, Theresa. "Business Rises, Though Ads Not a Favorite." *USA Today*, 11 March 2002, 9(B).

"Humphrey Has 70 30 Margin Over Miller." *Washington Post*, 5 September 1964, 2(A).

"Humphrey, 'Speaking For Self,' Says Troop Pullout Is Possible." *Los Angeles Times*, 23 September 1968, 20(A).

Humphrey, Hubert. "Investing in People." Campaign speech delivered in Charleston, W.V., 3 October 1968. Annenberg/Pew Archive of Presidential Discourse. Philadelphia: Annenberg School for Communication, University of Pennsylvania, 2000. CD-ROM.

Huntington, Samuel. *Political Order in Changing Societies*. New Haven, Conn.: Yale University Press, 1968.

Ives, Nat. "Putting Out the Message that Registering and Voting Should Have a Place in the Youth Culture." *New York Times*, 13 July 2004, 15(C).

———. "Commercials Have Expanded into Short Films with the Story as the Focus." *New York Times*, 21 April 2004, 8(C).

———. "Marketers Discover Election Day, Embracing Get-out-the Vote Efforts for Young People as a Way to Reach Potential Consumers." *New York Times*, 22 March 2004, 13(C).

Iyengar, Shanto. *Is Anyone Responsible? How Television Frames Political Issues*. Chicago: The University of Chicago Press, 1991.

Jamieson, Kathleen Hall. *Eloquence in an Electronic Age*. Oxford: Oxford University Press, 1988.

———. *Dirty Politics: Deception, Distraction, and Democracy*. New York: Oxford University Press, 1992.

———. *Packaging the Presidency: A History and Criticism of Presidential Campaign Advertising*. New York: Oxford University Press, 1992.

———. "The subversive effects of a focus on strategy in news coverage of campaigns." In *1–800 president, by the Twentieth Century Fund Task Force on Television and the Campaign of 1992*. New York: Twentieth Century Fund Press, 1993. At www.tcf.org/task_forces/tv_1992_campaign/Jamieson.html (accessed 17 July 2004).

Jamieson, Kathleen Hall, and Erica Falk. "Civility in the House of Representatives: The 105th Congress." Report number 26 from the Annenberg Public Policy Center, March 1999. At www.annenbergpublicpolicycenter.org/03_political_communication/civility/REP26.PDF.

"Jersey Held Safe for Eisenhower; '52 Margin Expected to Be Cut Democrats Say New Crisis is Helping Party." *New York Times*, 5 November 1956, 28(A).

Jhally, Sut. *Advertising and the End of the World.* Northhampton, Mass.: The Media Education Foundation, 1998. Film.

Johnson, Jerry. "Seeking Votes and Building Brands Have Much in Common." *PR Week,* 26 January 2004, 8.

Johnston, Pamela Conover, and Stanley Feldman. "The Origins and Meanings of Liberal/Conservative Self-Identification." *American Journal of Political Science* 25, no. 4 (November 1981): 617–45.

Just, Marion R., Ann N. Crigler, Dean E. Alger, Timothy E. Cook, Montague Kern, and Darryl M. West. *Crosstalk: Citizens, Candidates, and the Media in a Presidential Campaign.* Chicago: University of Chicago Press, 1996.

Justice, Glen. "Despite New Financing Rules, Parties Collect Record $1 Billion." *New York Times Online,* 25 October 2004. At www.nytimes.com/2004/10/26/politics/campaign/26money.html.

Kapferer, Jean-Noel. *Strategic Brand Management: Creating and Sustaining Brand Equity Long Term.* London: Kogan Page Ltd., 1997.

Keefe, Bob. "Advertisers Leaving No Space Unexplored: Spider-Man's Ballpark Gig Joins the Ongoing March of Ad Creep." *Austin American Statesman,* 8 May 2004, 1, 16(A).

Keith, Bruce E., David B. Magleby, Candice J. Nelson, Elizabeth Orr, Mark C. Westlye, and Raymond E. Wolfinger. *The Myth of the Independent Voter.* Berkeley: University of California Press, 1992.

Keller, Kevin. "The Brand Report Card." *Harvard Business Review* 1 (January 2000): 147–57.

Kendall, Willmoore, and Austin Ranney. *Democracy and the American Party System.* New York: Harcourt, Brace, 1956.

Kennedy, Edward. "Address to the Democratic National Convention." New York City, N.Y., 12 August 1980. Accessible via the John F. Kennedy Library and Museum, at www.jfklibrary.org/e081280.htm (accessed 20 October 1999).

Kennedy, John F. "Speech." Buffalo, N.Y., 28 September 1960. Annenberg/Pew Archive of Presidential Discourse. Philadelphia: Annenberg School for Communication, University of Pennsylvania, 2000. CD-ROM.

———. "Campaign Speech at the Auditorium Coliseum." Indianapolis, Ind., 4 October 1960. Annenberg/Pew Archive of Presidential Discourse. Philadelphia: Annenberg School for Communication, University of Pennsylvania, 2000. CD-ROM.

———. "Campaign Address, Delivered at the Biltmore Hotel." New York, N.Y., 12 October 1960. Annenberg/Pew Archive of Presidential Discourse. Philadelphia: Annenberg School for Communication, University of Pennsylvania, 2000. CD-ROM.

Kenski, Henry C., Sharon Jarvis, Tom Reichert, and Christie Van Reit. "Perot: Media Framing." Paper presented to the Speech Communication Association, New Orleans, La., November 1994.

Kernell, Samuel. *Going Public: New Strategies of Presidential Leadership.* 3rd ed. Washington, D.C.: Congressional Quarterly Press, 1997.

Kesler, Charles. "Who Needs Political Parties?" *IntellectualCapital,* 16 May 2000. At www.intellectualcapital.com.

Key, V. O. *Politics, Parties, and Pressure Groups.* 5th ed. New York: Crowell, 1964.

———. *Public Opinion and American Democracy.* New York: Alfred A. Knopf, 1961.

Knapp, Mark L. *Social Intercourse: From Greeting to Goodbye.* Boston: Allyn & Bacon 1978.

Kowalczyk, Liz. "For Kids, a Steady Diet of Food Ads TV, Net Marketing Blitz Studied for Links to Childhood Obesity." *The Boston Globe,* 24 February 2004, 1(C).

Kotler, Philip. *Marketing Management,* 11th ed. Upper Saddle River, N.J.: Prentice Hall, 2003.

Kress, Gunther, and Robert Hodge. *Language as Ideology.* London: Routledge & Kegan Paul, 1981.

Krippendorff, Klaus. *Content Analysis: An Introduction to its Methodology.* Newbury Park, Calif.: Sage, 1980.

Kurtzman, Laura. "California Gubernatorial Nominee Starts to Shy Away From Conservative Label." *San Jose Mercury News,* 7 March 2002.

Ladd, Carl Everett. *The American Polity: The People and Their Government.* 3rd ed. New York: W. W. Norton, 1985.

———. "Of Political Parties Great and Strong: A Dissent." *American Enterprise* 5, no. 4 (July/August 1994): 60–70.

Lakoff, George. *Moral Politics: How Liberals and Conservatives Think.* Chicago: University of Chicago Press, 2002.

———. "Metaphor, Morality, and Politics, or, Why Conservatives Have Left Liberals in the Dust." *Social Research* 62, no. 2 (1995): 177–214.

Larson, Charles U. *Persuasion: Reception and Responsibility.* 8th ed. Belmont, Calif.: Wadsworth Publishing, 1998.

Leibovich, Mark. "The Image of Security: Homeland Chief Tom Ridge, Keeping Up His Appearances." *Washington Post,* 22 May 2003, 1(C).

Leonhardt, David. "Is Madison Avenue Taking 'Get 'em While They're Young' Too Far?" *Business Week,* 30 June 1997, 62.

Lemann, Nicholas. "The Word Lab; The Mad Scientist Behind what the Candidates Say." *New Yorker* 76 no. 35 (16 October 2000): 100–108.

———. "The Controller." *New Yorker* 79, no. 11 (12 May 2003): 68–84.

Lewinski, Marcel, et al. *Consent of the Governed: A Study of American Government.* Glenview, Ill.: Scott Foresman, 1987.

"Lieberman Castigates GOP; Gore's Appearance with Daughter Provides an Emotional Spark." *Chicago Tribune,* 17 August 2000, 1(A).

Lieberman, David. "Studies Show Increase in Television Ads, Promos." *USA Today,* 15 February 2002, 2(B).

Lindbloom, Charles. "The Market as a Prison." *The Journal of Politics* 44, no. 2 (May 1982): 324–36.

Linz, Juan J., and Alfred Stepan. *Problems of Democratic Transition and Consolidation.* Baltimore, Md.: Johns Hopkins University Press, 1996.

Littlejohn, Stephen W. *Theories of Human Communication.* 3rd ed. Belmont, Calif.: Wadsworth Publishing, 1989.

Lodge, Milton, and Ruth Hamil. "A Partisan Schema for Information Processing." *American Political Science Review* 83, no. 2, (1986): 399–419.

Lowi, Theodore. *The End of Liberalism.* 2nd ed. New York: W. W. Norton & Company, 1979.

———. "The Party Crasher." *New York Times Magazine,* 23 August 1992, 28, 33.

Lowi, Theodore J., and Benjamin Ginsberg. *American Government: Freedom and Power.* New York: W. W. Norton, 1990.

Luntz, Frank. Cover letter, "Language of the 21st Century," 1994.

———. "Perovian Civilization: Who Supported Ross and Why." *Policy Review* (Spring 1993): 18.

Mack, Ann. "Politicians Log On." *Media Week* 26 (2004): 24–28.

Madison, James. *Federalist No. 10.* In *The Federalist Papers,* by Alexander Hamilton, John Jay, and James Madison. London: Penguin, 1987.

Maisel, L. Sandy, Kara Z. Buckley, and Louis Sandy Maisel. *Parties and Elections in America: The Electoral Process.* Lanham, Md.: Rowman & Littlefield, 2004.

Malone, Julia. "Re-Election Campaign Hopes Shindigs Unite Supporters." *Austin American Statesman,* 29 April 2004, 25(A).

———. "In Campaign Waged One Voter at a Time, GOP Gave Bush not Only Electoral Vote but 3.5 Million Majority of Popular Vote." *Austin American Statesman,* 4 November 2004. At www.statesman.com/news/content/auto/epaper/editions/thursday/news_14982e64728e21f2001a.html.

Man, Anthony. "Conservative Democrats Challenge GOP's Caricature of their Party." *South Florida Sun-Sentinel,* 23 April 2004. At www.sun-sentinel.com/.

Mandese, Joe. "Consumers Understand, Reject TV Ad Model; Deem Ad-skipping Indispensable." *Media Post's MediaDailyNews,* 10 March 2004. At www.knowledgenetworks.com.

Matus, R. "Vote for Perot: He Addresses Issues." *Salinas Californian,* 10 October 1992, 6(A).

McCarthy, Michael. "Critics Target 'Omnipresent' Ads; Advertising Spreads into Non-traditional Venues." *USA Today,* 16 March 2001, 6(B).

McCombs, Maxwell, and Donald Shaw. "The Agenda-Setting Function of Mass Media." *Public Opinion Quarterly* 36 (1972): 176–85.

McGovern, George. "Campaign Speech." Alameda County, Calif., 4 September 1972. Annenberg/Pew Archive of Presidential Discourse. Philadelphia: Annenberg School for Communication, University of Pennsylvania, 2000. CD-ROM.

Merritt, Richard. *Symbols of American Community.* New Haven, Conn.: Yale University Press, 1966.

Menefree, Selden. "The Effect of Stereotyped Words on Political Judgments." *American Sociological Review* 1 no. 4 (1936): 614–21.

Miliband, Edward. "Meet-up at the White House?" *New Statesman,* 25 August 2003, 19.

Mondak, Jeffrey. "Public Opinion and Heuristic Processing of Source Cues." *Political Behavior* 15, no. 2 (June 1993): 167–92.

———. "Source Cues and Policy Approval: The Cognitive Dynamics of Public Support for the Reagan Agenda." *American Journal of Political Science* 37, no. 1 (February 1993): 186–212.

Mondale, Walter. "What Kind of People Are We." Remarks at Merrill, Wis., 3 September 1984. Annenberg/Pew Archive of Presidential Discourse. Philadelphia: Annenberg School for Communication, University of Pennsylvania, 2000. CD-ROM.

———. "Principles." Mondale Rally, Duluth, Minn., 30 October 1984. Annenberg/Pew Archive of Presidential Discourse. Philadelphia: Annenberg School for Communication, University of Pennsylvania, 2000. CD-ROM.

Moore, James, and Wayne Slater. *Bush's Brain How Karl Rove Made George W. Bush Presidential.* New York: John Wiley & Sons, 2003.

Morgan, Adam. *Eating the Big Fish: How Challenger Brands Can Compete against Brand Leaders.* New York: John Wiley & Sons: 1999.

Morris, Dick. *Behind the Oval Office: Winning the Presidency in the Nineties.* New York: Random House, 1997.

———. *The New Prince.* Los Angeles, Calif.: Renaissance Books, 1999.

Murray, Brian H. *Defending the Brand: Aggressive Strategies for Protecting your Brand in the Online Arena.* New York: AMACOM, 2003.

Nelson, Michael. "Why Americans Hate Politics and Politicians." *PS: Political Science and Politics* 28, no. 1 (March 1995): 72–78.

"New York Liberals Fully Back Truman." *Christian Science Monitor,* 2 September 1948, A3.

Newman, Bruce. *The Mass Marketing of Politics: Democracy in an Age of Manufactured Images.* Thousand Oaks, Calif.: Sage, 1999.

———. *Marketing of the President: Political Marketing as Campaign Strategy.* Thousand Oaks, Calif.: Sage, 1994.

Nie, Norman, Sydney Verba, and John Petrocik. *The Changing American Voter.* Cambridge: Harvard University Press, 1979.

Niemi, Richard, and Herbert Weisberg. *Controversies in Voting Behavior.* Washington D.C.: Congressional Quarterly Press, 1984.

Nierenberg, Gerard I., and Henry H. Colero. *Meta-Talk.* New York: Simon & Schuster, 1981.

"Nixon Advocates Regional Summits to Combat Soviet." *New York Times,* 15 October 1960, 1(A).

"Nixon Appeals To Swing Voters." *Washington Post,* 10 October 1956, 2(A).

"Nixon Is Acclaimed on 5th Trip South; Kennedy in Chicago." *Washington Post,* 25 September 1960, 1(A).

"Nixon Urges Democrats In Texas To Vote For Ike." *Washington Post,* 10 October 1956, 2(A).

Nixon, Richard. "Campaign Speech." Charleston, W.Va., Civic Center, 27 September 1960. Annenberg/Pew Archive of Presidential Discourse. Philadelphia:

Annenberg School for Communication, University of Pennsylvania, 2000. CD-ROM.

——. "Campaign Speech." New York, N.Y., Columbian Republican League Luncheon, Commodore Hotel, 5 October 1960. Annenberg/Pew Archive of Presidential Discourse. Philadelphia: Annenberg School for Communication, University of Pennsylvania, 2000. CD-ROM.

——. "Remarks on Accepting the Presidential Nomination of the Republican National Convention." 23 August 1972. Annenberg/Pew Archive of Presidential Discourse. Philadelphia: Annenberg School for Communication, University of Pennsylvania, 2000. CD-ROM.

——. "Remarks to the Student Body of Rio Grande High School." Rio Grande City, Tex., 22 September 1972. Annenberg/Pew Archive of Presidential Discourse. Philadelphia: Annenberg School for Communication, University of Pennsylvania, 2000. CD-ROM.

"Nominee Raps Tactics; Lauds Maryland Slate." *Washington Post*, 21 September 1956, 1(A).

Noonan, Peggy. "Will the Real John Kerry Please Stand Up?" *Wall Street Journal*, 22 July 2004. At www.wsj.com.

Norpoth, Helmut, and Jerry Rusk. "Partisan Dealignment in the American Electorate." *American Political Science Review* 76, no. 3 (September 1982): 522–37.

Nunberg, Geoffrey. "The Liberal Label: The Substance Is Alive and Well, But the Brand Is in Trouble." *The American Prospect* 14, no. 8 (1 September 2003): 36.

"One Last Hurrah for Pat Lucey." *Chicago Tribune*, 3 October 1980, 1(A).

Orren, Gary. "The Changing Styles of American Party Politics." In *The Future of American Political Parties: The Challenge of Governance*, ed. J. L. Fleishman, 4–41. Englewood Cliffs, N.J.: Prentice Hall, 1982.

O'Shaugnessy, Nicholas. *The Idea of Political Marketing*. Westport, Conn.: Praeger, 2002.

——. *The Marketing Power of Emotion*. New York: Oxford, 2003.

——. *The Phenomenon of Political Marketing*. New York: St. Martin's Press, 1990.

"Parties Reign, In Independent Age Voters Increasingly Register 'Independent,' But Two Parties Buoyed By Money And Fired Up Voters." *Christian Science Monitor*, 1 August 2000, 1(A).

Patterson, Thomas E. *Out of Order*. New York: Vintage, 1994.

——. "Bad News, Period." *PS: Political Science and Politics* 29, no. 1 (March 1996): 17–21.

Pennebaker, James, Matthias Mehl, and Kimberly Niederhoffer. "Psychological Aspects of Natural Language Use: Our Words, Our Selves." *Annual Review of Psychology* 54 (2003): 547–77.

"Perot Reconsiders Withdrawal from Presidential Race." *Washington Post*, 23 September 1992, 12(A).

Petrocik, John. "Issues and Agendas: Electoral Coalitions of the 1988 Election." Paper prepared for the delivery at the Annual American Political Science Association Meeting, Atlanta, Ga., 31 August–3 September 1989.

Petrocik, John. "Issue Ownership in Presidential Elections, with a 1980 Case Study." *American Journal of Political Science* 40 (1996): 825–50.

Petrocik, John, William L. Benoit, and Glen J. Hansen. "Issue Ownership and Presidential Campaigning, 1952–2000." Paper presented to the annual meeting of the American Political Science Association, San Francisco, 30 August–2 September 2001.

Pfau, Michael, and Hank Kenski. *Attack Politics: Strategy and Defense.* New York: Praeger, 1990.

"Politics: The Strategy; Clinton Pursues Party Sweep Without Whispering a Hint." *New York Times*, 23 October 1996, 1(A).

"Poll Finds Growing Voter Confusion." *Los Angeles Times*, 18 October 1976, 1(A).

"Polls Show Shifts Aiding Reagan." *New York Times*, 1 October 1980, 1(A).

Polsby, Nelson. *Consequences of Party Reform.* Oxford: Oxford University Press, 1983.

Pomper, Gerald. *Passions and Interests: Political Party Concepts of American Democracy.* Lawrence: University of Kansas Press, 1992.

———. "Comments by Practitioners and Scholars." In *The Politics of Ideas: Intellectual Challenges to the Party After 1992*, edited by John Kenneth White and John Clifford Green, 101–2. Lanham, Md.: Rowman & Littlefield, 1995.

———. "The Alleged Decline of American Parties." In *Politicians and Party Politics*, edited by John Grey Geer. Baltimore: Johns Hopkins University Press, 1998.

Popkin, Samuel. *The Reasoning Voter.* Chicago: University of Chicago Press, 1991.

Powell, Bonnie Azab. "Framing the Issues: UC Berkeley Professor George Lakoff Tells How Conservatives Use Language to Dominate Politics." *UC Berkeley News*, 27 October 2003. At www.berkeley.edu/news/media/releases/2003/10/27_lakoff.shtml (accessed 15 July 2004).

"Pro-Kerry NEA Plans 'House parties' vs. Bush." *USA Today*, 6 July 2004, 9(D).

"Prospects Looking Up for a Head to Head Debate." *Washington Post*, 16 October 1980, 1(A).

Putnam, Robert. *Bowling Alone: The Collapse and Revival of American Community.* New York: Simon & Schuster, 2000.

———. "Bowling Alone: America's Declining Social Capital." *Current* 373 (June 1995): 3–10.

Quindlen, Anna. "A Leap into the Possible." *Newsweek*, 9 August 2004, 60.

Rahn, Wendy. "The Role of Partisan Stereotypes in Information Processing About Political Candidates." *American Journal of Political Science* 37, no. 2 (1993): 472–96.

Rahn, Wendy, John Aldrich, and Eugene Borgida. "Individual and Contextual Variations in Political Candidate Appraisal." *American Political Science Review* 88, no. 1 (March 1994):193–99.

Rahn, Wendy, and Kathleen J. Cramer. "Activation of Political Party Stereotypes: The Role of Television." *Political Communication* 13 (1996): 195–212.

Rapoport, Ronald R. "Partisanship Change in a Candidate-Centered Era." *Journal of Politics* 59, no. 1 (February 1997): 185–99.

Ray, Alastair. "Television—Clearing up the Commercials Clutter." *Financial Times*, 29 June 2004, 4.

"Reagan, Anderson to Aim at Each Other in Debate, Not Carter." *Los Angeles Times*, 21 September 1980, 4(A).

Reagan, Ronald. "Speech to the Republican National Convention." Detroit, Mich., 17 July 1980. Annenberg/Pew Archive of Presidential Discourse. Philadelphia: Annenberg School for Communication, University of Pennsylvania, 2000. CD-ROM.

———. "A Vital Economy: Jobs, Growth and Progress for Americans." Televised Campaign Address, 24 October 1980. Annenberg/Pew Archive of Presidential Discourse. Philadelphia: Annenberg School for Communication, University of Pennsylvania, 2000. CD-ROM.

———. "A Vision for America." Television Address, 3 November 1980. Annenberg/Pew Archive of Presidential Discourse. Philadelphia: Annenberg School for Communication, University of Pennsylvania, 2000. CD-ROM.

———. "Campaign Speech Delivered to Reagan Bush Rally." Waterbury, Conn., 19 September 1984. Annenberg/Pew Archive of Presidential Discourse. Philadelphia: Annenberg School for Communication, University of Pennsylvania, 2000. CD-ROM.

"Reagan's Age Muddles His Thinking; Anderson." *Chicago Tribune*, 16 September 1980, 6(A).

Reich, Robert. *Why Liberals Win Will the Battle for America*. New York: Knopf, 2004.

Ries, Al, and Jack Trout. *Positioning: The Battle for Your Mind*. New York: McGraw Hill, 2001.

Remy, Richard. *United States Government: Democracy in Action*. New York: Glencoe, 1993.

Robinson, Michael, and Margaret Sheehan. *Over the Wire and on TV: CBS and UPI in Campaign '80*. New York: Russell Sage Foundation, 1983.

Rodgers, Daniel T. *Contested Truths: Keywords in American Politics since Independence*. Cambridge, Mass.: Harvard University Press, 1987.

Rosenstone, Steven J., Roy Behr, and Edward H. Lazarus. *Third Parties in America: Citizen Response to Major Party Failure*. Princeton, N.J.: Princeton University Press, 1984.

Sabato, Larry. *The Party's Just Begun: Shaping Political Parties for America's Future*. Glenville, Ill.: Scot, Foresman and Company, 1988.

Sanchez, J. M. "Mediocrity at the Helm: Evaluations of the President in Political Science Textbooks." *Social Science Journal* 33, no. 1 (1996): 97–112.

———. "Old habits Die Hard: The Textbook Presidency Is Alive and Well." *PS: Political Science & Politics* 29, no. 1 (1996): 63–67.

———."Awaiting Rehabilitation: The Carter Presidency in Political Science Textbooks." *Presidential Studies Quarterly* 27, no. 2 (1997): 284–97.

Sanders, Arthur. "The Meaning of Party Images." *Western Political Quarterly* 41 (1988): 583–99.

Schaffner, Brian F., and Matthew J. Streb. "The Partisan Heuristic in Low Information Elections." *Public Opinion Quarterly* 66, no. 4 (winter 2002): 558–81.

Schattschneider, E. E. *Party Government.* New York: Holt, Rinehart and Winston, 1942.

Schlesinger, Joseph A. "The New American Political Party." *American Political Science Review* 79, no. 4 (December 1985): 1152–69.

Schmitter, Phillipe, and Terry Karl. "What Democracy Is . . . and Is Not." In *The Global Resurgency of Democracy*, 2nd ed., edited by Larry Diamond and Marc Plattner, 49–62. Baltimore, Md.: Johns Hopkins University Press, 1996.

Schudson, Michael. *Advertising: The Uneasy Persuasion.* New York: Basic Books, 1986.

———. *The Good Citizen: A History of American Civic Life.* New York: The Free Press, 1998.

Schumpeter, Joseph A. *Capitalism, Socialism and Democracy.* New York: Harper and Row, 1942.

Sherman, Christopher. "Along Political Spectrum, 'Progressive' Label is Claimed by Everyone." *Daily Record*, 29 October 2002.

Shesgreen, Deidre. "Little Attraction to Third Parties in Polarized Country." *Austin American Statesman*, 31 October 2004, 7(A).

Smith-Howell, Deborah. "Using the Past in the Present: The Rhetorical Construction of the Presidency." Doctoral dissertation, University of Texas at Austin, 1993.

Snyder, James M., and Michael M. Ting. "An Informational Rationale for Political Parties." *American Journal of Political Science* 46, no. 1, (January 2002): 90–110.

Sorauf, Frank, and Paul Allen Beck. *Party Politics in America.* 6th ed. Glenview, Ill.: Scott, Foresman and Company, 1988.

"Sparkman Charges GOP Uses Fear Philosophy; Old Thinking Men Have No Vision of Their Country's Future." *UP Wire Report*, 19 October 1952.

"Sparkman Rips McCarthyism." *AP/UPI Wire Report*, 10 September 1952, 19(A).

"Spot Check by NBC News Finds Reagan Is Leading." *AP-UPI*, 29 September 1980.

Stevens, H. "Perot Vote Necessary." *Fall River Herald News*, 26 October 1992, 4(A).

"Stevenson Asks Truth From GOP; Accuses Administration of Withholding Facts From Public on World Situation." *AP-UPI Wire*, 7 September 1956.

"Stevenson Assails Party 'Apostates; Tells South to Guard Economic and Political Gains by Ignoring the Dissidents." *New York Times*, 12 October 1952, 1(A).

Stevenson, Aldai. "Speech to the Democratic National Convention." 26 July 1952. Annenberg/Pew Archive of Presidential Discourse. Philadelphia: Annenberg School for Communication, University of Pennsylvania, 2000. CD-ROM.

———. "Campaign Speech." Palisades Park, N.J., 9 September 1956. Annenberg/Pew Archive of Presidential Discourse. Philadelphia: Annenberg School for Communication, University of Pennsylvania, 2000. CD-ROM.

———. "Campaign Address entitled 'Tough Issues.'" Albuquerque, N.Mex., 12 September 1952. Annenberg/Pew Archive of Presidential Discourse. Philadelphia:

Annenberg School for Communication, University of Pennsylvania, 2000. CD-ROM.

———. "Campaign Speech." Elkins, W.Va., 4 October 1956. Annenberg/Pew Archive of Presidential Discourse. Philadelphia: Annenberg School for Communication, University of Pennsylvania, 2000. CD-ROM.

———. "Concession Statement." 6 November 1956. Annenberg/Pew Archive of Presidential Discourse. Philadelphia: Annenberg School for Communication, University of Pennsylvania, 2000. CD-ROM.

Stolberg, Sheryl Gay. "Washington Talk; Seeking the Words that Will Win Back the House." *New York Times*, 10 September 2003, 20(A).

Stone, Walter, and Ronald Rapoport. "It's Perot Stupid? The Legacy of the 1992 Perot Movement in the Major-Party System, 1994-2000." *PS Online*, March 2001. At www.apsanet.org/PS/march01/stone.cfm.

"Style Counts, Strategists Say." *Washington Post*, 1 November 2000, 16(A).

Tarrance, V. Lance, Walter DeVries, and Donna L. Mosher. *Checked and Balanced: How Ticket Splitters Are Shaping the New Balance of Power in American Politics.* Grand Rapids, Mich.: Wm. B. Eerdmans Publishing Group, 1998.

Taylor, Chris, and Karen Tumulty. "MoveOn's Big Moment." *Time*, 24 November 2003, 32.

"The Main Event." *New York Times*, 7 September 1980, 1(A).

Thomas, Greg. "W Tries Boutique Hotel Feel at National Chain Level; Offers 'Whatever Whenever' Service." *Orleans*, 17 July 2003, 1(F).

Thomma, Steven. "Religion, Politics Go Hand in Hand." *Austin American Statesman*, 14 December 2003, 21(A).

Travis, Daryl. *Emotional Branding: How Successful Brands Gain the Irrational Edge.* Roseveille, Calif.: Prima Venture, 2000.

Trilling, Richard. *Party Image and Electoral Behavior.* New York: John Wiley & Sons, 1976.

Trout, Jack. *Big Brands Big Trouble: Lessons Learned the Hard Way.* New York: John Wiley & Sons, 2002.

"Truman Appeals for end of Split in Southern Party." *New York Times*, 20 October 1948, 1(A).

Truman, Harry. "Acceptance Address to the Democratic Nominating Convention." Philadelphia, Pa., 15 July 1948. Annenberg/Pew Archive of Presidential Discourse. Philadelphia: Annenberg School for Communication, University of Pennsylvania, 2000. CD-ROM.

———. "Radio Address Sponsored by the International Ladies Garment Workers Union Campaign Committee." Washington, D.C., 21 October 1948. Annenberg/Pew Archive of Presidential Discourse. Philadelphia: Annenberg School for Communication, University of Pennsylvania, 2000. CD-ROM.

———. "Address." Cleveland, Ohio, 26 October 1948. Annenberg/Pew Archive of Presidential Discourse. Philadelphia: Annenberg School for Communication, University of Pennsylvania, 2000. CD-ROM.

———. "Campaign Speech." St. Louis, Mo., 30 October 1948. Annenberg/Pew Archive of Presidential Discourse. Philadelphia: Annenberg School for Communication, University of Pennsylvania, 2000. CD-ROM.

Tucker, Joshua, and Ted Brader. "Congratulations, It's a Party! The Birth of Mass Political Parties in Russia, 1993–1996." Paper presented at the Annual Meeting of the American Political Science Association, Boston, Mass., 3–6 September 1998.

Tynan, Trudy. "New Words Define Times." *Austin American Statesman*, 4 July 2003, 27(A).

"U.S. Electorate Deeply Divided." *Chicago Tribune*, 5 November 1968, 1(A).

Uslaner, Eric. *The Decline of Comity in Congress.* Ann Arbor: University of Michigan Press, 1993.

Varoga, Craig, and Mike Rice. "Only the Facts: Professional Research and Message Development." In *The Handbook of Political Marketing*, edited by Bruce Newman, 243–56. Thousand Oaks, Calif.: Sage, 1999.

Viguerie, Richard, and David Franke, *America's Right Turn: How Conservatives Used New and Alternative Media to Take Power.* Chicago: Bonus Books, 2004.

"Voter Turnout of 60% to 78% Expected in Area." *Washington Post*, 4 November 1980, 1(A).

"W. Hotels or W. the President?" *NewYorkish*, 6 July 2004. At www.newyorkish .com/newyorkish/2004/week28/index.html.

Ward, Ian. "'Media Intrusion' and the Changing Nature of Political Parties in Australia and Canada." *Canadian Journal of Political Science* 26, no. 3 (1993): 478–508.

"Warren Says GOP can Bring Unity to Anxious Nation." *New York Times*, 17 September 1948, 1(A).

Wattenberg, Martin P. *The Decline of American Political Parties, 1952–1988.* Cambridge, Mass.: Harvard University Press, 1998.

"Wearing Out the L-Word." *New York Times*, 31 August 2003, 26(A).

White, John K. "Reviving the Parties: What Must be Done?" In *The Politics of Ideas: Intellectual Challenges to the Party after 1992*, edited by John Kenneth White and John Clifford Green, 4–27. Lanham, Md.: Rowman & Littlefield, 1995.

Whitney, D. Charles, and Lee Becker, "'Keeping the Gates' for Gatekeepers: The Effects of Wire News." *Journalism Quarterly* 59 (1982): 60–65.

Whorf, Benjamin. *Language, Thought, and Reality.* New York: John Wiley, 1956.

Will, George F. *Men at Work.* New York: Macmillan, 1990.

———. "The Politics of Participation." *Washington Post*, 29 July 1999, 29(A).

Williams, Raymond. *Keywords: A Vocabulary of Culture and Society.* New York: Oxford, 1976.

Wilson, James Q., and Karlyn Bowman. "Defining the Peace Party." *Public Interest* 153 (fall 2003): 69–79.

Winters Lauro, Patricia. "According to a Survey, the Democratic and Republican Parties Have Brand-Name Problems." *New York Times*, 17 November 2000, 10(C).

Woodward, Gary. "Reagan as Roosevelt: The Elasticity of Pseduo-Populist Appeals." *Central States Speech Journal* 34 (1983): 44–58.

Zaller, John. *The Nature and Origins of Mass Opinion.* Cambridge: Cambridge University Press, 1992.

———. "The Rise and Fall of Candidate Perot: Unmediated Versus Mediated Politics (Part I)." *Political Communication* 11, no. 4 (1994): 357–91.

———. "The Rise and Fall of Candidate Perot: The Outsider Versus the Political System (Part II)." *Political Communication* 12, no. 1 (1995): 97–124.

INDEX

ABOUT THE AUTHOR

Sharon E. Jarvis (PhD, 2000) is an assistant professor of communication studies and associate director of the Annette Strauss Institute for Civic Participation at the University of Texas at Austin, where she teaches and conducts research on political communication. She is a coauthor of *Political Keywords: Using Language That Uses Us*, and her work has appeared in *Journal of Communication, Political Psychology, American Behavioral Scientist, Political Communication, Communication Quarterly, Communication Studies, Journal of Computer Mediated Communication*, and the *Howard Journal of Communications*. She has been the recipient of numerous teaching honors, including the Texas Exes Teaching Award, the Eyes of Texas Teaching Award, and Outstanding Professor in the College of Communication. In 2005, she received the Friar Centennial Teaching Award, the largest undergraduate teaching honor at the University of Texas.